Boosting
Self-Esteem
FOR
DUMMIES®

Boosting Self-Esteem FOR DUMMIES®

by Rhena Branch and Rob Willson

A John Wiley and Sons, Ltd, Publication

Boosting Self-Esteem For Dummies®

Published by
John Wiley & Sons, Ltd
The Atrium
Southern Gate
Chichester
West Sussex
PO19 8SQ
England

E-mail (for orders and customer service enquires): cs-books@wiley.co.uk

Visit our Home Page on www.wiley.com

For general information on our other products and services, please contact our Customer Care Department within the U.S. at 877-762-2974, outside the U.S. at 317-572-3993, or fax 317-572-4002.

For technical support, please visit www.wiley.com/techsupport.

Wiley also publishes its books in a variety of electronic formats. Some content that appears in print may not be available in electronic books.

British Library Cataloguing in Publication Data: A catalogue record for this book is available from the British Library

ISBN: 978-0-470-74193-1

Printed and bound in Great Britain by TJ International, Padstow, Cornwall

10 9 8 7 6 5 4 3

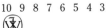
WILEY

About the Authors

Rhena Branch: Rhena has her own private practice and also teaches and supervises on the MSc at Goldsmith's University London. Rhena has co-written CBT and REBT textbooks as well as self-help books. She treats general psychiatric disorders with special interest in eating disorders and anxiety disorders.

Rob Willson: Rob runs his own private practice and is involved in supervising and teaching on the MSc in CBT and REBT at Goldsmith's University London. Rob has co-authored several self-help books and has appeared on both radio and television. He's currently involved in research into the treatment of body dysmorphic disorder.

Authors' Acknowledgements

Rhena Branch: I extend a very big thank you to Felix and Atticus (my two teenage sons) for being patient whilst I wrote yet another book that neither one of them is likely to read soon. Also thanks to Rob for his input and help, especially in the final hour.

I also wish to acknowledge and thank all those excellent CBT practitioners and mental health professionals out there for providing literature and research to draw upon. And of course, my gratitude to all my patients over the years for teaching me so much about the ways we humans work.

I also probably need to apologise to a few friends for being inaccessible over the past few months (you know who you are) and to my dogs for being remiss in the rambling walks department.

Also, thanks to the Wiley team for your expert guidance.

Rob Willson: Thank you to Rhena for being the driving force behind this book.

As ever, I'm indebted to my patients for sharing with me their thoughts, feelings and strategies.

Publisher's Acknowledgements

We're proud of this book; please send us your comments through our Dummies online registration form located at www.dummies.com/register/.

Some of the people who helped bring this book to market include the following:

Acquisitions, Editorial and Media Development

Project Editor: Steve Edwards

Content Editor: Jo Theedom

Commissioning Editor: Samantha Spickernell

Publishing Assistant: Jennifer Prytherch

Development Editor: Kathleen Dobie

Copy Editor: Andy Finch

Technical Editor: Rameez Ali

Proofreader: David Price

Executive Editor: Samantha Spickernell

Executive Project Editor: Daniel Mersey

Cover Photos: © Photodisc/Alamy

Cartoons: Ed McLachlan

Composition Services

Project Coordinator: Lynsey Stanford

Layout and Graphics: Samantha Allen, Reuben W. Davis, Christin Swinford

Proofreaders: John Greenough, Susan Moritz

Indexer: Christine Karpeles

Brand Reviewer: Jennifer Bingham

Contents at a Glance

Table of Contents

Introduction

. . . .

*L*ow self-esteem probably brings more people to therapy than any other problem. Many people are aware that the opinion they have of themselves could be better. In our clinical practice we see people from all walks of life, from different personal and professional backgrounds, and of all races, ages and creeds, complaining of the same thing: low self-esteem. In fact, low self-esteem is such a commonly reported problem that we've written a whole book about defining what *healthy* self-esteem is and telling you how to get it.

Unfortunately self-doubt and poor self-appreciation seem to go hand-in-hand with being human. Even if you have generally healthy and good self-esteem, you probably have times in your life when you feel down and have denigrating ideas and thoughts about yourself. It seems to us that very few people (if any) escape feelings of low self-esteem at some point in their lifetimes. So, even if you think that you're the only person on the planet who feels as badly about him or herself as you do, we can reassure you: that's most certainly not the case.

Self-esteem is frequently misunderstood. You may think that it's all about being successful and confident or being able to make your mark on the world. But that doesn't account for the swathe of individuals in the world who have little wealth or power and yet still manage to think well of themselves. Healthy self-esteem isn't about what you have, what you've achieved or even about what you can do; it's an internal understanding of yourself as a complex, unique and intrinsically valuable person regardless of external factors.

This book helps you to better understand what low self-esteem really is and how it may be affecting your life. We aim to give you a better understanding of the nature of healthy self-esteem and how you can achieve it. Whether you suffer from chronic low self-esteem or just seem to get occasional bouts of it, we believe that the information in this book can benefit you.

About This Book

This book can be used as a form of self-help on its own or in conjunction with seeing a therapist or other type of mental health professional. You can use the information in this book to help yourself develop healthy self-esteem or to understand and support a loved one. If you're a psychology student or even a fully trained therapist, you're likely to find something of use to you in these chapters.

This book includes the following information:

- ✔ Definitions of low self-esteem and descriptions of the many different ways it can manifest in your life.

- ✔ Explanations of common emotional and behavioural problems that people with low self-esteem typically experience.

- ✔ Cognitive behavioural techniques to help you change your negative thoughts and take on board more helpful ways of thinking and behaving.

- ✔ Lots of practical exercises that you can do to help improve your self-esteem, your overall mood and your day-to-day functioning.

- ✔ Examples and case studies that represent the actual problems and circumstances of people we have treated. The names, however, are entirely fictional and not direct reflections of any particular clients.

- ✔ Additional information that can help you to understand yourself better and improve the ways in which you relate to other people in your life.

The methods outlined throughout this book are based on *cognitive behavioural therapy* (CBT) principles. CBT is a popular, effective, scientifically researched and well-respected psychotherapeutic method used in the treatment of many different kinds of emotional and psychological problems. So you can rest assured that the advice we offer has scientific validity and has been proven to work.

We wrote this book to give you hope that you can find a way out of the trap of low self-esteem. No matter how severe your self-image problems are, you can do a lot to make meaningful improvements. We also hope you find using this book at least a little bit interesting and entertaining. So we ask you to read on and urge you to keep an open mind about new ideas and techniques.

Conventions Used in This Book

To make this book easier to read and to highlight key points, we use the following conventions:

- ✔ *Italics* introduce new terminology, highlight differences in meaning between words or underline key aspects of a sentence or an example.

- ✔ We attempt to use a roughly equal number of male and female examples throughout the book in the interests of gender equality.

- ✔ **Bold** text is used to show the action part of numbered lists and practical exercises.

What You're Not to Read

This book is yours, you paid for it, so you can read whatever you like. Right down to the fine print on the opposite side of the title page if you feel so inclined (may be a bit dull, however). Seriously though, this book is written in such a way that you can dip in and out of it as the mood takes you. Each chapter is self-contained and so you don't need to read them in sequential order. If the information in a particular chapter is enhanced in another chapter, we make a reference to that chapter.

Just to give you a few basic guidelines on what you may not need or want to read, here's a little extra advice:

- ✔ Our acknowledgments are important to us but very possibly not to you. We tried to resist being sentimental but they may well make you sick if you've just had a large dinner.

- ✔ *Sidebars*, those grey boxes full of text, contain some interesting and useful information that isn't an essential part of the topic at hand. So if you aren't drawn in by them, you don't miss anything critical if you give them a miss.

- ✔ The index makes for pretty boring reading; however, it can be very useful if you want to know where to find information on a specific topic. Otherwise you can read it straight through as a possible strategy for combating insomnia.

Foolish Assumptions

Oh, if we had but a penny for every foolish assumption we ever made in our lives. Well, we can tell you that we'd be rich enough not to need to write books for a living!

In the process of writing this book, we made some assumptions about the people (like your good self) who are going to read it:

- ✔ You suffer from low self-esteem or you know someone who does and are interested in finding out ways to overcome it.
- ✔ You're willing to take in new information and to try out new techniques in the interests of improving your self-esteem.
- ✔ You have healthy self-esteem and are interested in finding out how to keep it that way.
- ✔ You're a human being and therefore will find something within this book that's useful and resonates with your personal experiences.
- ✔ You're a *For Dummies* junkie and have collected every title in the series.

If any of these assumptions apply to you, then read on...

How This Book Is Organised

This book is divided into 6 parts and 19 chapters. The table of contents includes subheadings for each chapter that clarify which subjects you can expect each chapter to deal with. We lay out the main points contained in each part of the book in the next sections.

Part 1: Understanding Self-Esteem

This part gives you a basic understanding of what both low self-esteem and healthy self-esteem are and how to spot the differences. These chapters explore common but often unhelpful ways people assess their own worth and offer more useful alternatives. Some of the more common psychological problems associated with low self-esteem are defined and explained.

Part II: Acknowledging That You're Okay As You Are

This part is all about discovering how to appreciate yourself just as you are. We look at some of the ways that you may be undermining your own self-esteem and how you can strive to accept yourself as a complex, vibrant and ever-changing human being.

This part also deals with negative self-focus and provides practical exercises to help you take control of your attention. We explore body image problems and suggest ways to become more comfortable and content with how you look and with who you are. Finally, we look at goal-setting and personal development as a way of enhancing your enjoyment of life and appreciation of yourself.

Part III: Taking On New Techniques

Roll your sleeves up and apply some elbow grease. In this part of the book we help you explore your past with a view to finding out how it continues to inform your personal beliefs today. We also offer some advice and practical exercises that encourage you to treat yourself with care and compassion. In Chapter 11 we urge you to behave like a scientist and get busy with the business of proving your own worth to yourself. Doing so may sound easy, but it involves a fair amount of effort on your part.

Part IV: Looking at the Ripple Effects of Low Self-Esteem

Your poor self-esteem obviously has some very negative effects on you. Low self-esteem also has implications for the people in your life who love and care about you. In this part, we examine the effects of your low self-esteem on your personal and professional relationships. We look at how you can stop the rot and make your love, work and family life relationships more fulfilling.

Part V: Living Like You Mean It

If you want to feel better about yourself, you need to act in better self-enhancing ways. This part is all about getting to grips with personal commitments and values. Living in accordance with how you want to feel and think about yourself is extremely important to improving your self-esteem. In this part we help you to identify what's truly important to you and to make plans about how to reflect your values through action.

Part VI: The Part of Tens

This part of the book acts like a quick 'ready reckoner' for how to recognise healthy self-esteem in yourself and in others. This recognition is useful because it leads you towards actions and ways of thinking that you can benefit from. In Chapter 19 we discuss ten ways to boost your self-esteem and coax you further along the path towards embracing healthy self-esteem.

Appendix

The Appendix gives you a list of organisations through which you can find professional help from a CBT therapist. It also has recommended additional reading and some useful websites that you may want to have a closer look at.

Icons Used in This Book

We use the following icons throughout this book to highlight certain types of information.

This bulls-eye flags up useful tips to help you get the most out of the practical exercises and information in the book.

This icon is a gentle but persistent signal to bear important points in mind.

This icon alerts you to possible traps and pitfalls along your path to developing healthy self-esteem.

This icon means that we're about to give you an example to illustrate a point or principle that we just discussed.

This icon indicates a chance for you to put new techniques into action. It may involve putting pen to paper or may indicate more direct behavioural action.

Where to Go from Here

Reading this book from cover to cover will probably be very good for your self-esteem; it would certainly be good for ours! Just kidding. As we explain in Chapter 1, that's not really how it works (still, it got a chuckle out of us). In fact, healthy self-esteem comes not from what you do or achieve necessarily, but from how you fundamentally think of yourself. Your sense of personal worth can be very solid and robust, even if you're not setting the world on fire every day. Your achievements may give your confidence a boost (and make you feel good) but your intrinsic worth is a constant that you can learn to appreciate even when you're not busy doing great things.

You're probably best advised to meander through the table of contents and turn to the chapters that interest you the most or seem to address your particular low self-esteem difficulties. Or both, why not? In for a penny, in for a pound.

When you've used this book, you may want to get even more help with improving your self-esteem by seeing a skilled and qualified CBT therapist for a few sessions. If your difficulties with poor self-esteem are mild to moderate, this book may be enough to help you overcome them. If you have very severe and chronic low self-esteem this book helps put you on the right track, but you may also benefit from some professional input and support. Turn to the appendix for information on where to find a qualified CBT therapist.

Part I
Understanding Self-Esteem

'Nobody takes any notice of me or
of anything I say.'

In this part . . .

You get a clear understanding of the nature of healthy self-esteem and how it differs from low self-esteem. We help you identify thoughts and ideas that can perpetuate feelings of low self-esteem and point you towards healthier ways of thinking about your self-worth. We also discuss some of the more common psychological problems associated with poor self-esteem and suggest strategies for tackling them.

Chapter 1

Explaining Self-Esteem

- -

In This Chapter

▶ Understanding the components of healthy self-esteem

▶ Accepting yourself and others

▶ Trusting your own judgement

- -

Many people know that the opinion they have of themselves can be better. In our clinical practice, we see all sorts of different people from all walks of life battling with self-esteem issues. Difficulty appreciating personal worth is such a core issue that it can be said to apply legitimately to every single human being on the planet in one way or another and at one time or another. In fact, low self-esteem is such a commonly reported problem that we've written a whole book about defining healthy self-esteem and telling you how to get it.

Pause for a moment and think about your own definition of 'self-esteem'. Maybe you think that having good self-esteem means being ever confident and happy. Or perhaps you link healthy self-esteem with success, wealth, achievement, attractiveness and popularity. If so, you aren't alone. These qualities have an undeniable 'feel good' factor but they don't necessarily guarantee healthy self-esteem.

Assuming that self-esteem is determined by external factors is a very common misconception. In this chapter (and to a greater extent in Chapter 2) we help you understand that true self-esteem is based on much more than confidence or success.

Even the person who seems to have everything can be suffering with low self-esteem. Equally, a person with little wealth or obvious success can have very healthy self-esteem.

Defining Healthy Self-Esteem

Healthy self-esteem is having an enduring sense of yourself as a fundamentally valuable and worthwhile individual. This view translates into treating yourself with compassion and appreciation and not relying on outside opinions to think well of yourself.

We use the term *healthy self-esteem* instead of *high self-esteem* because we want you to think of your worth as a constant, rather than as something that goes up and down depending on circumstance.

Some examples of what we mean by *enduring healthy self-esteem*:

- Accepting yourself even when you're faced with failure.
- Liking who you are while simultaneously striving for personal development (have a gander at Chapters 8 and 14 for more details).
- Thinking that you're worthwhile and lovable even when a long-term relationship ends.

A lot of people also make the faulty assumption that having good self-esteem makes them impervious to a crisis of confidence or unpleasant feelings. Even if your self-esteem is very robust, you still experience times when your confidence wobbles in your ability to do certain things. Plus, you still experience negative emotions when bad things happen, no matter how healthy your self-esteem happens to be.

Considering common foundations for self-esteem

Very often people assume that their worth is based purely on what they can achieve or what the rest of the world approves of and is impressed by. However, important factors such as your personal values, character traits and unique personality are more accurate and healthy measures.

You may also believe that your level of self-esteem is determined entirely by the quality of your childhood relationships with your parents. Although this idea certainly contains *some* truth, it's not the whole story. Many different types of experiences contribute to your understanding of yourself. Even individuals who have had very negative childhood experiences often manage to develop a robust sense of their own worth. So you're not strictly at the mercy of your past (Chapter 10 is all about this topic).

Rejecting futile strategies for improvement

You may have tried many different strategies to elevate your self-esteem with limited or short-lived success. Common but often problematic strategies people use to try and raise their self-esteem include:

- ✔ Driving themselves to improve their status through professional, academic or financial success.

- ✔ Judging themselves on what others seem to think of them.

- ✔ Striving for approval from other people, such as parents, peers and authority figures.

- ✔ Trying extremely hard to avoid failure and mistakes.

We're not suggesting that these kinds of endeavours are necessarily bad for you. However, linking your self-worth exclusively to such external factors leaves you vulnerable to low self-esteem whenever you're unable to meet your demands. And some strategies inadvertently keep you locked in a cycle of self-judgement and recrimination.

Knowing You're in Charge of Your Self-Esteem

You may believe that self-esteem is something you have or don't have. But in fact the way you feel about yourself is something that you can work towards improving. Good solid self-esteem requires continuous effort and nurturing. Just as responsible parents make efforts to engender a sense of significance and worth in their children, so you can do the same for yourself (investigate Chapters 9 and 15 for more on generating self-esteem through language and having values, respectively).

Throughout this book you find lots of useful information and advice to help you build reliable ways of recognising your own worth.

A note of encouragement

We understand that although you probably genuinely want to develop a more positive opinion of yourself, the whole process can be pretty daunting. Some of the subjects discussed in this chapter and in the rest of the book may be pretty unfamiliar. Many of the techniques we suggest are potentially uncomfortable and challenging.

We'd like you to know that we're really rooting for you. We believe that no matter how severe your low self-esteem issues are, you have reason to be optimistic. The stuff this book contains represents a lot of basic common sense and we've seen it work for lots of people over the years. We don't deny that it takes some hard work and stubborn persistence but the results really will be worth it. We kindly urge you not to give up too soon and to really give it an honest shot. That's why we include plenty of information to help you supercharge your motivation.

Happy reading!

Giving up the rating game

Human beings like to assess things and give them an overall rating: 'that was a great film', 'this meal is terrible' and so on. And assigning static values to certain tangible things can be useful, even things whose values can fluctuate, such as property, products and possessions.

You may find, however, that you give your whole self a global rating (or value) based on a few aspects or even one aspect of yourself – your behaviour at work or your social performance to name but two possibilities. Although this way of assigning value seems to make sense, it's actually very problematic; the result is that your opinion of yourself goes up and down like a yo-yo depending on your most recent experience. For example, if you receive a work promotion, you may decide: 'I'm such a winner!', but then two days later you fail your driving test and conclude: 'I'm such a loser!'. Neither label is accurate or true. Actually the reality is that you're a human being capable of both success *and* failure. No one is wholly good or wholly bad. Everybody has good, bad and neutral aspects to their whole selves.

A fundamental part of developing enduring healthy self-esteem is to stop giving yourself an overall rating on the basis of one or more parts of your overall self (we talk more about this aspect in Chapter 4). Equating 'I've done something bad' with 'I'm a bad person' is inaccurate and overly simplistic: you're throwing the baby out with the bathwater.

You have many hundreds (upon thousands, upon millions!) of various features about yourself, and so trying to give yourself a single, all-encompassing rating – such as 'good' or 'bad', 'weak' or 'strong', 'a success' or 'a failure' – is wholly nonsensical.

Figure 1-1 illustrates just how many different bits and pieces comprise a whole person (and these aspects are just the ones we can fit on the page!) Take a look at the illustration and think about yourself for a minute. How many different things make you the person you are?

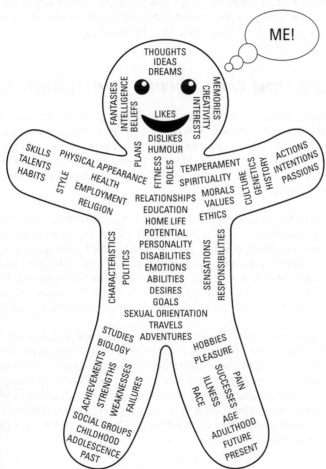

Figure 1-1:
The many aspects of one person.

Instead of trying to categorise your entire person as if you're sorting rotten fruit from unblemished, don't give yourself a rating at all. You're far too complex and multidimensional for that.

You can justifiably rate individual facets of yourself and work to improve on them if doing so is possible, but be clear and specific. Be strict about judging only the value of individual aspects of yourself or your actions – not your entire being. This discrimination allows you to be fair and realistic about what you do or fail to do. Being highly specific in your judgements means that you retain your sense of basic worth while being displeased or dissatisfied with certain parts of yourself. This book expands on this key principle and shows you how using it can promote self-development and enable you to make positive lifestyle changes (explore Chapter 15).

Recognising the vibrant ever-changing you

Some things are static, but you aren't. A chair is a chair and will always be a chair until it becomes firewood. A car is a car until it becomes an old wreck of a car and eventually a heap of car parts. But you change and grow throughout your entire life whether you plan to or not. And because you're a human being, you will at some stage die and become food for worms (sorry if that seems too direct!).

In that interim between birth and death (and we sincerely hope that the interim is long and happy) you perpetually evolve: your interests develop, you age, you acquire new skills, your priorities shift, new friendships are forged, your health changes and so on. Some changes are good and others are less desirable, some within your control and others without. Still, the upshot is that you're *not* a static creature. Nothing that lives – trees, animals or bacteria – remains exactly the same from starting point to end point.

Speaking of points, the one we're trying to make here is that no one can accurately measure or evaluate something that's in a constant state of flux. Therefore stop trying to decide whether you're thoroughly good or bad, adequate or inadequate. You're never going to be able to sustain one global view of yourself because you're always changing. Try thinking of yourself as a work in progress rather than a finished product. As you discover through reading this book, (whatever your age) you always have time for deliberate and positive action.

I'm Okay and You're Not So Bad Yourself

Accepting yourself and accepting other people go hand in hand. One reinforces the other. Everyone has room for growth and improvement. However, assuming responsibility for your own personal development is important, as is letting others take control of their own.

If you can live and work alongside others while accepting them as fallible creatures, you stand a good chance of being able to live with your own faults too. Likewise, you're more readily able to admire and appreciate things in others when you're practised at doing the same with yourself (and vice versa).

We often describe self-esteem as two sides of a coin. Truly holding a compassionate attitude towards yourself, even when things aren't going your way or when you seem to making mistake after mistake, is of enormous help in being able to do the same for others.

When you have healthy self-esteem, you probably enjoy good relationships with other people. Table 1-1 shows some of the attitudes you're likely to exemplify when you have healthy self-esteem and esteem for others.

Table 1-1	Healthy Attitudes towards Yourself and Others
Attitudes towards Yourself	*Attitudes towards Others*
You give others the right to be wrong.	You give yourself the right to be wrong.
You recognise your own faults and weaknesses and still value your own humanity.	You can appreciate that others may hold different opinions, values and beliefs to your own.
You don't see yourself as intrinsically inferior or superior to others.	You observe others with a sense of appreciation or admiration without putting yourself down by comparison.
You maintain your own viewpoint even when others disagree with you.	You take into account the opinion of others and use new information to refine or modify your own opinion if appropriate.

(continued)

Table 1-1 *(continued)*

Attitudes towards Yourself	Attitudes towards Others
You have a healthy desire to be liked and approved of by others but not at the cost of your own ideals, values and personality.	You enjoy the company of others and are also able to enjoy time spent on your own.
You can receive and give a compliment.	You can give and receive constructive criticism.
You rarely denigrate yourself for your mistakes or misdeeds.	You rarely denigrate others for their mistakes or misdeeds.

Clearly, many of the items in this table are 'easier said than done', and some are easier to act in accordance with than others. After all, no one is perfect. In fact, if you're able to say honestly that every item applies to you, you really don't need this book.

We revisit these concepts throughout this book and give you assistance in turning them into regular habits.

Living with Your Limitations

Everybody is dissatisfied with certain aspects of themselves. Some of these aspects you can change and others you just have to live with. For example, you can strive to become more organised, fitter, better educated or to improve your social skills. On the other hand, you're unlikely to have much success trying to make yourself taller, super extroverted if you're naturally shy, or a mathematical genius if maths just isn't your best subject.

You benefit from being realistic about self-development. And your self-esteem benefits when you concentrate your energies on improving in areas where you're most likely to reap results.

You may believe that you just can't change certain things about yourself because doing so seems too hard. But *hard* doesn't equal *impossible*. Feelings and thoughts arising from low self-esteem often prevent people from embarking on a journey from their problems towards recovery. Getting to grips with your individual difficulties (take a peek at Chapter 3) and setting yourself realistic goals is something that we investigate throughout this book. (You can take a look at goal-setting in Chapter 8.)

You can find out how to appreciate plenty of things about yourself (peruse Chapter 6 for more information) and work to maximise or overcome certain aspects of yourself via your own steam. However, if you have quite a severe specific problem – such as addiction, anxiety, phobias or other psychological problems – you may need some professional help, too. The Appendix at the end of this book lists sources of support and recommends additional reading.

Appraising your attributes

Several self-help books and magazines talk about boosting your self-esteem by becoming stronger, younger-looking, wealthier or more popular. The problem we have with this approach is that it conveys the message that you're not worthwhile just as you are. The implication is that the only way to be happy with yourself is to become more impressive to other people.

Although we're all for being goal-orientated, we believe that lasting self-esteem comes from *appreciating what you have*. Instead of focusing solely on what you lack or want to attain, we encourage you to take stock of your good points and maximise them. Why? Quite simply, you feel better about yourself when you concentrate your attention more on what you have going for you than on what you don't.

Again, we don't mean to suggest that anything is wrong with self-improvement – not at all. In fact we strongly recommend it throughout this book. But as a starting-off point, have a look at the positive side of things. If your self-esteem is already at a low ebb, you're at risk of putting yourself down further when you don't take time to look at your good stuff.

We continually emphasise the importance of making changes for the right reasons. Too many people believe things such as: 'If only I could get a good job then I'd have some worth' or 'If only I was more attractive with a devoted partner, I'd have some self-esteem'. These types of ideas are all kinds of wrong. First, they obliquely suggest that only certain types of people in certain situations *deserve* to have healthy self-esteem. Second, things like getting a nice job or a lovely partner can certainly enhance your enjoyment of life and boost your confidence in some areas, but your basic sense of personal worth may remain untouched. You may find that you just move the goalposts. Third, if you do get what you want and do feel better about yourself, your self-esteem is still likely to fall through the floor if you lose the job or the dashing partner.

When you choose a goal or start a plan of self-improvement, make sure that you're doing so purely because you want the benefits. Aiming for goals because you believe that reaching them makes you more worthwhile is a low self-esteem pitfall of the highest order. You're worthwhile right now. So think about things you want to do or change to improve your experience of life.

Managing making mistakes

No one likes making mistakes, certainly no one we've ever met! But everyone does it. Do you know anyone who has *never* made both serious and minor errors in his life? Didn't think so. Mistakes are normal and permissible behaviour among humans. Yet so many people refuse to accept this reality.

Terror about making errors is largely due to what you decide your blunders *mean*. The following examples show some of the unhelpful ways people think about making mistakes, even small ones:

- I can't stand other people knowing that I messed up.
- If I make a big mistake, the result will be total disaster.
- If I'm in a responsible role, mistakes are unacceptable.
- If I were a worthwhile person, I'd get things right.
- I'll never be forgiven for making a mistake.
- Intelligent people don't make mistakes.
- Making mistakes means I'm useless.
- Making silly little mistakes proves I'm an idiot, because they can be avoided.
- Mistakes are a sign of laziness.
- My mistakes are more serious than other people's.
- Other people will think I'm stupid, incompetent or inadequate.

Looking at these common ways of thinking, it's hardly surprising that so many people live in fear of making mistakes. Happily, none of these attitudes is true. Refuse to indoctrinate yourself with such low self-esteem-generating twaddle.

You can't avoid errors altogether (unless you stop living) but you can take the fear out of making them. Bear in mind that if you try overly hard to avoid making mistakes, you may end up also avoiding taking any risks and holding yourself back from doing things that you want to do.

Here's a list of healthy attitudes towards human error – we recap on this a lot throughout this book:

- ✔ Big mistakes are as easy to make as little ones.
- ✔ I prefer to avoid mistakes but I'm a human being and therefore I shouldn't expect to never make any.
- ✔ Many mistakes are repairable in some way.
- ✔ Many mistakes turn out to have hidden benefits.
- ✔ Mistakes are an integral part of discovering a new skill.
- ✔ Mistakes can have very serious consequences but are never the end of the world.
- ✔ No one, no matter how intelligent, is immune to human error.
- ✔ Owning up to my mistakes is likely to prevent me from feeling ashamed of them.

Respecting Your Own Judgement

When your self-esteem isn't great, assuming that other people know better than you is all too easy. The opinions they hold must be more valid than your own, you think. But beware: that's your self-doubt speaking. It tells you: 'Listen to other people! Who the hell do you think you are making your own mind up about stuff!? You're not capable!' If you want to have healthy self-esteem, the time has come to talk back.

Getting vocal

If your internal voice of self-doubt tells you to keep quiet, defy it! Stifling your opinions in social situations for fear of being disagreed with is common among people with poor self-esteem. Such self-censorship may seem like the safest strategy, but the result is that you feel even worse about yourself because you're not getting involved in conversations. You end up feeling left out and isolated. Plus, you're depriving others of the chance to get to know you.

Worse things exist than having your opinion disagreed with. Do you agree with everything you hear your friends discuss? Probably not, whether you speak up or keep your view to yourself. So if you don't expect to agree with everything you hear other people say, why should you think that someone disagreeing with you is so terrible?

Instead of censoring everything you utter, speak your mind. Overcoming the fear of being disagreed with or causing offence is covered throughout this book. In particular we look at ways to challenge negative thoughts associated with low self-esteem in Chapters 5 and 11.

Putting your peers' opinions into perspective

Getting an objective opinion about decisions, plans and so on is often very helpful. Friends can be really useful sources of advice and guidance. However, if you're full of self-doubt, you may well rely too heavily on what other people say and dismiss your own ideas.

The more you turn to others before deciding a course of action, the more you undermine your faith in your own decision-making capabilities. You *can* make up your own mind about important stuff if you give yourself the chance. Your peers are unlikely to have extra information or special powers that render their views superior to your own.

Give yourself a chance to see how your own choices work out. Part of developing healthy self-esteem is realising that you can cope with any negative consequences arising from decisions you've made.

Spending (or dare we say wasting) a lot of time worrying about and second-guessing how others view you is part and parcel of low self-esteem. A term often used to describe excessive worry about being thought of badly by others is *fear of negative evaluation* or FNE for short (turn to Chapter 6 for more on this). In this book we discuss how you can care about other people's opinions (sometimes very much), and yet cease worrying and allowing FNE to interrupt your life.

Chapter 2

Exploring the Effects of Low Self-Esteem

In This Chapter

▶ Looking at psychological disorders perpetuated by low self-esteem

▶ Considering professional help

▶ Understanding low self-esteem as a symptom of other problems

▶ Overcoming overwhelming emotions associated with low self-esteem

*L*ow self-esteem is extremely invasive and can distort your view of every aspect of your life. Frequently, distorted negative thoughts about yourself are symptoms of other problems such as depression or anxiety disorders. At other times, very low self-esteem can cause the development of this type of psychological problem. The situation becomes a 'chicken and egg' conundrum: self-deprecating thoughts lower your mood and decrease your energy and motivation until all these negative thoughts make you depressed or anxious and you're caught in a vicious circle. Breaking the cycle of bad thoughts and bad feelings is difficult but can be done. So don't lose hope!

In this chapter we discuss some of the psychological disorders you may experience if you have self-esteem problems. Although providing in-depth information on how to overcome such disorders is beyond the scope of this book, we do offer some useful information to get you started. (We also include a reading list and resources for professional help in the Appendix.) This chapter also examines some of the most common emotional problems that you may run into and offers strategies for out-running them.

Looking at the Many Ways Low Self-Esteem Can Manifest

You can feel and act on low self-esteem in a number of ways. Critical thoughts about yourself may lead you to:

- ✔ Avoid situations or other people.
- ✔ Endure excessive worry or anxiety.
- ✔ Experience low mood.
- ✔ Feel the temptation to drink excessively or rely on drugs.

 You may try a variety of behaviours to help alleviate the unpleasant feelings caused by your low self-esteem, but sometimes the strategies you use can cause even greater problems in the long run. The disorders we discuss in the next sections are made worse by continued social withdrawal, avoidance, substance misuse and excessive worry. Low self-esteem is often both a potential cause *and* a symptom of these disorders.

These disorders are complex and can vary greatly in severity. Indeed complete books have been written on each of these disorders and we can't cover them in depth in this chapter. We include them here in order to help you do three things:

1. **Recognise the symptoms or defining features of these disorders.**

2. **Give you some useful tips and encouragement to get further support if you recognise symptoms in yourself.**

3. **Understand that your low self-esteem may be a symptom of another problem.**

Digging out depression

Depression is a mood disorder characterised by a persistent low mood that's present most of the time. Depression is very unpleasant and can be extremely debilitating; it's also among the most commonly experienced psychiatric problems today.

The key diagnostic features of depression include:

- ✔ Depressed mood for most of the day, for more days than not (over a period of two weeks or more).

- ✔ Feelings of hopelessness, helplessness and dread. (*Dread* can include feeling like something is wrong but you can't quite put your finger on what it is.)

- ✔ Insomnia or sleeping all the time.

- ✔ Loss of interest and enjoyment derived from previously rewarding activities.

- ✔ Low energy and fatigue.

- ✔ Low self-esteem.

- ✔ Poor appetite or overeating.

- ✔ Poor concentration and difficulty making decisions.

Seeking help is smart

If your problems seem too severe for you to deal with on your own, get help sooner rather than later. If you've been battling symptoms of depression, Body Dysmorphic Disorder (which we cover in more detail in the later section 'Busting body-image problems'), eating disorders or anxiety (or any other emotional or psychological problem) for two months or more, you probably can benefit from some professional support. Symptoms that begin to interfere with your work, relationships and day-to-day functioning are also indications that you need to seek further help.

Your GP is a good first port of call. He or she may be able to prescribe appropriate medication or refer you to a psychiatrist who can. Cognitive behavioural therapy (CBT) is widely considered to be the most effective psychotherapy treatment for general psychiatric disorders. Often CBT and medications are used in conjunction. Your GP may be able to refer you for CBT treatment. If not, you can also contact the professional bodies listed in the Appendix to find a CBT therapist in your area. Ensure that you select a qualified and accredited therapist. Looking for a therapist with experience of working with your specific difficulties is also a good idea. (If you're interested, you can read more in *Cognitive Behavioural Therapy For Dummies* (Wiley), by yours truly.)

Don't allow your low self-esteem to stop you seeking the help you need. You may have thoughts like: 'Other people need help more than I do' or 'I'm wasting people's time'. Ignore your critical internal musings. You deserve help and support as much as anyone else. Also, don't let feelings of embarrassment or shame get in the way. You're not the only person with your type of problem; otherwise all those experts who are used to hearing about all sorts of difficulties wouldn't exist! Most GPs and mental health professionals are sympathetic and understanding about whatever you're experiencing.

If you have three or more of the symptoms in this list you may have depression. If your symptoms have been present for several weeks, a period of months or even longer, you're even more likely to be depressed. You can use the techniques discussed in this chapter and the rest of the book to help overcome your depressed feelings. However, when you feel overwhelmed and self-help seems to be too daunting or of minimal impact, see your GP.

Mild or moderate episodes of depression can sometimes resolve themselves of their own accord without the need for professional help. In other cases, however, the symptoms can drag on for much longer and the help of a medical professional can be invaluable.

If you're depressed, you may feel slightly brighter at certain times of the day or notice that your mood is much lower at specific times. Some depressed people report that mornings are the worst and evenings are more bearable. Others experience the symptoms the other way around.

Because low self-esteem is a diagnostic criterion of depression, a lot of your negative thoughts about yourself may diminish as your depression is treated. Recognising that low self-esteem is a key symptom of depression may help you to understand that your negative thoughts about yourself are produced by your depressed state and aren't accurate reflections of reality.

You can use the following tips to help pull yourself out of depression. They may not magically transform your mood but they certainly don't do you any harm and may well prevent your depression from worsening.

✔ Take regular exercise such as swimming or walking. Aim for about 20 minutes a day if you can (the more vigorous the exercise, the more 'feel good' chemicals your brain releases).

✔ Make a schedule of daily tasks and go from one task to the next however daunting it may seem. You may have to grit your teeth and pull yourself through the motions at first. Include household chores such as washing up and opening the post. Allocate a specific time slot to each task.

✔ Regulate your sleep pattern. Try to get up, dressed and out of the house by a certain time every day, regardless of how dreadful you feel. Things tend to look brighter when you're out of bed and out in the world. Avoid naps during the day because they can disrupt your sleep at night and in some cases lower your mood further. Take scheduled rests instead.

✔ Eat well. Take regular healthy meals and drink plenty of water.

✔ Be wary of using alcohol for temporary relief. Excessive drinking can become a problem itself and increase depressive symptoms in the longer term.

✔ Engage with others. Friends and family may be able to help out practically or emotionally. Being with people can distract you fr your negative thoughts and shift your perspective for the better. Even if you find generating conversation difficult and think that you're a 'wet blanket', socialising is often far better for you than being on your own with your negative feelings and thoughts.

✔ Consider psychotherapy (see the earlier 'Seeking help is smart' sidebar and the recommended reading in the Appendix) and/or medication. Certain forms of depression respond very well to the right kind of medication. Many different types of antidepressants are available, and so if you've tried one before that didn't work or the side effects were unpleasant, another type may suit you better. Don't hesitate to talk to your GP if your symptoms are severe.

If you're having suicidal thoughts and feel at risk, let a close friend or family member know and seek professional help *immediately*.

Grappling with grief

Grief is an extremely profound and ubiquitous human experience. You can't get through life without experiencing a significant loss sometime along the way – at least we've never met such a fortunate person. Because it impacts everyone, grief is a very big topic.

We don't claim to cover all there is to be explored about grief in this section but instead focus on the points that can tie into self-esteem issues.

The pain of grief associated with the loss of a loved one is natural and normal. Some of the symptoms that accompany a normal grief reaction bear similarities to those of clinical depression (see the preceding, 'Digging Out Depression' section). Common symptoms reported by people faced with bereavement include:

✔ Profound sadness and tearfulness

✔ Loss of interest in previously enjoyed activities

✔ Social withdrawal

✔ Agitation

✔ Reduced ability to function (carry out daily activities)

✔ Sleep disturbances

✔ Changes in appetite

✔ Feeling disconnected or separate from the rest of the world

In the majority of cases these symptoms gradually resolve themselves without the need for professional treatment or medication.

Natural recovery time depends somewhat on the nature of the loss and the circumstances surrounding it. In most cases the symptoms begin to diminish within about two to four months, although it can take longer.

Usually the bereaved individual slowly re-engages with the routine of everyday life and re-invests in other relationships as she adjusts to the loss of her loved one. The acute pain experienced immediately after the loss starts to dull and becomes more tolerable, although painful emotions are likely to resurge when memories are triggered by events like birthdays, anniversaries or other types of reminders.

Some of the types of losses people often find most difficult to adjust to and recover from typically include:

- ✔ Very sudden loss through accidents or previously undetected illnesses
- ✔ The death of children (or friends and relatives younger than the bereaved person)
- ✔ Death by suicide
- ✔ Death occurring from violence
- ✔ Multiple losses (such as the loss of several family members through accident)

Sometimes the grieving process can get complicated, not only in cases like those just listed but also in response to any loss, whatever the circumstances. Complicated grieving can often give rise to problematic, painful emotions, such as guilt, depression and anxiety, which may interrupt natural adjustment and recovery.

How does this relate to self-esteem? Many people have mixed emotions in response to a loved one's death. People may feel relieved, angry, sad and hurt all at the same time. Often people assume that they should not bear any ill feeling towards the deceased or continue to enjoy life in their loved one's absence.

Here are two examples of how natural grief can get complicated and impact on self-esteem:

✔ Gavin's mother died of cancer after a long period of illness. Because his brother lives abroad and his father died ten years before, Gavin acted as a carer for his mother. He looked after her virtually every day for a year until she eventually entered a hospice a few weeks before her death. Gavin reduced his work hours and really limited his social life in order to provide essential care for his mum. Gavin's mum was in a lot of pain prior to her death and was often ill tempered and hard to please.

She also missed her other son living abroad and often complained to Gavin that she'd be happier if only she could see him. Though Gavin loved his mother dearly they had a difficult relationship when he was growing up. His mother seemed to prefer Gavin's brother and often seemed disappointed with Gavin's accomplishments. Gavin experienced his mother as critical and disapproving for much of his life. When his mother died, Gavin began experiencing a lot of conflicting emotions:

- Relieved that his mum is at peace and no longer in pain.

- Guilty about feeling personally relieved that he no longer has to devote all his time to looking after her.

- Hurt that his mother wanted so much to see his brother and seemed to disregard how much Gavin was doing for her.

- Angry and resentful about the sacrifices he made to care for his mother.

- Deeply saddened about losing his mother.

- Anxious about doing anything his mother would disapprove of, despite the fact that she is no longer alive.

All these emotions are normal and understandable. But Gavin doesn't think so. He believes that he should not bear any residual ill feelings towards his mother and that he should only feel sadness. Gavin thinks that his mixed feelings mean that he's a bad son and a wicked person. He also makes things more difficult for himself by frequently assessing his actions, both personally and professionally, according to what he imagines his mother would think about them.

Because of his self-recrimination for having mixed feelings about his mother's death, Gavin's self-esteem suffers. He thinks that if he were a worthwhile, decent person he'd only have feelings of loss and would focus on pleasant memories. Gavin's tendency to imagine his mother disapproving of many aspects of how he lives his life means that he lacks confidence in his ability to make reasonable decisions. He chips away at his own self-esteem by concluding that if he were worthwhile and capable then he'd be sure that he was doing things that would win his mother's approval.

✔ June was involved in a road traffic accident. She was driving the car and survived the crash with few serious injuries. June's sister, who was a passenger in the car, was killed. In the months that followed the accident June felt tremendous grief over the loss of her sister with whom she was very close. Two years later, June still misses her sister very much. She often thinks about what her sister would be doing now had she also survived the crash.

Although June knows that investigations have indicated that the accident was not her fault, she experiences intense guilt almost daily. June also feels depressed although she has a satisfying life and is soon to be married.

Some of the thoughts that underlie June's guilty and depressed feelings:

- Whenever June is having a good time she remembers her sister and feels guilty. June thinks that she shouldn't be enjoying herself and that she is selfish to do so because her sister isn't alive to share in it.

- Conversely, whenever she is in a low mood June also feels guilty because she tells herself that she should be living life to the full on behalf of her dead sister.

- June feels guilty about getting married and starting a family because her sister died before she was able to do the same.

- June's depressed feelings come from her belief that she is somewhat responsible for her sister's death and because she can't accept that what happened was a deeply unfortunate and regrettable but random event.

Because she was the driver of the car, June is mistakenly taking responsibility for the death of her sister. Because she keeps thinking of the accident as her responsibility, she feels both guilty and depressed. June believes that if she lets go of her self-blame she will be betraying her sister. June also keeps using her sister's untimely death as a yardstick for deciding how she ought to feel in situations.

June feels bad and worthless for engaging in life when her sister can't do the same. Yet she also puts herself into a double bind by telling herself that she should be living on behalf of her sister. Guilt and self-blame take a toll on June's overall sense of worth. June's self-esteem is likely to remain poor until she accepts the circumstances surrounding her sister's death and gives herself permission to enjoy life despite the tragic death of her sister.

As these two examples illustrate, grief and loss can influence the way you think about yourself and have implications for your self-esteem.

You can help yourself overcome complications arising from grief by reminding yourself of these points:

- Feeling a mixture of emotions in response to the loss of a loved one is normal and doesn't mean that you're doing anything wrong or unnatural.

- The loved ones you've lost would most probably wish you to enjoy your life.

- You can't do someone else's living for her, no matter how deeply you miss her. So you're best off focusing on living your own life and throwing yourself into your own experiences.

- If you crave the approval of someone who is no longer alive you'll probably benefit from letting go of that now. Trying to live up to the standards or expectations of someone who is no longer around only serves to keep you perpetually focused on your loss. It also destabilises your self-esteem because you can never get approval from someone who is no longer alive. Basing your self-worth on the hypothetical opinions of a deceased person is strikingly similar to doing the same with someone yet living. Both are faulty ways of deciding how to feel about yourself (more on this in Chapter 6).

As we say, we can't cover every possible grief reaction in this brief section. So much depends on the circumstances of the loss. However, if you're having trouble adjusting to a recent bereavement or you think that part of your low self-esteem issues are related to a loss, you may wish to see a professional to help you resolve things and move on. Many therapists will have experience of helping people make sense of loss and process associated emotions. There are also specialist services that deal exclusively with grief. You can find sources for professional support in the Appendix of this book.

Sussing out social phobia

If you suffer from low self-esteem you probably worry a lot about the impression you make upon other people. You may imagine social rejection lurking around every corner. You may feel so anxious about going into a social setting that you avoid doing so or become a bag of nerves when you do. On top of that you may also fret about others noticing your shaking hands, faltering speech or sweating and thinking that you're weird. These symptoms of the recognised psychiatric disorder called *social phobia* or *social anxiety* can be very disabling and distressing.

Avoiding social interaction entirely is difficult and so most socially anxious people develop coping mechanisms or *safety behaviours*, which help them to feel safer in situations where they believe that they're being scrutinised or negatively judged.

Unfortunately, although safety behaviours may make you feel better in the short term, in the long run they keep you trapped in your anxiety because they prevent you from realising that you *can* survive anxiety without using them. They also stop you recognising that many of the negative predictions you make about social interaction (that you're going to be rejected or ridiculed, for example) don't actually happen. (See Chapter 11 for more information about testing out negative predictions.) Common safety behaviours include:

- ✔ Avoiding direct eye contact when involved in conversation.
- ✔ Avoiding unfamiliar social settings and meeting new people.
- ✔ Drinking alcohol to quell nervousness.
- ✔ Fidgeting with things such as your phone, clothing or other objects to hide your awkwardness.
- ✔ Keeping to the outside of a social group (sitting in corners or out of the limelight).
- ✔ Keeping your opinions to yourself and being vigilant about not saying anything offensive or silly.
- ✔ Monitoring yourself for obvious signs of anxiety, such as sweating, blushing, shaking and so on.
- ✔ Preparing what you're going to say in your head.
- ✔ Taking friends, family or partners to accompany you in social situations.
- ✔ Thinking a lot about how others see you and guessing about their opinions of you.
- ✔ Trying very hard to 'fit in'.

Many more possible safety behaviours exist. Try making a list of all the things you do (including what you do in your head) in order to cope with your anxiety in social situations. The knowledge gained gives you a good starting point for managing your anxiety more effectively.

Trying very hard to stop anxiety is what tends to keep it going. If you drop your safety behaviours and just tolerate your anxiety until it reduces of its own accord (which it does over time) your confidence eventually increases.

Wanting others to accept and like you is natural and normal, especially people whose opinions you value and respect. However, *everyone* liking you simply isn't possible. You can't be everyone's cup of tea without sacrificing all the idiosyncratic features that make you unique.

When you have social anxiety, you're highly likely to place too much importance on what others think of you. Practise adopting some of the statements in the following list to help you put the opinions of others into a more helpful perspective:

- ✔ I'd like to be accepted by everyone I meet but I don't *need* to be.
- ✔ I don't want people to think I'm weird but if they do, that's too bad, I'll live.
- ✔ I don't like people judging me negatively but it doesn't make me less worthwhile as a person.
- ✔ I hate being thought of as weird but it's certainly not the worst thing in the world.
- ✔ I really dislike the idea of people thinking bad things about me but I can stand it.
- ✔ I can choose to reject people's opinion even if they think badly of me.
- ✔ I'm still a basically okay person even if someone dislikes me.

Social anxiety can become a real obstacle to getting on with your life. Over time severe social avoidance can lead to depression. Psychotherapy can really help, as can properly prescribed medication. If your anxiety is interfering significantly with your daily functioning, consider seeking professional support (check out the earlier 'Seeking help is smart' sidebar and the recommended reading in the Appendix).

Busting body-image problems

Body-image problems are common among men and women alike. Although you may dislike or downright despise aspects of your appearance, *Body Dysmorphic Disorder* (BDD) is a somewhat different kettle of fish. People suffering from BDD typically become preoccupied with one aspect of their appearance and experience extreme distress as a result. BDD goes beyond average body-image problems to the point of being all consuming and, when severe, interferes greatly with normal life. (We take a closer look at body-image problems in Chapter 7.)

Symptoms of BDD include:

- Preoccupation with an *imagined* defect in appearance (skin, teeth, facial features, hair, scars and face shape are common areas of focus). Even if a slight flaw or imperfection does exist, the BDD sufferer's concern about it is extreme and excessive.

- Worry about the physical imperfection, causing extreme distress and preventing the sufferer from engaging in normal activities, such as socialising, school, work and, in extreme cases, leaving the house.

- Reassurance from others that the defect doesn't exist or is very insignificant fails to help end the BDD sufferer's worry and distress.

- Increase in desperation, depression and shockingly poor self-esteem. People with BDD often think of themselves as repulsive, monstrous or hideous because of their perceived appearance. They may also go to great lengths to try to hide the perceived flaw.

Common coping strategies include:

- Attempting to get rid of the defect by using cosmetic remedies or personal grooming tools (often causing damage to the area).

- Avoiding being seen by others and hiding away indoors.

- Checking the defect in the mirror almost constantly or avoiding mirrors.

- Dressing to mask the area of dissatisfaction and draw attention to other parts of the body.

- Feeling and touching the area of dissatisfaction to check if it has changed or worsened.

- Seeking repeated reassurance from others that the imperfection isn't obvious (although never feeling reassured no matter what others say).

- Taking excessive amounts of time to get ready to go out in public (sometimes hours).

- Wearing heavy make-up.

The problem with trying to mask, detract attention from or fix a physical dissatisfaction is that the behaviour keeps you focused on it all the more. The perceived defect becomes bigger and more important in your mind, and your distress is likely to get worse rather than better. As with many anxiety disorders, your attempts to cope with your worries about your appearance actually perpetuate the problem.

Happily, BDD is steadily becoming more recognised as a disorder and help is out there. If you think that you have symptoms of BDD, get some professional help (see the 'Seeking help is smart' sidebar earlier in this chapter and the recommended literature in the Appendix). A course of self-help may be sufficient if your symptoms are mild, but don't hesitate to seek professional therapy if you think you need to.

People with BDD often consider plastic surgery. In many cases this fails to solve the problem because the surgery results fail to satisfy or the sufferer thinks the problem has been made worse. In some cases the focus of preoccupation and dissatisfaction shifts to another part of the body. We strongly advise leaving drastic measures such as surgery alone until you have some appropriate therapy.

Exorcising eating disorders

Like the other disorders discussed in this chapter, eating disorders can be mild, moderate or severe and exist in many forms.

Prizing the rail-thin unreality

More girls than boys fall prey to conditions in which they try to get their bodies to an unnatural and unhealthy thinness, although eating disorders such as anorexia and bulimia nervosa are on the rise in young males. Eating problems are generally spotted more readily in females and may be overlooked in males (by family members and health professionals) because they just don't expect to find them. Males are sometimes also more reluctant to disclose an eating disorder because they're commonly viewed as a 'female problem'. Boys and men may be diagnosed with other disorders such as depression when really they primarily suffer from an eating disorder. If you're male and you think you have an eating disorder, do seek help. The conditions involving an unhealthy relationship with food are strikingly similar in both sexes. Most professionals are very sympathetic and understanding about eating issues, whatever your gender.

Looking at how eating disorders show themselves

Eating disorders come in different types. Common eating disorders include:

✔ **Anorexia nervosa:** a condition in which you restrict your food intake and may exercise excessively in order to burn off calories and lose weight.

✔ **Bulimia:** a condition in which you tend to have recurrent binge-eating incidents in which you consume large amounts of food. Afterwards you may induce vomiting to purge yourself of what you've eaten. Or you may have periods of restricting food intake, in order to make up for a binge, but not induce vomiting.

A primary diagnostic criterion for eating disorders is 'undue influence of body weight and/or shape on self-evaluation'. In other words, if you have an eating disorder (however severe) you probably judge your worth on your weight and your body shape to the exclusion of other aspects of yourself.

Discovering how to appreciate your whole self and not just your physical self is one part of overcoming an eating disorder.

If your eating issue is fairly mild you may be able to recover entirely through self-help. On the other hand, you may think that you need some professional help to get you back on the straight and narrow with your eating. Check out the following list of behaviours and symptoms and see how many apply to you:

✔ Being underweight for your age, height and build.

✔ Being very fearful of gaining weight or becoming fat.

✔ Binge eating.

✔ Constantly checking and thinking about your body weight and shape.

✔ Eating as few calories as possible per day despite hunger pangs, headaches or fatigue (some anorexic people eat less than 500 calories per day).

✔ Examining your body for signs of fat or checking that you can feel or see certain bones to reassure yourself that you haven't gained any weight.

✔ Exercising to excess and solely for the purpose of weight loss (excessive exercise means more than an hour or two per day). Also, exercising in a strict and ritualistic manner such as doing jumping jacks before bed.

✔ Feeling very guilty and angry when you eat a forbidden food or have too many calories.

✔ Inducing vomiting to purge food from your body.

✔ Missing menstrual periods (in women).

✔ Obsessively counting calories and/or weighing portions.

✔ Restricting your diet to certain foods that you think are safe because they contain few calories.

✔ Saving up calories for certain foods or meals.

✔ Vicarious eating. This involves feeding other people and encouraging them to eat foods you won't allow yourself to eat.

✔ Striving to lose more weight despite being at a low weight for your age, height and build.

✔ Using laxatives to purge food from your body.

✔ Using rituals around eating such as being strict about mealtimes, chewing your food a certain number of times, always leaving a bit on your plate or refusing to eat in public.

✔ Weighing yourself every day or several times per day.

If you recognise even one or two of these symptoms, you may have a serious eating problem. Bingeing, purging and being chronically underweight can result in serious health problems. Being underfed can lead to depression and other mental health difficulties. Don't allow your fears about gaining weight to stop you seeking medical and psychological help: often, the earlier you get help, the easier your recovery.

Consuming for comfort

Whilst some people under-eat because they prize a thin body too highly, others over-eat. Common reasons for eating too much or binge eating include:

✔ To combat feelings of loneliness or boredom

✔ To quell uncomfortable emotions like anxiety, guilt, anger and sadness

✔ As a reward for getting through a difficult task or experience

✔ Habit

Comfort eating is a term commonly used to describe the nature of over-eating. If you suffer from low self-esteem, you may eat to try to escape from negative thoughts about yourself and to alleviate nasty feelings (just as other people may turn to cigarettes, alcohol or drugs).

The problem is that you may also give yourself a very hard time for lacking self-discipline around food and for being overweight. So the food solution becomes a self-esteem depleting problem in the long run. Carrying too much weight and having poor nutritional eating habits can also have serious health implications.

Over-eating is very common and though it may not seem to carry as much psychiatric clout as eating disorders that involve self-starvation, health professionals take it very seriously. If you think that you eat for comfort, speak to your GP and ask to be referred to a dietician. You may also want to get some extra help and support from a therapist experienced in working with people who over-eat.

Examining Excruciating Emotions

You've probably already noticed just how toxic low self-esteem can be. It pollutes your thinking to such an extent that you may feel you've little room in your head for any other form of thought. (You may want to read Chapter 5 for extra information about dealing with negative thoughts.) Unfortunately, a lot of unpleasant emotional experiences arise with negative thinking. The more extreme and negative your view of yourself, the more intense and disabling your emotions are likely to be. On a positive note, the more work you do on developing healthy self-esteem, the less emotional discomfort you're prey to.

Shooting down shame

Shame is a really corrosive emotion associated with the idea (or reality) that something undesirable has been publicly revealed about you. The information revealed may be of little importance or interest to other people, but you're *personally* deeply ashamed of it and assume that everyone is going to shun you. You may feel like crawling under the carpet, digging a hole and diving into it, or running away.

Shame is an *interpersonal* emotion, which means that it requires an audience to take hold; and that audience can be just one other person or a group of people with whom you're associated.

You can be ashamed of just about anything – aspects of your past and current flaws, failures, mistakes, rejections or behaviour can all be potential sources of shame.

If your self-esteem is low, you may be ashamed of many things about yourself or your life (past and present). Low self-esteem readily creates shame because you assume that you're not worth much in the first place. If other people find out undesirable things about you then you may believe that they 'see you for what you really are'. The chances are that you're attaching major importance to relatively minor events. Even if the event is a major one, you're probably shaming yourself because you think that the event *defines* you.

Life events or aspects of yourself (however major) are only ever one part of your whole self.

Here are just a few broad examples of common shame subjects:

- Events from the past (even as far back as early childhood): Details about your family history, domestic or other forms of abuse, adoption, abortion, having been in prison, coming from a deprived background, being a victim of crime.

- Mental or emotional health problems and physical illness (past or present).

- Mistakes, rejections and failures (past or present): Being dumped, failing an exam, being fired, being divorced, being bullied, having financial debt or going bankrupt, being involved in an accident.

- Personal conduct (past or present): Social *faux pas*, poor job performance, losing your temper, treating another poorly, being pushed around, showing fear or crying in public, letting others down.

Because shame causes you to hide away from others, you may not recognise attempts to make you feel better. Your friends, family or colleagues may be trying to forget about the recent event and get back to normal ways of relating. Or the information revealed may not have changed their view of you at all and they're behaving perfectly normally. But unless you remain within the group you can't accurately judge the situation. Instead you're left with your own thoughts about what other people may be thinking about you in light of your recent disclosure or behaviour. Hiding away with your negative thoughts can lead to further shame and make the situation worse than it needs to be.

Instead of hiding away, remain in contact with the social group in question. Allow yourself time to get over the incident but try to get back to normal as soon as possible by following these tips:

- Allow people to raise the issue for further discussion but don't get drawn into making excuses or excessive justification. Sometimes talking openly about something you feel ashamed of can help to dissolve your shame and give you a more balanced perspective on things.

- Keep your head high and make eye contact.

✔ Pardon yourself (or anyone else responsible for making the information public) and resist any urge to punish or seek revenge.

✔ Remind yourself that the information or event is probably far more important to you than to other people.

✔ Respond positively to attempts to get back to normal ways of relating.

✔ Tolerate your uncomfortable feelings and realise that however strongly you may be feeling right now, that feeling's going to pass.

✔ Treat yourself with compassion. You're only human after all. Everyone has their own 'shameful secrets' and so you're no different from anyone else.

The event itself isn't what makes you feel ashamed. Instead, your shame results from what you decide the event means about you. Even if others react differently towards you for a period of time after something 'secret' has been revealed, you can choose not to feel ashamed. By refusing to condemn yourself you can turn shame into healthy regret, a far less painful emotion.

Get a piece of paper and write at the top the event of which you're ashamed, whether it's recent or from long ago. Record your shame-producing thoughts in one column. In another column, try to construct a more balanced and accepting counter-argument. The examples in Table 2-1 may help you along.

Table 2-1 Sample Shame and Self-Acceptance Statements

Shame Thought	Self-Acceptance Argument
This makes me a freak.	No it doesn't. I'm a fallible human being and having negative experiences is normal. It's also normal to feel badly about them but they don't mean anything about my worth and they don't make me a freak.
This shouldn't have happened.	Well, unfortunately it did. I can't undo the past – all I can do is accept it, come to terms with it and move on with my life. Being ashamed just keeps me trapped in bad feelings and memories.
I'll never live this down.	Of course I will. It may be uncomfortable for a while but it will pass. Instead of dwelling on the event and thinking bad things about myself, I can focus on my present and my future.
If people find out, I'll be rejected.	I don't know for sure that people will reject me. People may be far more understanding and compassionate than I think. This event probably means a lot more to me than it does to anyone else. It would be painful if some people were to reject me but I can still carry on and enjoy my life.

Shame can often prevent people from getting help for more serious problems. You may be ashamed of your depression because you think that you should be able to get over it on your own or that being depressed makes you 'weak'. You may think that your haunting worries about some aspect of your appearance make you a superficial person. You may worry that others agree with your concerns about your looks or mock you. Or you may believe that something's deeply wrong with you for having such problems. Stamp on your shame-producing thoughts before they stop you in your tracks.

Eroding embarrassment

Embarrassment shares some similarities with shame but generally is less intense and doesn't last as long. In fact, a little embarrassment can be healthy because it helps you to behave in socially acceptable ways.

People with low self-esteem, however, can be very easily embarrassed and find the experience much more uncomfortable than those with healthy self-esteem. If you're someone who's very prone to feelings of embarrassment you may try to avoid situations that bring attention upon you. This avoidance means that you miss out on some enjoyable aspects of life such as socialising and also that you keep your opinions to yourself and are reluctant to ask questions or attempt new activities.

You can make yourself less susceptible to embarrassment through regular practice. Try biting the bullet and taking risks such as cracking a joke, offering your opinion on a contentious subject, deliberately asking a stupid question, singing karaoke *really badly*, dancing like an untamed thing or taking up a sport such as roller-skating that holds huge potential for lots of embarrassing spills. Discover how to laugh at yourself by not taking yourself or your performance too seriously. Putting yourself into lots of 'embarrassing' situations on a regular basis can really help you to see the lighter side of gaffs and 'foot in the mouth' moments. Remember that looking foolish and behaving foolishly doesn't make you a fool. Repeated practice may help you understand that you *can* recover from embarrassment and move on unscathed.

Gouging out guilt

Guilt generally comes after breaking your moral code in some way. You may have done something that you believe is wrong or bad or failed to do something that your moral code dictates is right and proper. The first scenario is called a *sin of commission* and the second is called a *sin of omission*. Both can lead to feelings of guilt.

Guilt can paralyse you and prevent you from making appropriate amends for your misdeed. Most people who suffer from frequent bouts of guilt hold a rigid belief that they must *never* transgress their moral code at anytime and further conclude that they're bad people when they do so. Having a strong moral code needn't be detrimental to your emotional health. Guilt can be very painful; it leads to self-recrimination and punishment. You may believe that you're 'unforgivable' and that your reprehensible behaviour can't be made better. In addition, guilt may lead you to hide away or to beg for forgiveness. Rarely does guilt encourage you to try to remedy the situation in a measured and effective manner.

People with more robust self-esteem generally hold a more realistic belief such as, 'It's bad to break my moral code but it's possible to do so. I'm still a worthwhile person even if I sometimes do the wrong thing.' This flexible way of thinking tends to lead to strong but healthy feelings of remorse when you do break your moral code. Remorse can be intense but it encourages you to make amends and forgive yourself.

People with low self-esteem also often take undue responsibility for events in their lives or blame themselves entirely for other people's reactions. If you're one of these people you may find that you often feel guilty about things that upon reflection aren't your fault at all. Practise being more objective about your actions and take into account other factors that may have contributed to the event. Chapter 13 includes a section on using a responsibility pie chart that can also be used to combat guilt.

Guilt is particularly corrosive to self-esteem. Serious effort may be necessary to overcome years of guilt-producing beliefs, but you can succeed if you're prepared to work at it.

The next time you feel very guilty about something you've done or failed to do, use the following list to help you move from grotesque guilt to reasonable remorse:

- ✔ Adopt a flexible personal rule about transgressing your moral code that allows for your human fallibility such as: 'Ideally I won't break my moral code', 'I strongly desire to keep to my moral code', 'Keeping my moral code is highly preferable' or 'I strive to always uphold my moral code'.

- ✔ Apologise or make up for your sin if possible and appropriate. Accept forgiveness from others and don't seek punishment.

- ✔ Condemn your sin but *not* yourself. Use arguments such as: 'A bad deed does not a bad person make', 'I'm worthwhile despite wrongdoing', 'What I've done is wrong but I deserve forgiveness' and 'All human beings are imperfect and capable of committing bad deeds'.

Feeling the burn of blushing

All human beings have the capacity to blush. Blushing or going red is a normal physical response often associated with shame, embarrassment and guilt. You may also blush from pleasure, nervousness or pride.

Blushing is a pretty standard thing to do but many people have a real problem with it. For some, this problem develops into a full-blown phobia. We don't claim to know all the possible reasons why people have a fear of blushing, but we've heard quite a few explanations from our clients. Different people have said that blushing:

✔ Causes people to notice that I blush and they think I'm weird.

✔ Causes teasing, which is intolerable.

✔ Draws people's attention to my anxiety.

✔ Is a sign of immaturity.

✔ Is a sign of weakness.

✔ Makes me look inept and inadequate.

✔ Makes me look unattractive.

✔ Shows others that I have no confidence in myself.

✔ Shows that I'm vulnerable and people may take advantage of that.

The thing about blushing is that the more you try to control or stop it, the more self-conscious you become and (not surprisingly) the more likely you are to blush! Like other physical feelings and emotions, blushing passes naturally if you let it do so.

Focus on any behaviours you use to reduce blushing, and try to drop them. Splashing water on your face, wearing lightweight clothing or wearing heavy make-up are all common strategies.

The more you interfere with your blushing the more aware of it you become. Just let it be. Many people assume that they go much redder than they actually do because they focus so much on the sensation of blushing that they assume they must be absolutely puce! Chapter 5 has some useful tips about finding out how to focus your attention where you want it.

Chapter 3

Working Out Your Self-Worth

*H*uman beings are complex and ever-changing, going through several developmental stages from birth to death. Throughout your life your aspirations, knowledge, abilities, priorities, interests and personal ideology alter according to new experiences and increased maturity. No doubt your living circumstances have changed more than once as well.

As you grow and develop, you become responsible for meeting your own basic survival needs, your work life becomes more prominent and your relationships change. During this development, you may come to judge yourself based on your success in one particular area or domain. This tendency can be perilous to your self-esteem because things can go wrong due to external events beyond your control as well as through your own actions.

In this chapter, we encourage you to investigate whether or not you're putting too much emphasis on one or two domains to the exclusion of others, and doing your self-esteem damage in the process. We also look at how society tends to assess individual worth and point out ways to develop your own assessment criteria. This chapter aims to help you become the boss of your own self-opinion.

Figuring Out What Makes You Worthwhile

Based on the ever-changing nature of living, you probably understand that many different facets of your being make you who you are today. All too frequently, however, people focus on one facet of themselves and decide that this singular feature sums them up entirely. This focus is reflected in statements such as: 'I'm a lawyer', 'I'm a single mother', 'I'm an alcoholic', 'I'm a criminal', 'I'm a family man', 'I'm unemployed' and so on. Broad areas of your life that encompass one or more important roles you play (such as parent and partner) are called *domains*.

The truth is that however prominent a particular aspect of yourself or your lifestyle may be, you're never just one thing. Instead, you're an elaborate composition of all the different dimensions of your existence: past, present and future. This section helps you to understand the dangers of judging your worth on the 'success' of particular domains in your life.

So, although judging your overall worth on one area of your life or a set of behaviours is common, it's also overly simplistic because it fails to account for all the other millions of features that comprise you. Far better for your psychological wellbeing is to understand that just through being alive you have intrinsic worth and value.

Digging into domains

Basically, the word *domain* describes broad areas of your life. Figure 3.1, which shows the most common domains, makes this point clear.

Understandably you strive to keep all domains of your life ticking over nicely. Equally understandably, you're at your most content when your basic needs are adequately met and you're experiencing satisfaction in all the other domains illustrated in Figure 3-1. That's perfectly normal and fine.

However, if you aren't able to keep things hunky-dory in all domains and you unrealistically expect that you should be able to, your self-esteem may well suffer. We say 'unrealistically' because some of your domains are bound to take the occasional knock. For example, you may lose your job, have an argument with your spouse, your house may burn down, you may become ill or fall out with a close friend – life happens. We sincerely hope these bad events don't befall you (or us for that matter!), but the reality is that no one is immune to negative events. Certainly do what you can to minimise the risk of bad things happening, but even your best efforts to protect yourself from tragedy and mishap don't guarantee immunity. (Check out Chapter 8 for more on personal development.)

Falling into the trap of focusing almost exclusively on one or two domains of your life is all too easy – for example, linking your self-esteem to success in work and love. Significant drawbacks exist to identifying yourself too closely with one or two domains of your life:

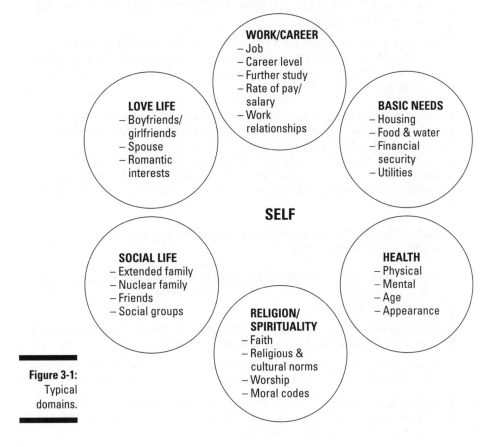

Figure 3-1:
Typical
domains.

✔ You may end up blaming yourself for events outside of your control. For example, you can't anticipate or control your house flooding or the company you work for going bust, and so your self-worth may take a hit if it's tied to providing a nice home or bringing in a certain amount of money.

✔ You may fail to acknowledge successes in other domains of your life that can help you to appreciate life more fully and keep a balanced perspective. For example, if work is slow and you're late with the mortgage, you may not appreciate that your family's close and your health is good.

✔ You may focus so much on one area of your life that other areas are neglected. For example, you may work all hours and miss out on time with your family.

✔ You may pay so much attention to a single domain that your self-esteem plummets when something goes wrong in that domain. For example, if you focus on success at work, being made redundant may lead you to think less of yourself.

Working out whether you're linking your self-worth to only one or two domains can be an important first step in developing healthy self-esteem. When you understand what you're doing, you can work on viewing yourself more holistically. And when you don't expect to be able to keep certain domains constantly in tip-top shape, and instead pay equal attention to all domains, you can strive to be more realistic and remind yourself that you're only human.

To determine whether you're focusing on just one or two domains, ask yourself the following questions:

✔ Do I blame myself for difficulties in particular domains and fail to take into account other factors, such as chance, economic climate and the actions of others?

✔ Do I ignore or discount positive stuff going on in other domains when I experience difficulty in one particular domain?

✔ Do I place more importance on being successful in one domain than on the others? Do I expect to always keep *all* my domains in perfect order?

✔ Do I say things about myself such as: 'It's all my fault', 'I should've known better', 'Life's against me', 'I must deserve bad luck' or 'I'm cursed', when bad things happen?

If you answered 'yes' to all (or even one) of these four questions, you may benefit from challenging your way of thinking. Answering the following questions (for which we provide space in Table 3-1) can help you get a more accurate picture of what may be behind some of your domain-specific difficulties. Figure 3-2 provides examples to help you better understand how to challenge self-destructive thinking when bad things happen.

* **What exactly is the difficulty I'm experiencing? Be specific.**

    My wife left me.

* **What could I have done differently to prevent this event from happening?**

    Again, be precise. You may be able to take legitimate responsibility for some aspects of the event but be wary of blaming yourself for everything that happens. Even if you did play a part in the event you can find out things from the experience rather than merely punishing and mentally abusing yourself.

    I could've paid more attention to the state of our relationship instead of throwing myself into work.
    I could've been more attentive and affectionate on a daily basis.
    I could've paid her more compliments and showed her more appreciation for looking after our home and children.

* **What aspects of the event are outside of my control? Keep your answers precise.**

    Think about aspects of the event that you may think are your fault but may in fact be nothing to do with you.

    My wife's decision to end the marriage is ultimately her own.
    There were clues that she was unhappy but I had no way of knowing that she was thinking of leaving.
    I have little or no control over my wife's feelings about me; even if I'd done my best to be a more attentive partner she may have still fallen out of love with me.

* **However painful the event has been, what lessons can I take from it?**

    Try to think of both immediate and longer-term life lessons.

    I've discovered that I can survive being rejected by my partner even though it's extremely painful right now.
    In future relationships I'll make extra efforts to keep open communication because understanding how one another feels is important.

* **How would I treat a friend in the same situation who was putting him/herself down for what has happened?**

    Whether your wife has left you or your house been flooded, when bad things happen often you benefit from a bit of compassion. You may well find that you can be compassionate and understanding towards others but are usually harsh and critical toward yourself. Try dumping this double standard.

    I'd remind him that he did a lot of good things in his marriage.
    I'd console him.
    I'd encourage him to think optimistically about his future.
    I wouldn't condemn him for his mistakes.

* **What's going well in other domains of my life?**

    Search out as many positives as you can. Doing so can make the difference between being justifiably distressed about *one* specific aspect of your life and becoming unnecessarily depressed about the *whole* of your life.

    Work is enjoyable and my job is secure.
    My home is secure.
    I'm in pretty good health.
    I have a handful of good friends I can rely on for support.
    My children are doing okay and my wife and I will continue to look after them well even if we're no longer married.

Figure 3-2:
A sample of how to suss out domains.

Use Table 3-1 to record your own experience.

Table 3-1	Analysing Your Domain Difficulties
Question	*Your Response*
What difficulty am I experiencing? Be specific.	
What could I have done differently to prevent this event from happening?	
What aspects of the event are outside of my control?	
What life lessons can I take from this experience?	
How would I treat a friend in the same situation?	
What is going well in other domains of my life?	

You're a complex creature and much better off believing that you're basically worthwhile, regardless of specific difficulties in specific domains. Instead of judging yourself as 'good' or 'bad', reserve such judgments for the events, circumstances and situations you encounter.

You can evaluate your own actions but leave your self-esteem intact by stubbornly refusing to condemn your whole self on the basis of your mistakes or misdeeds. Blaming and berating yourself is unlikely to make you a better problem solver and serves only to make you feel even worse.

Blame implies shame, punishment and self-denigration. *Responsibility*, on the other hand, implies personal accountability and the potential to make amends and recover from your mistakes. You can hold your head up high while taking responsibility for part of a bad event. Take responsibility for your actions (or inactions) that contribute to an undesirable event but also uphold your view of yourself as a fundamentally worthwhile human being. Feeling badly about bad events is normal (and pretty much unavoidable), but you choose whether your entire self-esteem disappears down the plughole. (Chapter 4 offers more tips on how to take responsibility without blaming yourself.)

Life is full of random events, some good and some bad, utterly outside of your control. Blaming yourself for things you have no control over batters your self-esteem and shakes your belief that you can cope with problems.

Combating common criteria of worth

You don't have to look very hard to find loads of examples of value-laden messages in the media. Advertising material is riddled with implied or direct messages about how to judge yourself and the grounds on which you can think of yourself as 'worthy'.

Take a moment to consider some of the images on billboards, television advertisements and in magazines: a businessman who uses a cold remedy that enables him to attend an important meeting; vitamins engineered for 'today's hectic lifestyle'; bikini-clad women draped over cars or clutching the latest mp3 player to their bosoms; the 'super-mum' who keeps an immaculate house and a smile on her youthful face; the feminine boss who is sexy and stylish, and yet also a hard-headed businesswoman; men with six-pack abs promoting chocolate and soft drinks . . . the list goes on and on. You may end up thinking, 'Look at that guy on the TV with the gorgeous girlfriend and the slick car . . . now he's a real success. That guy *deserves* to have good self-esteem!' Even school systems can be overly focused on getting good results and conspicuously adulate high achievers. Woe betide the average student. In light of such a barrage of messages about who's 'worthy' and who isn't up to scratch, you can understand how easily your self-esteem suffers.

Recognise that many advertisements are designed to make you feel dissatisfied with your life and yourself. Why? So that you buy the product in an attempt to raise your drooping self-esteem.

Do the products work? Mostly not, or only temporarily. Getting a new car, a promotion or even a facelift may artificially inflate your self-esteem for a while, but the effects are rarely long-lasting because when you attempt to bring yourself up to a perceived standard, you're telling yourself at base level that you're not worth much. You're (perhaps unwittingly) buying into the ridiculous idea that your internal worth can be measured by external criteria and that until you meet certain criteria you've no business having any self-esteem at all. Well, we say that's hogwash; rubbish; tripe; codswallop; drivel; poppycock!

Table 3-2 is a list of common worth criteria propagated by the media. Notice that many are superficial and fleeting, whereas others are outside the reach of the average person. Even those that can be attained by the mere mortal imply that your worth is dependent upon always meeting that criterion, which is nigh on impossible.

Table 3-2	Media-Driven Worth Criteria
Value	*Value*
Being good-looking	Being ambitious and determined (a real 'go-getter')
Being youthful or looking youthful	Being in strict control of your emotions
Being sexy	Being stylish and trendy (or a 'trend-setter')
Having wealth and material possessions	Leading a busy life (being 'in demand' and 'a mover and a shaker')
Being famous	Having a high-powered job
Being tough	Being a rebel or a 'gangster' (being notorious)
Being fit and muscular (men)	Being thin (women)
Being recognised for artistic achievement (music, writing, acting or art)	Being popular
Receiving academic accolades	Being recognised for athletic achievement (being 'the best' and 'a winner')
Having power and influence (entre-preneurs, bosses, politicians, world leaders)	Being super-competent; being talented in many areas; being respected by members of your peer group (especially adolescents)
Being a genius	Being a recognised martyr or a humanitarian, spiritual or religious figure

Gather examples of value-laden messages you see around you. Take note of the ones that you typically find yourself 'buying into' and strive to de-program yourself: Instead of relying on worth criteria outlined by the media and society, think about your own personal values and standards. Resist the propaganda! Chapter 15 deals with living in line with your values.

Casting a critical eye over your own worth criteria

So what's the antidote to socially imposed low self-esteem? Well, ideally you abandon the criteria listed in the preceding section and construct your own worth criteria instead. We don't mean to suggest that anything's wrong or unhealthy about achieving success, taking care of your appearance or gaining material possessions. Indeed, these things can help you to feel good and carry many benefits with them. However, in order to build enduring self-esteem you have to see them for what they are – achievements, successes, bonuses, attributes but *not* indicators of worth.

Attempts to evaluate your overall worth are somewhat misguided. Because you're alive and capable of further development and change, viewing yourself as a work in progress makes more sense.

Instead of making judgements about whether you're a good or bad person, evaluate how well you're living: Are you living in a manner that enhances you, your significant others and the world around you? Table 3-3 lists qualities that often promote a sense of well-being.

Table 3-3	Qualities of a Life Lived Well
Quality	*Quality*
Being polite	Being trustworthy and honest
Being considerate and thoughtful of others	Looking after the environment and/or animal welfare
Caring for your family and friends	Taking responsibility for your health
Being law-abiding	Rejoicing in the company of others
Earning a living	Having personal goals or projects
Striving for knowledge	Being reliable
Contributing to the kind of world you want to live in	Supporting charities and altruistic causes
Having appreciation and gratitude	Having compassion
Accepting that many things in life are uncertain	Treating others as equals
Striking a balance between work and leisure	Being true to your values
Finding out things from mistakes	Making amends for misdeeds
Displaying forgiveness	Being open to new experiences and people

This list is by no means exhaustive; feel free to add more of your own points.

You can use points from the list in Table 3-3 to build up your own 'living well' checklist. When you've done that, refer to your checklist instead of trying to assess your overall worth on the basis of more problematic criteria like those promoted by advertisers.

Be wary of using your 'living well' checklist against yourself. If you're used to giving yourself a hard time you may decide: 'I'm not meeting my own criteria for living well so that must prove that I'm a total loser.' That's your old self-critical habits talking. Realise that you can't meet all the items on your checklist all the time. Instead, use it as a guide to keep yourself on track and feeling good. If you find that you're neglecting certain things in your life simply make efforts to address these aspects and leave your self-worth out of it!

Judging How to Judge Success

If you suffer from low self-esteem you may well be a very harsh judge of yourself and your efforts. You may set the bar unrealistically high for yourself, thinking that only total success at any given goal or endeavour counts, discounting minor achievements and disregarding partial successes. Such unrealistic expectations just get in your way.

Part of having a healthy self-opinion is the ability to enjoy the journey towards a goal. A lot of useful discovery can come from pursuing goals, even if you don't get the ultimate outcome you want (we talk more about goal setting in Chapter 8). Try to value your efforts and not just the end results.

Take note of your 'living well' checklist (see the preceding section) and count meeting the items on it as successes. Also try to be more flexible in your thinking about what constitutes 'success'. For example, you don't have to become a golf pro for your golf lessons to be successful. You don't need to get an A in an exam for it to count as an achievement. Even if you don't score a passing grade, attending classes, studying and giving the task your best shot can all be counted as successes.

Unfortunately, having healthy self-esteem doesn't immunise you against unpleasant feelings about negative events; but it does spare you the extra pain inflicted by self-denigration. Emotions associated with poor self-esteem, such as depression, hurt, guilt, shame and rage, are profoundly uncomfortable and may cause you to give up. So remind yourself that even with healthy self-esteem, feeling sad, disappointed, remorseful, regretful and even angry is normal and appropriate when things don't roll your way. These emotions are uncomfortable but ultimately they can spur you onto constructive action.

Living up to your potential . . . or not

We often hear our clients say that they haven't 'lived up to their potential'. What they usually mean is that they think they *should* have done better in life. 'Potential' is a slippery concept, and really means the possibility or likelihood of becoming something. You may have been told as a child that you had potential to become a musician or a doctor, for example. However, for a variety of reasons this may not have happened. Putting tremendous pressure on yourself not to 'waste your potential' is common. But how do you know for sure when you have or haven't met your potential? How does one go about measuring potential? Maybe you met your potential in a given area and didn't even know it! Or, perhaps you have hidden potential, as yet undiscovered! Very often people refer to their 'potential' as a way of expressing dissatisfaction with themselves and their achievements.

Instead of worrying about whether or not you live up to your potential, recognise how tricky pinning down that term can be. We all have potential in lots of different areas but this doesn't mean that we *must* use it all up in order to be happy or indeed successful. Focusing on your desires and aspirations is more useful than dwelling on the vague notion that you may be wasting (or have wasted) your potential.

Building a baseline

Coming up with an easily remembered and realistic self-accepting statement is a useful tool for combating low self-esteem. Every time you catch yourself defaulting to self-damning thoughts, you can challenge and replace them with your prepared self-accepting statement, also called a *baseline statement* because it ideally becomes the baseline you return to whenever you're faced with negative events.

Your baseline statement can be worded any way you like but ensure that it includes a validation of your intrinsic worth.

Intrinsic worth is based on the idea that, as a human being, you have fundamental value and potential. You have the right to be on this planet living your life alongside everyone else. Low self-esteem frequently leads you to forget this point and view yourself as less valuable than those around you. Your baseline statement aids you in challenging such thoughts and recognising that you have personal worth *even* when things go less well than you want them to.

Your baseline statement needs to be something that you can imagine yourself truly coming to believe in, and also needs to allow for good, less good, neutral and downright bad aspects of your character, personality and behaviour and events in your life. Your baseline may be something like the following:

- ✔ I have fundamental value.

- ✔ I'm a complex person capable of success and failure.

- ✔ I'm a fallible human being just like everyone else.

- ✔ I'm basically a worthwhile individual.

- ✔ I'm unique.

When you've constructed your own baseline statement, write it down. Tape it to a mirror or somewhere you see it often. Repeat your baseline statement regularly and act as though you truly believe it. Reviewing your statement and acting in ways that are consistent with your new way of thinking help to make it an automatic response. It's like rewiring your brain for the better. The more you act in ways that reflect how you *want* to think about yourself, the more you come to *believe* it. If you want to truly believe that you're capable of both success and failure, for example, allow yourself to take risks and make mistakes. Or if you're embracing the idea that you're a worthwhile individual, treat yourself respectfully and make good eye contact in social settings. Have a look at your baseline statement and identify ways you'd be acting differently and more positively if you really believed that it were true. Next, build these behaviours into your daily life.

The more you practise your self-accepting baseline belief, the more readily you can enjoy success and bounce back from failures.

Your self statement isn't about saying things like 'I'm great' or other overly positive Pollyanna-ish statements. Veering into grandiose ways of thinking about yourself is no antidote to low self-esteem. First, you're going to have a very hard time believing them. Second, believing that you're 100 per cent good is as senseless as believing that you're 100 per cent bad. Both positions are too extreme and don't allow for behavioural variation or deviation.

Thinking globally and acting locally

When you have an overall view of yourself as being worthwhile, you don't need to fear failure or rejection. Your self-esteem remains intact despite negative events because you understand that individual failings don't make you an overall failure. Similarly, a specific rejection doesn't mean that you're unlovable. Instead of putting yourself down, you recognise that you're okay – even though you may want to improve aspects of yourself or your life.

Although success may feel good and failure may feel bad, your basic worth remains unchanged by such events.

When your self-esteem is stable, you're probably less anxious about taking risks. Holding an overall positive view of yourself enables you to target specific (or local) aspects of your life for development and improvement. Applying for a job, asking someone for a date, taking up a new hobby or developing a new skill become less daunting because you're not telling yourself that you're worthless if things don't work out.

Sometimes people worry that if they stop judging themselves on specific behaviours they're going to become complacent and less motivated to achieve. This situation is rarely, if ever, the case. On the contrary, your drive for personal development is likely to increase. Think about this scenario: If you believe that failing a job interview means that you're worthless, you may want to avoid the interview entirely. And, if you do attend the interview, your performance is driven by fear of failure. On the other hand, if you believe failing the interview would be bad but that you remain a person to be valued, your performance is likely to be driven by a healthy desire to get the job.

Part II
Acknowledging That You're Okay As You Are

In this part . . .

You discover lots of reasons to appreciate yourself just as you are right now, and we provide practical advice on how to feel happier with your personality and your looks. We also help you to take control over your attention and stifle low self-esteem mind babble, and we provide useful information about making positive changes for all the right reasons.

Chapter 4

Judging Yourself Compassionately, Accurately and Objectively

· ·

In This Chapter

▶ Getting down to specifics

▶ Judging your behaviour and performance fairly

▶ Understanding the different roles you play

· ·

*P*eople with low self-esteem often find that making sense of their individual shortcomings and behaviour is difficult without resorting to rash negative conclusions about themselves as a whole person. When you select just one poor action, undesirable characteristic, bad experience or failing, and conclude that you're unworthy (or less worthwhile than other people) as a result, you're making the part-whole error.

The *part–whole error* is judging your whole self – past, present and future – on the basis of one singular aspect of your existence. The error is like carpet-bombing your entire house just because you painted the kitchen the wrong shade.

In this chapter we examine several of the more common part-whole error traps and show you ways to sidestep them in the interest of promoting and preserving your self-esteem. A key part of developing healthy self-esteem is taking on board new skills and habits.

Getting Good at Going for the Specifics

Specificity is key to thinking of yourself in more realistic and optimistic ways. A massive part of what perpetuates low self-esteem is failing to be very, very, *very* clear and precise about whatever aspect of yourself you dislike or are displeased with.

If you simply write yourself off for every mess-up you make, you batter your own self-esteem and hinder your chances of improving things for yourself in the future. You're also likely to experience some pretty profoundly unpleasant emotions such as depression, guilt and shame (see Chapter 2 for more information about unhealthy emotions).

Fortunately, you can be specific about your personal dissatisfactions and continue to like yourself at the same time. Being specific about your actions, experiences and characteristics also allows you to feel more hopeful about making possible improvements.

Accurately assessing your actions

People with poor self-esteem all too easily condemn themselves on the basis of one or more of their actions. You may typically become very upset and put yourself down when you make an error or a poor decision, fail, embarrass yourself, break your moral code or fall short of meeting a personal standard.

Falling into the trap of judging the whole of yourself on just a few actions can lead to helplessness and resignation. You may ask yourself: 'What's the point in trying anymore? I'm such a screw-up.' This kind of thinking throws the proverbial baby out with the bathwater. Sure, you may have messed up in a particular situation on a particular day but that doesn't mean that you're destined to do so forever!

Getting pernickety about the details is important in order to safeguard your self-esteem. When you get highly specific about your undesirable behaviours, you go into problem-solving mode instead of passive resignation. Sometimes you can make amends or rectify your behaviour and other times you just have to accept what you've done, take what you can from it and move on.

Being specific about your undesirable actions helps you to feel appropriately annoyed, regretful, disappointed or sad about them, but also allows you to keep your basic self-esteem intact.

Table 4-1 offers questions to help you accurately assess your actions, and some sample answers.

Table 4-1	Assessing Your Actions
Question	*Sample Answer*
In what specific way have I failed?	*I didn't get the job I was interviewed for on Friday.*
What exact error did I make?	*I forgot my husband's birthday.*
With what specific aspect of myself am I dissatisfied?	*I drink too much alcohol in the evenings.*
What precisely did I do wrong?	*I shouted at my daughter and made her cry.*
In what exact area would I like to improve?	*I want to lose a stone in weight.*
In what way have I fallen short of my ideals and standards?	*I didn't contribute to the fund-raising event for my preferred charity.*
In what specific way have I broken my moral code?	*I lied to my girlfriend about going out with my mates at the weekend.*
In what precise way have I committed a social *faux-pas*?	*I swore in front of the vicar at the church meal.*
Exactly what did I say or do that was stupid or silly?	*I gave last month's figures at the team budget meeting.*
What specific poor decision did I make?	*I decided to invest in company shares and lost money.*

The next time you realise that you're calling yourself a 'failure', 'loser', 'stupid' or even more colourful names, stop in your tracks. Try instead to really isolate exactly what's bothering you by using the questions in Table 4-1. When you've worked out exactly what you're displeased with, you can decide whether or not taking remedial action is possible.

Even if you can't fix the problem, you can still maintain your self-esteem by reminding yourself that you're an imperfect, fallible human being. You can see the lessons from your mistakes more effectively when you're not preoccupied with beating yourself up for making them in the first place.

Making individual judgements

You – and everyone else – often sum up yourself and other people with one-word descriptions, such as 'I'm a smoker', 'I'm a nurse', 'He's a real joker' and 'She's a headmistress'. This tendency is common and normal because it provides a quick and simple means of getting a message across. You don't mean that so and so is a nurse and that sums up the whole person. Instead you're describing one aspect of that person; in this case her occupation. But because each person – including you – is a vibrant, multi-faceted individual, giving anyone an accurate one-word description is impossible. To do so fails to take into account millions upon billions upon zillions of other descriptive features.

If you have low self-esteem, however, you may assign to yourself single-word descriptions that are hurtful and all encompassing, such as 'I'm lazy', 'I'm a failure' or similar things. People suffering with poor self-opinion commonly focus on one part of their personalities, actions or experiences and draw global conclusions about themselves.

For example, consider this statement: 'Failing one important exam means that I'm a total failure forever.' Sound familiar? You may say this kind of thing only in the privacy of your own mind or you may even say it out loud to other people. Here are just three very good reasons for dumping this kind of global self-rating:

- ✔ It's neither true nor consistent with reality because you've probably passed exams in the past and have the potential to pass more in the future.

- ✔ It's overly extreme and harsh. Calling yourself a total failure on the basis of one failed exam is *way* over the top and far too punishing.

- ✔ It makes you feel really dreadful. Making harsh negative judgements about yourself erodes your self-esteem like caustic soda in a blocked drain.

One way of beginning to dump negative global self-judgement is to view yourself holistically. As a human being, you're an assemblage of positive, negative and neutral features and experiences. Try seeing negative aspects of yourself for what they are – a small part of your whole. All your failings and successes are only a little bit of you in the grand scheme of things. One individual part, whether positive or negative, doesn't constitute your entire self.

Figure 4-1 illustrates how the whole of you comprises many different smaller parts:

- ✔ The large 'I' is you as a whole person.
- ✔ The '–' symbols represent negative attributes or experiences.
- ✔ The '+' symbols represent positive characteristics or experiences.
- ✔ The 'o' symbols represent neutral things about you and your experiences.

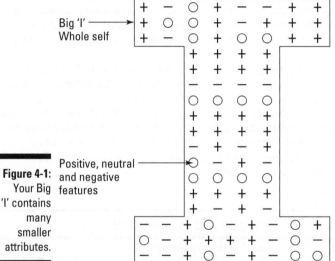

Big 'I' → Whole self

Positive, neutral and negative features

Figure 4-1: Your Big 'I' contains many smaller attributes.

Ideally, Figure 4-1 makes clear that giving any living creature an accurate global evaluation is virtually impossible, with too many factors to take into account. Instead of labelling and judging yourself overall, make efforts to judge only specific individual aspects of yourself. You can identify areas that you're dissatisfied with and target them for change while still thinking of yourself positively. Chapter 8 deals with self-development more fully.

You can make your own Big 'I' on any piece of paper. Aim to include *at least* an equal number of positive, neutral and negative points. In the interest of developing your self-esteem, make a special effort to include as many positive things as you can think of within your Big 'I'. Doing so helps to give you a more balanced perspective of yourself and counterbalance some negative points that you may be dwelling upon.

Low self-esteem generally leads you to home in on your mistakes and limitations. Be aware that you may tend to ignore, minimise or utterly dismiss your good points. Discovering how to recognise and celebrate your strengths is a key part of developing healthy self-esteem.

Washing your mouth out with soap

Don't underestimate the effect that self-talk can have on your general mood and self-esteem. If you aim to improve your self-esteem, you need a change in your attitude towards yourself. The language you use when thinking and talking about yourself is very important. People with poor self-opinion frequently put themselves down and assign negative labels to themselves.

In order to stop chipping away at your own self-esteem through abusive self-talk, you need to catch yourself in the act, which can be difficult. You may be so used to calling yourself names and degrading yourself that you aren't even aware of how often you do it, and when you do it, it happens so quickly that you're taken by surprise. Have a look at the first column in Table 4-2 to see whether your negative self-talk takes the form of any of these short statements or labels; and then practise replacing such statements with ones like those in the second column.

Table 4-2	Negative and Positive Self-Talk
Self-Abusive Talk	*Self-Accepting Alternative*
I'm a loser.	I sometimes lose and sometimes win.
Nobody likes me.	I'm likeable.
I'm useless.	I'm capable.
I'm weak.	I have strengths.
I'm a failure.	I'm fallible and make mistakes like everybody else.

Notice that self-accepting alternatives aren't extremely positive or grandiose statements like 'I'm great!' or I'm a winner!'. This approach isn't just an exercise in positive thinking; instead it's an exercise in thinking more realistically and optimistically about yourself and your capabilities. Saying 'I'm great' is another global label (albeit a positive one) and no human being is 100 per cent great any more than they're 100 per cent bad.

Generally, your self-accepting alternative attitudes need to:

- ✔ Be something that you can really believe to be true about yourself.
- ✔ Leave you room for error and disappointment in your performance or experience (without condemning yourself).
- ✔ Encourage you to carry on even when things go poorly or you find a situation difficult.
- ✔ Allow you to maximise and improve upon your existing strengths.
- ✔ Give a fair and objective representation of what has actually happened.

Put a ban on profane and obscene language! Using swear words to describe (or more to the point, degrade) yourself when you suffer from low self-esteem is all too common. Would you use that kind of language towards someone you care about? Stop cursing yourself and start being more self-compassionate. Try treating and talking to yourself as you would a loved one; your self-esteem will thank you.

You can get adept at catching your negative statements and changing them through practice. You just need to be on the look out for names you may be calling yourself and quickly say 'No!'. Then substitute that thought, name or label for a self-accepting alternative.

Record how often you take yourself to task (whether in your own head or out loud) in any given day. With a better idea of just how often you engage in this kind of self-berating, you may find that nipping it in the bud is easier. Try keeping a daily diary of frequency over a week. Make determined efforts to resist degrading yourself in the first place and to challenge and replace damaging thoughts when you spot them. After the week is up, review your diary and look for signs of improvement. Monitor how you speak to yourself and replace extreme negative messages with more objective assessments of what's actually going on. As you get better at talking politely to yourself, keep a record of how you're affecting your mood. You're likely to notice an improvement in how you feel as you get into the habit of talking to yourself respectfully and fairly.

Mathilde went to a wedding for a friend but knew few of the other guests. During the dinner she attempted to make small talk with other guests at her table. The result was silence and she felt awkward. In her head she told herself, 'I'm totally screwing this up, I'm such a social failure.' Not surprisingly, Mathilde felt even more anxious about socialising and thoroughly discouraged.

However, she arrested her negative self-talk and replaced it with a more encouraging and accurate assessment of what was going on at her table of wedding guests. She challenged her initial negative thoughts and replaced them with a fairer new thought: 'Okay, this is awkward but it's not my job to make the whole table at ease. I have got social skills and I'll just do the best I can in this situation.' Consequently, her anxiety diminished and she was able to enjoy herself.

Do you know anyone who constantly puts herself down and calls herself bad names? Not the most attractive habit, is it? You may find yourself almost visibly wincing when you hear someone being very self-denigrating. Stopping the name-calling once and for all can give your social confidence a real boost and also improve the impression you make on others around you.

Knowing Your Role and Knowing Your Whole

You play many different roles in your life. For example, you may play a variety of roles in different aspects of your life: partner in your primary relationship with another person; boss or subordinate in your job; parent to your children; child to your parents; sibling; friend and so on. Different roles bring out different aspects of your personality and no doubt you act differently in accordance with each role. Each individual role is a smaller part of your whole self. Figure 4-2 shows some roles a person may play.

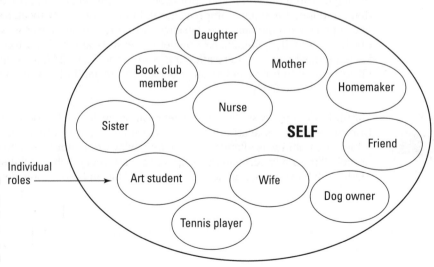

Individual roles →

Figure 4-2:
Role recognition reminder.

Just as you can make the mistake of negatively judging your whole self on one isolated action or characteristic, you may also condemn your whole self for failing in one of your roles. To avoid damaging your self-esteem by assuming that your role equals your whole, try the following attitudes and actions out for size:

- ✔ Recognise the many different roles you play within your overall life. No single role defines you totally. Even if a role is very important to you, it's still possible to under-perform and make mistakes within it. Avoid holding unrealistically high expectations for your performance in an important role. Expecting yourself to behave perfectly only sets you up for failure and disappointment. You can keep your high standards and strive to do the best you possibly can but it also makes sense to leave a margin for error.

- ✔ Focus on the bigger picture by acknowledging the other roles you play too. If things are going poorly in one role (be it spouse, worker, partner or friend), take stock of the things you do well and positive contributions you make within other roles. Keeping a holistic view of yourself as a person playing many roles may help you to resist judging your entire self unfairly on the basis of role-specific difficulties.

- ✔ Understand that roles are broad and involve various behaviours, tasks, skills and responsibilities. Rather than deciding that failing in one aspect of a role equals total failure within that role, be fair. Define your areas of weakness or difficulty within a given role very clearly, and write them down. Look for ways you can improve your behaviour or skills and take action. Doing this can help you to focus on improvement rather than dwell on failure.

- ✔ Make a note of the tasks and responsibilities that you carry out *successfully* within the role you're concerned about. Even when it seems like you're making a pig's ear of your performance in a role, chances are you're doing some things well and neglecting to acknowledge them. No matter how trivial a task or other aspect of a role may seem, if you do it well, make a note of it. Looking at the positive *as well as* the negative things you do can give you a more objective perspective of your overall role performance.

Fredrick is an accountant. Recently he received a lukewarm appraisal from his manager. Fredrick focused on the negative feedback he received and concluded: 'I'm a rubbish accountant and a real loser.' Not only is Fredrick negatively judging himself as an accountant, he's also calling himself an overall 'loser' for doing poorly in his appraisal. Fredrick is neglecting to acknowledge other roles in his life and is hinging his entire self-concept on his performance in this one specific role. Even though Fredrick's work is important to him and therefore constitutes a key role in his life, he can still choose to think differently about his overall worth despite receiving a middling appraisal.

Instead of negatively judging the whole of himself on his performance in his accountancy role, Fredrick puts his work appraisal into context by deliberately reminding himself of his other life roles. By doing this, Fredrick helps himself avoid making faulty 'role=whole' conclusions. His assessment of himself may look like this:

> 'I got a poor appraisal and that may mean that I'm underperforming at work. However, I'm still a worthwhile person. Many other roles in my life are going well. Even though being an accountant is important to me, it's not all there is to me. I can do my best to improve my accountancy skills and see if my career truly lies in that direction. Even if I fail at being an accountant I can find other means of supporting myself and my family.'

Whether Fredrick succeeds as an accountant or not, he can still keep his self-esteem intact by seeing himself in one of the following ways:

✔ Unsuccessful as an accountant but still a worthwhile person.

✔ Lacking in certain accountancy skills but still potentially a good accountant.

Taking this kind of balanced attitude helps Fredrick to retain his overall sense of worth while acknowledging his poor appraisal. This approach helps him to think in a problem-solving manner rather than becoming depressed and hopeless.

If you suffer from low self-esteem, ask yourself whether you jump to negative conclusions about your performance within a given role, based on criticism or errors.

Low self-esteem may prevent you from making good use of constructive criticism (find more in Chapter 13 about how to handle and use feedback). You may be a very harsh critic of yourself within a given role and refuse yourself permission to get things wrong and make poor decisions. Therefore even well-intended or mild criticism can leave you feeling extremely upset and make you rashly conclude that you're rubbish.

Don't mistake failings in a particular role for being utterly unsuccessful in that role. Typically roles comprise lots of different tasks and responsibilities, some of which you find easier to manage successfully than others. It's unlikely that you're *utterly* no good at any single role.

Take another look at Fredrick's work appraisal example. Just because he didn't get great feedback from his manager doesn't automatically mean that he hasn't got a future as an accountant. The feedback he was given may be a useful guide to areas of his work he can target for improvement and may highlight training needs.

Look at failings within a specific role with these thoughts in mind:

✔ Getting very specific about your performance problems within a role helps you to see things more accurately. Name the difficulty you're having very clearly and descriptively. Think of it as using surgical precision – you need to pinpoint the problem area without hitting any of the other functioning organs.

✔ Being objective involves trying to see the situation from an outsider's perspective. Objectivity allows you to dispassionately review the facts without being negatively biased by your personal feelings. Imagine how you'd look at your situation if it were happening to someone else. Focus only on the facts as you see them.

✔ Being fair involves looking at the good and the bad aspects of your role performance. Low self-esteem often leads you to blow the negative stuff out of proportion and dismiss anything positive. Fairness is about taking a step back from your feelings of low self-esteem and forcibly focusing on your positive and neutral actions too. When you're being fair, you're more likely to get a balanced picture of what you're doing that's good, bad and neutral within your role.

Rolling along with changing roles

As you live and grow, your roles are likely to change and develop. Sometimes you get more responsibility within a role through something like getting a promotion at work or buying a property. Or you may gain a new role like becoming a parent.

When roles develop you can feel out of your depth for a while until you get used to changes. You may need to learn new skills or enhance existing ones before you feel confident in that role again. New roles such as being a parent involve lots of skills and duties that you may never have used before.

If you have low self-esteem, you may have trouble adjusting to new or changed roles because you expect to feel confident and capable instantly. Your low self-esteem can lead you to draw erroneous negative conclusions about your overall utility and worth when you find role-related tasks awkward or difficult.

Don't allow your low self-esteem to railroad you into thinking that you're not up to the task at hand. Remind yourself that adjustment takes time and that it's common to have a crisis of confidence when faced with unfamiliar situations. Be patient with yourself and coach yourself along through role transitions. If you need some extra support, talk to friend or a therapist.

This example shows how Joseph remains specific, objective and fair about his self-criticism in the context of his fatherly role and identifies constructive action: Joseph missed his daughter's school assembly twice in a row due to work. He also rarely takes her out at the weekend because he likes to play golf with his friends and unwind. Some weeks he works late every night and misses her bedtime, seeing her for only a few minutes in the morning. Lately, Joseph has been feeling guilty about neglecting his daughter. He's started having thoughts like: 'I'm a terrible father and my daughter deserves better.'

Joseph challenges his thoughts about being a terrible father by getting specific about the behaviour he's displeased with:

Question	*Joseph's Answer*
Which role is affected?	Being a father.
What part of my performance in this role am I disappointed with?	Not spending enough time with my daughter.
Can I take steps to improve my performance in this role?	Yes. I can get home early at least once a week and put her to bed. I can also make sure that I put her next school assembly in my diary and take time off work to attend.
Do I do some things well within this role that I may be overlooking?	Yes. I provide well for my daughter and I spend a lot of time playing with her during holidays. I always give her a hug and a kiss in the morning and tell her that I love her. I also usually do a bit of homework with her on Sunday evenings.

Answering these questions allows Joseph to see himself as a father who does both desirable and undesirable things. His self-esteem remains solid despite acknowledging the shortcomings in his parenting. Joseph also highlights a few things he can do to improve his relationship with his young daughter. You can apply the same questions to your situation to help you get specific, fair and objective. Just write them out on any old piece of paper and answer them fully like Joseph does.

(Check out Chapter 3, where we discuss in more detail the concept of judging your worth on singular areas of your life.)

Being bad at one thing

Realising that you're not terribly good at something (or in fact that you're downright bad) is never a 'feel good' experience. And the feeling is even less pleasant when that thing is important to you.

Remember Fredrick from the preceding section? He's not likely to feel on top of the world if he tries to act on his manager's feedback and discovers that he's simply not cut out for a career in accounting. No matter how compassionate and self-accepting his thoughts are about it, he may still feel badly. However, he can get over the setback more quickly and move on to other things by thinking in a self-accepting manner, such as: 'I'm human, I fail and make mistakes just like anyone else. I'm fundamentally a worthwhile person.'

Part of living as a human being with healthy self-esteem is being able to accept your limitations. You don't have to like them, but you do need to accept them in order to avoid low self-esteem. It's easier said than done but it *can* be done if you're prepared to put in some effort. Here are a handful of helpful how-to hints:

- ✔ Admit your limitations to yourself and to others. Shame grows in the shade of secrecy. Hold your head high and simultaneously speak out about your personal failings, mistakes, shortcomings and limitations. Remember that nobody is perfect and that you've got nothing to be ashamed of.

- ✔ Allow others to normalise your experiences by listening to what they have to say about their own personal limitations. Sharing experiences can remind you that you're not the only person on the planet who sometimes fails, behaves poorly or makes errors. Also, other people's reactions to your reported failings are often far less extreme and damning than your own. Try to view the situation from a friend's perspective and adopt her more objective response.

- ✔ Use descriptive factual language when talking about your limitations both to others *and* to yourself. Be strict about refusing to use abusive or condemning language, which only feeds low self-esteem and hinders problem solving. Try to take a more compassionate and forgiving attitude towards yourself when facing up to your limitations.

- ✔ Once you accept a specific shortcoming or limitation, think about how you can adjust and learn to live with it. Rather than beating yourself up about it, plan ways to make the most of life regardless. If you're naturally shy for instance, you can still enjoy socialising but you may just need to accept that stand-up comedy isn't the job for you.

Feelings of sadness, regret, disappointment or annoyance in the face of failures are consistent with healthy self-esteem. Feelings of depression and shame go hand in hand with low self-esteem. To keep your self-esteem robust, acknowledge and accept your limitations, then make adjustments. When you accept your limitations (without deciding that you're useless or a failure), you're more likely to feel appropriately sad or disappointed about them, but not intensely depressed or ashamed.

Being good at one thing

Realising that you're good at something (particularly something that's important to you) tends to feel pretty darn good. And that's great. Being able to recognise and rejoice in your strengths is an important component of building healthy self-esteem. You can capitalise on your strengths in your work, home and social life but only if you're willing to acknowledge them.

We don't suggest that you go around bragging or blowing your own horn. People who do that tend to be masking insecurities. But we do suggest that you give yourself plenty of well-deserved credit and accept compliments gracefully. (You can find more information on taking compliments in Chapter 12.)

When someone says that you did well, simply respond with a 'thank you'. Don't let yourself fall into old habits of minimising or dismissing compliments by saying things like: 'Oh, well anyone could've done that'. Credit where credit is due.

Keep a positive self-information log. Make a note of any compliments you receive and record things that you do well. You can use this list to help you challenge self-defeating thoughts and fight back against low self-esteem. Remember to be specific about your good points and desirable actions in the same way as with negative ones. The more specific you are about positive things about yourself, the more likely you are to remember them.

Your strengths and weaknesses, abilities and limitations all add up to make you a complex human being. No single good or bad feature renders you a globally good or bad person.

Just as not judging your self-worth on a singular bad point is important, avoid making a similar error by judging your self-worth on a single good point. When you base your self-worth solely on your ability to be good at one thing, you put your self-esteem at risk, because if, for any reason, you stop being good at it you're prone to self-denigration. We talk about this point further in Chapter 3.

Allowing for variations

As you become familiar with seeing yourself as a complex and vibrant being, you can take a closer look at what may affect your performance in various tasks and roles.

If you've had poor self-esteem for a long time, you're probably in the habit of assuming that everything that goes wrong in your life is totally your responsibility. But that's certainly not the case. In almost any situation, some contributing factors are outside of your control.

For example, imagine that you're late for a meeting and you decide that the whole thing is your fault and that you should have planned your departure better. But have you taken into account the traffic jam and the completely full car park? Did you even know about the diversion that made the traffic heavier or that parking would be so difficult to find? Sure, you could have left the house earlier if you'd known about these obstacles, but did you know? Clearly not, or you probably would have left more travel time.

Also be mindful of mitigating circumstances that may negatively impact on your performance. This time imagine that you've given a presentation that didn't go very well. You had difficulty making yourself heard and you forgot to mention some key points. Instead of taking total responsibility for making a poor presentation, have a serious look at any other circumstances that may have impacted on your performance. Perhaps your sleep was disturbed the night before by your infant. Maybe you've just recovered from flu and still feel a bit ropy.

Be wary of taking personal responsibility for conditions over which you've no control, and about ignoring mitigating circumstances that may prevent you performing to the best of your ability. Doing so may lead you to berate yourself unfairly and undermine your self-esteem.

Keeping your eyes open to underlying issues

Focusing narrowly on one mistake or failure in one role can prevent you from recognising and addressing a primary problem. You may be so busy focusing on your dissatisfaction with your work performance, irritability with your children or your unhealthy eating that you don't recognise these things as symptoms of an underlying issue.

Perhaps your temper is frayed because you're working too many hours. Maybe your work performance is suffering because you're pre-occupied by the need to have a heart-to-heart with your spouse about some aspect of your marriage. Are you binge eating out of boredom and would you benefit from pursuing a hobby?

Resisting the tendency to simply put yourself down can give you room to really examine what's going on in your life. Sometimes lethargy, irritability, avoidance, over- or under-eating and impaired concentration (to name but a few) are symptoms of clinical depression or anxiety. Don't ignore the possibility.

You may need to make some changes to your relationships, lifestyle or both. Also have a look at Chapter 2 and consider whether or not you may benefit from seeking professional advice and support. Keep in mind that part of building up a healthy and positive self-opinion is seeking out extra support when necessary.

Chapter 5

Finding a Functional Focus

- -

In This Chapter

▶ Choosing what you want to focus your attention on

▶ Getting skilled at ignoring unhelpful thoughts

▶ Practising steering your attention towards tasks and the environment

- -

*Y*ou've probably noticed for yourself that low self-esteem can really cloud your thinking. Your head may sometimes seem so full of negative thoughts about yourself that you find concentrating on anything else very difficult.

Unfortunately, negative thoughts produce a lot of uncomfortable, unhelpful and unpleasant feelings such as depression and anxiety. They also tend to reinforce your negative view about yourself and keep you locked into a cycle of low self-esteem. Your negative thoughts may feel so all-consuming and powerful that you think you don't stand a snowball's chance in Hades of overcoming or managing them. Also, you may come to believe that a lot of these thoughts are true reflections of reality, whereas in fact they're by-products of your poor self-opinion and low mood.

Fortunately, this chapter offers a way out of negative thinking. We explore ways of managing (and sometimes just stubbornly ignoring) what goes on in your mind.

Retraining Your Attention

Many of the thoughts and images that enter your head are totally random. Often you don't *choose* what to think. Unsolicited thoughts just seem to pop into your head automatically.

Your thoughts are provoked by multiple factors, such as how you're feeling, your beliefs about yourself, what's going on around you and things you hear, feel, see and smell (to name but a few factors).

The trouble is that along with low self-esteem come many negative, automatic thoughts, which may include things such as:

- ✔ Self-abusive or self-denigrating thoughts, such as: 'I'm weird' or 'I'm a failure'.

- ✔ Harsh judgements about your performance, like: 'I totally messed up that conversation' or 'I made a real idiot of myself in that meeting'.

- ✔ Pessimistic guesses about what others are thinking about you, such as: 'Everyone at this party thinks I'm an oddball' or 'That person is thinking that I'm boring'.

- ✔ Gloomy predictions about the future, such as: 'I'll be ignored by everyone at the pub; no one will want to talk to me' or 'I'll never pass the interview next week'.

- ✔ Comparisons in which you come off worse, for example: 'Pam is so beautiful, I look like a frog next to her' or 'Charles is so much more confident and capable than I am'.

- ✔ Thoughts about how bad you're feeling, such as: 'I'm so anxious, I can't stand it, I'm shaking like a leaf' or 'I'm so miserable, what's wrong with me? Why can't I just be happy like other people?'

- ✔ Mental images of yourself failing or things going badly, like seeing yourself standing alone in a corner at a party or getting flustered in an interview.

These thoughts produce negative feelings of depression or anxiety that in turn generate even more negative unwelcome thoughts.

Understanding negative thoughts for what they are – just thoughts – can be difficult. Your low self-esteem probably guides you into believing that they are facts, causing you to take them very seriously and get really involved with them. Without even realising it, you may start to engage with your negative thoughts and turn all your attention towards them, worsening your mood in the process.

You don't have to take negative thoughts about yourself so seriously. Instead you can choose to consider them 'mental drivel' or chatter that isn't important or worth paying much attention to.

Your attention is a bit like the steering wheel of a car: you can choose which direction to turn and swerve to avoid hitting an obstacle. But unlike using a steering wheel, discovering how to direct your attention takes a lot more effort and practice. Think of it as 'mental training' in the same way as you train your muscles at the gym: the more you work at steering your thoughts, the stronger your mental attention muscles become.

We based the following exercise on an attention-training technique developed by a chap called Adrian Wells from the University of Manchester. The aim is to help you strengthen your attention muscles so that you spend less time focused internally on unpleasant thoughts and feelings, though you need to be careful not to use it in an attempt to block out negative thoughts. The point is to choose to accept and tolerate unwanted mind matter rather than trying to stop it or silence it altogether.

We all have thoughts and feelings that we'd rather get rid of from time to time. However, research shows that the more you try to stop having certain types of undesirable thoughts, the more likely you are to experience them. A more effective solution is to practise letting your negative thoughts play themselves out but choosing to focus on other things instead. It's somewhat like filtering out background noise and focusing your attention on what's most important at the moment.

The exercise may seem a bit complicated at first but give it a go. Try doing it when you're not feeling too down or full of anxious thoughts. The best time to start practising taking control of your attention is when your mood is neutral or positive. Otherwise you're probably just making things harder for yourself.

1. **Collect five separate sounds that you can hear all at the same time.**

   Some ideas include: a radio, your dog snoring, traffic outside, birds chirping, a clock ticking, the hum of a vacuum cleaner, a dripping tap, the neighbours' music, construction work, the washing machine spinning and so on.

   Aim for sounds of roughly equal volume that don't drown out one another.

2. **Get comfortable in a chair. Keep your eyes open and focus on a specific spot (you can blink; no need to stare until your eyes water!).**

3. **Focus on each one of the sounds in turn giving each of them a roughly equal amount of time – 30 seconds or so.**

   As you focus on each sound, listen to it as if it's the only sound that matters. Disregard all the other sounds; the important sound is the one you're focusing on.

4. **Give all your attention to each sound and re-focus your attention as necessary as you go through all five sounds.**

   If you're distracted by a loud grunting snort from the dog when you're focusing on the radio, let it go as unimportant and re-focus on the radio. Likewise, if you get any distracting thoughts, just filter them out as if they are simply additional noise and re-focus on the sound at which you're targeting your attention.

5. **After focusing on each of the five sounds, rapidly shift your attention from one sound to another in a random order.**

   Make sure to focus all your attention on one particular sound before switching your attention to a different sound.

6. **Expand and deepen your attentional focus by taking in all the sounds simultaneously.**

   Try to identify and count all five of the sounds you hear like 'that's sound number 1 – my mutt snoring', 'that's sound number 2 – the radio', 'that's sound number 3 – the traffic' and so on, until you've identified all five sounds.

This exercise is meant to show you two important points:

✔ You have the ability to direct your attention towards whatever you decide is important and away from other distractions – be they sounds or thoughts.

✔ Through practice you can become more externally focused and less internally focused. People with low self-esteem and other emotional problems generally give most of their attention to how they feel and to their negative thoughts. Many people report that their mood and self-opinion improves when they get more into the habit of focusing on the external world.

Giving all your attention to negative thoughts about yourself (and the noxious emotions arising from such thoughts) does your self-esteem a lot of damage. Becoming more able to shift your attention on to external factors like tasks, sensations, sounds, other people and your immediate environment saves you from endless painful and unproductive self-focused criticism. Attention retraining helps you to view your negative thoughts as unimportant and unworthy of your attention. Over time your self-esteem will benefit from less negative self-focus.

Exploring CBT and mindfulness

If you think that you have a particular problem with worry and repetitive thoughts, you may want to consider having regular sessions with a Cognitive Behaviour Therapy (CBT) practitioner skilled in attention-retraining techniques. You can ask your GP for a referral or find a CBT practitioner via one of the professional bodies listing in this book's Appendix.

If you're interested in the mindfulness concepts we discuss in this chapter, you may want to investigate mindfulness meditation in more depth. Jon Kabat-Zinn has written books on the subject. Mindfulness meditation is based on Buddhist meditation practice, and though it's somewhat different to the exercises outlined in this chapter, many of the principles are similar. If you're interested in Buddhism, check out *Buddhism For Dummies* by Jonathan Landaw and Stephen Bodian, published by Wiley.

Don't expect perfection. Your self-esteem and your mood can start to benefit from even moderate improvement in your ability to control your attention.

Practise this exercise for a minimum of 10 to 15 minutes, ideally a couple of times each day for optimum benefit. Up to two months of regular practice may well be necessary for you to get really good and begin to experience the positive effects fully.

Giving negative thoughts the cold shoulder

Although you can't stop yourself having negative thoughts altogether, you can give them the cold shoulder. Refusing to 'engage' or 'get into a conversation' with the critical, low-self-esteem part of yourself is a very useful strategy. This approach, however, is *not* the same as trying to censor your thoughts, get rid of negative thoughts and images, or suppress upsetting memories. Trying to stop yourself having certain thoughts usually has the paradoxical effect of producing more of them – like trying not to think of an elephant after being told not to.

When we say to give your negative thoughts the cold shoulder, we mean more along the lines of being deliberately rude to your low self-esteem voice – just as you may get up and leave a conversation with someone who's being really negative and unpleasant or switch the TV channel from a programme you find boring or upsetting.

Many of the thoughts arising from your low self-esteem are probably very familiar to you. They're like rude, drunk guests turning up at a party. Just when everyone is having a nice civilised time they barge in and trash the place. Instead of trying to reason with these unwelcome thoughts or strong-arm them out the door, we encourage you to just ignore them. Easier said than done, we realise, because they're big, mean and ugly. But the more you refuse to get involved with them, the less powerful they eventually become.

When you find yourself getting absorbed in negative thoughts about yourself, your past or your future, stop for a minute and ask yourself these questions:

- ✔ Are these thoughts making functioning and getting on with tasks harder for me?

- ✔ Are these thoughts making me feel worse about myself?

- ✔ Are these the kind of thoughts I typically have when I'm feeling down about myself?

- ✔ Are the same thoughts going round and round in my mind?

We suspect that the answer to all four questions is a resounding 'Yes!'. In which case you know that these thoughts are bullies you definitely don't want to play with.

Some tips to help you break the habit of dwelling on negative thoughts include the following:

- ✔ **Put your brain to work.** Do something that requires a lot of close attention, such as solving a puzzle or working out your household budget. Any activity that takes up a lot of your brainpower is likely to interrupt negative thoughts.

- ✔ **Stop dwelling and start talking.** Give someone a call or strike up a conversation with someone nearby (don't talk about your negative thoughts or feelings, keep it light). Talking to other people can distract you from your thoughts and make you feel connected with the world again.

- ✔ **Shake your booty.** Go for a run, clean the house or dance to music. Vigorous exercise can shake nasty thoughts from your mind and also give you a feel-good buzz.

- ✔ **Make a break for the border.** A change of scene can help break the cycle of negative thoughts. If you're indoors, take yourself outside for a walk. If you're in bed, get up and go into another room for a while. Get up from your desk and do some filing or another task in a different area of your office.

✔ **Stimulate your senses.** Instead of focusing internally on all the negative stuff in your mind, force your attention outwards. Take a good look at your environment and whatever's going on around you. Make a mental note of different things you see, hear, touch, smell or taste. Really focus on your surroundings.

Imagine that you're a space traveller landing on an unknown planet. All the plants and animals are new and unfamiliar, even the atmosphere is different. You need all your attention to try to make sense of this new place. Use this metaphor to help you focus on your external environment. Imagine that you're seeing things for the first time and you have to take careful note of every detail.

Practising re-focusing

Even when you're in a low mood and full of self-denigrating thoughts, you forget about all that if you suddenly have to deal with a crisis. If a fire breaks out in your kitchen or you have to swerve wildly to avoid a car crash, your mind focuses entirely on dealing with the crisis. All other thoughts and feelings are suspended.

We're not suggesting that you seek out crisis situations to escape from the thoughts associated with low self-esteem. The point is that when your mind is absorbed in executing an important task, you leave little room for any other type of thought.

When you find yourself engaging with self-denigrating thoughts, you can purposefully turn your attention away from how you're feeling and back towards what you're doing. No matter how basic or trivial the task you're involved in is, you can give it your full attention. Look at the minute detail of what you're doing and really focus on it. If you're folding clothing, pay full attention to the feel of the fabric and the angle of the folds. If you're socialising, try to observe very closely the other people around you. Take in their conversation. Get involved and ask questions, then listen very attentively to the answers you receive. Imagine that you're going to be asked to be a police witness; you need to be able to recount lots of details about your environment and the people within it. Use your attention to gather lots of information about what's actually going on around you and how others look and behave. Being very externally focused helps occupy your attention and leaves less room for unhelpful negative thoughts. It also increases your confidence in your ability to manage and tolerate unwelcome activity in your head.

This technique can be particularly useful when you're feeling anxious. Instead of getting distracted by anxious feelings and thoughts, just let them play out in the background. Re-focus on your environment and the steps involved in completing your task. The task doesn't need to be large, like putting out a fire. Even walking across a room with a tray of drinks or making specific points during a meeting or presentation can be suitable re-focusing tasks.

When you suffer from low self-esteem, you sometimes make negative predictions about your performance and other people's responses to you. Focusing on tasks and taking note of your environment allows you to discover – perhaps with a pleasant surprise – that your predictions aren't borne out in reality. Looking outwards instead of inwards gives you a chance to take in previously neglected information; for example, noticing the fact that no one seems to be that interested in you carrying your tray of drinks, even though you originally predicted that the entire bar would look at and judge you.

Making Yourself More Mindful

Although we emphasise the importance of effort throughout this book, here we ask you to do absolutely nothing. Well, that's not strictly true; we want you to try to do nothing with your negative thoughts. And that does take practice and effort. Basically we're asking you to work hard at getting skilled at doing nothing. We hope that makes sense but if not, look at it this way: Rather than thinking about your negative thoughts by starting to dwell upon them and worry, just let them be. Accept that they're present and allow them to pass in their own time and choosing:

- ✔ Don't try to answer any 'why?' or 'what if?' questions.
- ✔ Don't try to suppress or get rid of any unpleasant thoughts.
- ✔ Don't judge your thoughts as important, dangerous or true.

The tips in the next sections are intended to help you to become adept at accepting all kinds of thoughts without interfering with them. You don't have to like all your thoughts and images but you can acknowledge and accept them. All thoughts pass eventually. However, if you anchor your attention onto certain negative thoughts, they tend to stay around longer and cause you emotional upset. The plan is to give them the minimum amount of attention so that they don't suck up more attention than they deserve.

Being present and attentive

Being present in the moment may seem pretty simple but in fact requires you to take deliberate and exclusive notice of what you're doing at any given time. Instead of going through the motions of everyday tasks while worrying or dwelling on negative mind chatter, pay ultra-close attention to whatever you're doing in the here and now.

You can practise being truly present during any type of task. Just filter out the extraneous thoughts and use all five of your senses to fully absorb the task you're involved in at that moment. If distracting thoughts come into your head, simply re-focus your attention onto your physical environment and your current activity.

For example, if you're washing the dishes, pay close attention to the feeling of the water and soap on your hands. Employ all your senses. Notice the smell of the washing-up liquid, the sound of your cloth on the surface of the plates, the gleam of clean porcelain and any tastes in your mouth, perhaps a faint soapy taste from the washing-up liquid.

Being sceptical about the truth of your thoughts

Becoming able to accept unwelcome thoughts without dwelling on them or considering them to be important facts can help you feel better. Negative thoughts about yourself can feel very true, but feeling that such thoughts are true doesn't make them true.

A thought about yourself like: 'I'm useless, nobody will ever want to be in a relationship with me' is no truer than a thought like: 'I can fly through the air like a bird'. No matter how much you focus on that second thought and feel it to be true, you're very unlikely to take actual flight!

Bad thoughts about yourself are probably harder to see as opinions or ideas and not facts because they're so painful. One way of trying to make your negative thoughts less important is to detach from them. If you can see the thought as separate from yourself you can more easily let it go rather than getting swallowed up by it. Reminding yourself of the following points can help you to be more sceptical about negative thoughts:

✔ **Your negative thoughts are often a by-product of your mood.** Being tired, run down or in a bit of funk provides fertile ground for negative thoughts to thrive. Although you can't always control your mood, you can recognise the unhelpful thoughts that frequently come along for the ride.

Instead of concluding that your poisonous thoughts are worthy of deeper investigation and attention, regard them as side effects of being in a low mood and a negative state of mind. When low-self-esteem thoughts encroach, refuse to give them any attention until your mood has improved significantly or you're better rested. Chances are they'll be much less prominent or even absent when you're in a more positive state of mind.

✔ **Your negative thoughts are most likely not true – they're just born out of habit.** Low self-esteem puts you in the habit of thinking about yourself in damning and abusive terms. Just because you think of yourself in a negative way habitually doesn't mean that those opinions have any basis in reality.

Rather than regarding your negative self-opinion as an accurate reflection of reality, remind yourself that you're simply locked into a very bad habit. Try deciding something like: 'There I go again thinking about myself in those old familiar and foul ways; these thoughts are best disregarded.'

✔ **You gain nothing by latching on to negative thoughts about yourself.** Dwelling on negative thoughts and feelings about yourself doesn't give you anything positive; instead it makes you lose confidence and undermines your self-esteem further. You may believe that if you pay attention to your negative thoughts, you discover novel ways of improving yourself or solving your problems. Don't be fooled – this is rarely (if ever) the case. Ninety-nine point nine per cent of the time you just come away feeling terrible and helpless. Think about it: Would you advise a friend to indulge in his self-defeating thoughts or would you strenuously urge him to ignore them? Apply the same advice to yourself that you'd give to a close friend plagued by self-denigration. You have plenty of time to think about self-improvement and personal development when you're in a more positive and objective frame of mind (see Chapter 8 for advice on setting personal goals).

✔ **Treating low-self-esteem thoughts as unimportant makes them lose their power over your feelings.** What gives negative thoughts about yourself power is the attention and importance you assign to them. The less prestige you award them, the less impact they'll have on your mood, behaviour and self-view.

Take a leap of faith and try concluding that uncharitable thoughts are nothing more than that: thoughts. They have no basis in reality and no useful information to impart. Use the following exercises to get better at regarding painful thoughts about yourself as dark clouds moving across the skyline.

Try challenging your negative thoughts by looking for facts and evidence in the world around you. Take in new information that may well contradict toxic ideas and beliefs you hold about yourself. Write down real hard provable facts that fly in the face of your insidious self-demeaning ideas. Make a real effort to fight back against your internal damaging propaganda.

Becoming a casual observer

A lot of information passes through your five senses every day. Much of it you choose to let pass you by without forming any judgements about it or giving it much importance. You can shake off loud noises from road works or easily forget a lot of the faces you see on a busy train platform. Information that doesn't hold any personal significance to you is relatively easy to merely observe and let go of. Negative thoughts arising from low self-esteem can, however, *seem* very important and true. It's much harder to allow such thoughts to pass through your mind without seizing on them and beginning to analyse them. Low self-esteem images and thoughts can be extremely pernicious even though most of them are distorted and untrue.

The following exercises are devised to help you master the art of treating destructive thoughts as unimportant chaff that you can merely observe and allow to pass through your mind. It takes practice – as you probably imagine. But becoming better at simply recognising the presence of negative self-denigrating ideas, thoughts and images *without* deciding to dwell on them can make a really positive difference to how you feel about yourself.

Sit in a comfortable chair and close your eyes. Imagine a blue sky full of clouds. The clouds are many different shapes and sizes and are moving swiftly across the sky. Now imagine that each cloud represents a thought or a mental image. Just observe the thought clouds floating past without trying to control them in anyway. Allow your mind to wander freely and don't try to block out anything that comes into your mind. Simply put it on a cloud and watch your thoughts sail across the sky.

Another exercise you can use to become better at detaching from negative thinking involves shifting your perspective from participant to observer. This exercise is a little bit trickier than the cloud metaphor and you may need to try it a few times before getting it down pat.

Get back into your comfortable chair and close your eyes. This time engage in a pleasant daydream, such as driving in a car with the top down on a sunny day, walking along a beach or sitting in front of a roaring fire sipping hot chocolate. Really get immersed in the daydream and visualise yourself there. Imagine yourself going through the motions of your daydream scenario. When you've got a clear image and are deeply participating in the daydream, try to switch your perspective to observer. Try to see the daydream continuing from your position in the present. Just watch it unfold, having taken a step back.

Chapter 6

Becoming Comfortable with Who You Are

In This Chapter

▶ Getting in touch with yourself

▶ Accepting yourself as a fallible human being

▶ Saying goodbye to behaviours that hold you back

▶ Having faith in your likeability

*I*mproving your self-esteem is an uphill struggle when you don't actually like the nuts and bolts of who you are. Many people refuse to make peace withtheir basic nature – who they are, what skills they have and what they look like. You may hanker to be wildly different in certain respects or perhaps even want to be a totally different person altogether.

You may assume that healthy self-esteem is an impossible dream for someone as flawed and imperfect as yourself. And if you insist on thinking along those lines and stamping 'reject' on your forehead, you're right. In this chapter we show you that healthy self-esteem isn't about changing the elemental scaffolding of your character or trying to swap your body or brain for a new one (lots of luck if that's your ambition). You can improve your self-opinion by accepting and showing a little appreciation for the vehicle that provides your transport through this life – you.

Wearing the Skin You're In

When you're comfortable with yourself, it shows and a person with healthy self-esteem is a very attractive thing to behold. Many people with a sound understanding and appreciation of their own individuality get a lot of positive attention. They're nice to be around because they emanate good psychological health. People enjoy the relaxed and approachable manner that those with healthy self-esteem possess. People also feel safe in the company of healthy self-esteem holders because they're usually accepting and non-judgemental.

Don't get the wrong idea. Having a good sense of your own worth doesn't turn you into some sort of transcendental guru with a beatific smile plastered on your face all day, every day. You're not rendered impervious to the slings and errors of everyday events simply because you have healthy self-esteem. You are, however, likely to be pleasant company. And surely that's a good thing.

Getting to know you

Getting to know yourself is a precursor to getting to like yourself. You need to be able to recognise yourself in a crowd, so to speak; pick yourself out in a line-up; know who you are even if you're stranded on a desert island with nothing familiar around you. Think about how well you probably know some of your friends and family. You can most likely describe them to a tee. Make an effort to get as deeply acquainted with yourself.

If you've been battling with low self-esteem demons for a long time, you may have forgotten who you really are. Low self-esteem can lead you to focus so much on your faults and limitations that you may be completely unaware of what makes you tick. You spend the majority of your time observing others and wanting to be more like them or trying to live up to unrealistic expectations (your own or those of others). All this effort can leave you little time to think about yourself.

Even if your opinion of yourself is well and truly on the floor, you stand to gain from getting re-acquainted with who you really are. You may be shocked to discover that you have a lot of personal opinions, values, tastes and ideas. (Getting in touch with your personal values is a subject we explore more fully in Chapter 15.)

In the interests of extracting your self-opinion from the pernicious tentacles of the floorboards, give yourself a chance to re-kindle a relationship with that person you see peering back at you in the mirror. Ask yourself the following questions and ones like them in order to re-discover yourself:

✔ What are my likes and dislikes?

✔ What kinds of topics really grab my interest in conversations or on the TV and radio?

✔ What makes me laugh or cry?

✔ What do I daydream about?

✔ What are some memorable things I've done or experienced in my life?

✔ What are some of my favourite things? ('Raindrops on roses and whiskers on kittens, bright copper kettles and warm woollen mittens . . .' – clearly we're working a musicals theme into this chapter, in this case Rodgers and Hammerstein's 'My Favourite Things' from *The Sound of Music,* which is always fun at Christmas.)

✔ What words would I use to describe myself to someone I've never met?

The purpose of this exercise is to *describe* yourself as you would a room or an object or another person, and not an exercise in *evaluating* yourself. Put any negative thoughts to one side for a minute and try to answer each question purely and objectively. If you experience difficulty answering some questions because negative thoughts about yourself cloud your thinking, take a deep breath, clear your mind and revisit those questions.

Imagine that you're giving an interview on radio or TV. The interviewer wants to know all about you and asks you questions to help the audience feel that they have insight into who you are. Be really self-focused for a minute or two and concentrate on how interested everyone listening to the interview is in finding out about *you*. What would you say? You can do this exercise in your imagination or put it down in writing.

Speculating about yourself

Years ago I was having a chat with two close friends ('I' being Rhena in this anecdote). We somehow got onto the topic of how we'd all manage if we were stranded on a desert island. Based on our different personalities we concluded that my friend Kate would be preoccupied with combining coconut milk and papaya to make some sort of aromatic, moisturising face cream. My other friend Jordan would start by looking for materials to make an architectural masterpiece of a hut. I would be scouring the beach for shells to make into jewellery.

Get together with some of your closest friends and have a light-hearted talk about what you'd all do in some sort of extreme situation. You may rediscover a lot about your personality and your likes and dislikes.

Getting to like you

When you're back on familiar terms with yourself, you have the opportunity to deepen the relationship. Knowing about your own personality and exclusive characteristics offers you a chance to embrace and celebrate them. You can start to revel in your own company and find the whole experience of getting to know and like yourself quite uplifting ('all at once am I several stories high, knowing I'm on the street where you live' . . . spot that musical. Ok, we'll tell you. The song is from Lerner and Loewe's *My Fair Lady*).

Give your low self-esteem thoughts a backseat and take some time to truly appreciate the things that make you who you are. The advice offered in the following sections can help you to get back to basics and discover how to appreciate yourself.

Getting Better at Being Good Enough

Whoever said that you *have* to be the *best* or that being average isn't good enough? Well, the chances are, a lot of people including your parents and teachers. You may have absorbed many messages from important people in your early life that perpetuate your self-esteem problems today (take a look at Chapter 10). Low self-esteem often sprouts its first tender roots in early experiences.

Ray grew up in a family that prized achievement. He was a fairly average student and generally got good marks, but whenever he came second in anything his parents wanted to know why he hadn't come first. Ray got the impression very early on that in order to impress his parents he had to come top of whatever he decided to do. Because Ray wasn't especially gifted academically, he rarely got the top grade. He often felt that he'd let his parents down and that nothing he did was good enough. Today Ray still tends to dismiss his achievements unless he's managed to be the best at something. He understands that his parents were probably only trying to encourage him to try his hardest but he still carries the sting of never gaining their approval for what he did achieve.

The painful irony is that Ray is good at lots of different things. But the demands that he places on himself to be 'the best' prevent him from getting satisfaction from his achievements. Ray never discovered how to accept simply being 'good enough' and therefore his low self-esteem is perpetuated by his idea that 'only the best will do'.

Perhaps you too believe that you have to do things nigh on perfectly for them to matter. Being the best at something – much less everything – is really difficult, and even if you do reach those lofty heights, the chances are that someone else is going to top you at some stage.

'Best' is not a permanent state. Even the best athletes, for example, eventually have to relinquish the mantle to a newcomer who's younger, faster and stronger.

In the interests of improving your self-esteem, re-adjusting your standards makes good sense. Work on accepting that you can't always get perfect results. Instead of insisting that you must always come out at the very top in all your endeavours, give yourself credit for arriving somewhere in the middle ranking. Being 'good enough' is often a massive achievement.

As you combat your need for excellence and perfection, which often just perpetuates your low self-esteem, make an effort to adopt different attitudes:

- ✔ Preferring to be the best is fine, but I can tolerate not reaching that standard.

- ✔ Doing everything less than perfectly doesn't make me a less worthwhile person.

- ✔ Having failings and making mistakes is part of being human.

- ✔ Doing something to the best of my ability is the most I can reasonably ask of myself.

- ✔ Managing to achieve whatever I can is good enough, and I don't have to think poorly of myself for not hitting the highest level.

- ✔ Being good enough is good enough for me.

Enjoying being average

How many geniuses do you know? Perhaps you can name a lot of people who are bright and talented, but how many actual Mozart or Einstein types have you met? How about supermodels, while we're on the subject? Got many of those in your workplace or social sphere? Sure, you can probably name lots of attractive people, but are they gracing the cover of this month's *Vogue* or *GQ* magazine? And how about Olympic standard athletes? Maybe you have some friends who run marathons or are really good at football, but are they lining themselves up for the 2012 Olympics? Are you close personal friends with many rock stars or film stars? Of course, you may be able, quite honestly, to answer 'yes' to some of these questions, but the vast majority of people give an equally honest 'no' to every question. Actually, whatever your answer to those questions it's kind of beside the point, which is that most people in the world *aren't* exceptional intellects or unusually gifted. Most of the planet's population are average in the looks, brains and abilities department – including you.

You may think, like many people, that in order to have self-worth you need to be exceptional in some respect (you can read Chapter 2 for even more information about the criteria you may use to judge your worth). But if you look around you at the hard evidence, most people are not exceptional to any marked degree.

So how come lots of average people have healthy self-esteem? Well, that's a very interesting question. The secret is that you don't *need* to be extra special to have personal worth and a good number of average people know that's the truth. You can be average in almost every respect and still choose to accept yourself as you are.

Being able to cherish your unique points and enjoy your run-of-the-mill average bits is at the very heart of healthy self-esteem. We firmly believe that all people have their own idiosyncratic 'selling points', or in other words, a unique and special personality. However, in the vast majority of cases, your unique attributes and talents are unlikely to capture the attention of the nation, as it were.

We encourage you to consider the crazy notion that even those people who are famous for being exceptional in some specific way have no more claim to worth than you do. We're all just people when everything is said and done. You can legitimately say that David Beckham, for example, is a more *valuable footballer* than you are; but you're wrong to decide that he's a more worthwhile *person* because of that one skill. And the same holds true for anyone else that you admire and may compare yourself to.

Being average is great – not just okay or all right, but great. The entire world is geared up for the average Tom, Dick and Harriet. So get out there and enjoy it!

In addition, bear in mind that the people who love you think you're very special – and they're right. Do you really need to be recognised by the rest of the world as something super-duper in order to feel worthwhile? Can you not try to be satisfied with being special to a select group? Or even to yourself, for that matter? We hope that you can, because doing so is great for your self-esteem.

We're not suggesting that anything's wrong at all with being above average in some way. It can certainly carry lots of perks. If you do happen to be conspicuously above average in some way, enjoy that too. Just beware of placing too much emphasis on special talents when assessing your self-worth. Otherwise you can make yourself vulnerable to a self-esteem crisis if you suddenly cease to be above average for some reason. Try to view your special skills, attributes and talents as a bonus and not as the sole foundation of your intrinsic human worth.

Preferring rather than demanding

If you suffer low self-esteem, you may make unrealistic demands of yourself, other people and the world. You may insist that you have to get approval from others, or perform very highly in order to consider yourself worthwhile. You may also hold demands that the world treat you fairly or be fair in general. Lots of luck with that.

Part of developing healthy self-esteem involves turning your demands into realistic preferences. Preferences allow you to have desires about your personal performance or about how others and the world treat you, while leaving room for the chance that your desires won't be met. Acknowledging the possibility of disappointment generally means you're more able to cope when you don't get what you want. Demands, on the other hand, lead you to feel demoralised (and promote self-recrimination) when they're not met.

In order to become a preference-based thinker you needn't forego your ideals, personal standards or strong desires. Instead hold on to your preferences but be conscientious about acknowledging the possibility that they may not be satisfied.

Watch out for language like *should, must, have to, need to* and *got to* in your actual conversation and in your thoughts. These phrases are generally a sure sign of inflexible demand-based thinking. Deliberately use words like *want, prefer, desire, wish, hope* and *ideally* instead. Also add a great big 'but' after your stated preference and an acknowledgement that things don't have to work out as you'd like them to. Some examples of what we mean are:

- ✔ 'I want people to like me but I accept that people don't have to like me.'

- ✔ 'I really don't want to lose my girlfriend but I'm not immune from her leaving me.'

- ✔ 'I dearly wish for my family to stay together but realistically they may not.'

- ✔ 'I prefer to pass this exam but there's no universal law that states I must pass.'

- ✔ 'I want people to treat one another with respect but regrettably they don't have to do so.'

- ✔ 'Ideally the project will be complete by next month but it doesn't absolutely have to be.'

These types of statements express strong desires but also help prepare you for the possibility that they won't be realised. Sticking to your preferences whilst resisting turning them into demands helps you to understand that you can cope with negative outcomes although it may be difficult. Recognising your ability to cope with and move on from bad things is empowering and feeds your self-esteem.

Enjoying being outstandingly ordinary

You may notice that people who seem to have a good solid, healthy sense of their own worth display many of the same characteristics. People with healthy self-esteem often:

- ✔ Are able to laugh at themselves (and generally have a good sense of humour).
- ✔ Look attractive, but aren't necessarily of superior good looks.
- ✔ Are interested in other people.
- ✔ Can enjoy their own company.
- ✔ Are grateful for and appreciative of everyday things.
- ✔ Tend to be even-tempered.
- ✔ Have a wide range of interests.
- ✔ Set and achieve realistic goals.
- ✔ Maximise their skills and talents.
- ✔ Look after themselves while also considering the needs of others.

As the qualities in this checklist indicate, people who have healthy self-esteem aren't unusual in any definable way. They don't have magical powers or superhuman gifts. What makes people with healthy self-esteem stand out is their *outstanding ordinariness*. They do an outstanding job of being wonderfully ordinary people, doing ordinary things.

Self-esteem doesn't come from being extraordinary; it comes from appreciating the ordinary everyday stuff about who you are and what you do. So, if you pause to think about it, healthy self-esteem is well within your reach. It's not an exclusive club; anyone can join. You just need to sign yourself up.

Rejoicing in regularity

Part of accepting yourself as a normal human being – and believing that you're fine just as you are – involves rejoicing in a regular kind of life.

You can feel good about everything you do to keep your daily life running smoothly: going to work, making dinner, looking after the children, walking the dog, chatting to the neighbours and even scrubbing out the loo are all worthwhile day-to-day duties.

People with chronic low self-esteem often totally neglect the relevance of what they do to maintain their everyday lifestyle. You may dismiss, ignore and underestimate the value of carrying out mundane actions, or make the common error of assuming that all that everyday stuff is just a basic requirement that doesn't deserve to be applauded. But if so, you're wrong.

People with healthy self-esteem give themselves credit for, and take a 'job well done' attitude towards, all those everyday tasks.

You don't have to be building the next Taj Mahal to take some straightforward satisfaction from your basic DIY or house-cleaning efforts. Okay, so maybe you *haven't* set the world on fire but more importantly you may have prevented your own home from catching fire.

For the sake of driving a good point home, we repeat once more that you don't need to be living a particularly glamorous lifestyle to develop healthy self-esteem.

Discovering the treasures hidden in the tedium

'I'm just going through the motions' is a phrase we often hear from clients hounded by low self-esteem. Well, those motions that they're 'just going through' are pretty darn important (and we'd use a stronger word than 'darn' if we thought the publishers would allow it).

Although many aspects of your daily routine can be tedious and repetitive, they really do matter. If you're feeling low and full of negative thoughts, you can help yourself get a better perspective on things by taking more notice of what you're actually doing at any given time. Try to turn your attention away from how bad you're feeling and focus on the nitty-gritty of your routine actions. Really take in all the detail and pay attention to the moment – be present.

For example, if you're travelling to work on the bus, make a special effort to look at the people around you. Look out the window and notice what's going on outside in the streets. Because your bus route is so familiar, you can all too easily get lost in your thoughts and ignore the outside world. Pretend that you're in a foreign city and that everything around you is new. Look at your surroundings as if you're seeing them for the first time rather than the hundredth.

Even if you're doing something as lacklustre as cleaning the bathroom, try giving it your full attention. Take in every sensation, like the feel of the sponge against the porcelain and the sound of the cleaner squirting out of the bottle. Stand back and take pride in the gleam of the freshly cleaned mirror.

When you make yourself more aware of routine actions and events you probably notice many little details that you normally miss through being absorbed in your own thoughts. You may see some random acts of kindness on the bus that give your mood a bit of a lift. Even the bathroom can suddenly look cleaner than ever before.

An antidote to feeling like you're just going through the motions is to pay extra close attention to each individual motion. It's a deceptively simple strategy that can help you to feel connected with your environment again. Even the tedious everyday tasks of running a household and travelling to and from work can be gratifying if you choose to lavish them with a bit more attention. (If you find this idea interesting, read Chapter 5 where we discuss attention and focus in more detail).

'He rakes and trims the grass, he loves to mow and weed. I cook like Betty Crocker and I look like Donna Reed. There's plastic on the furniture to keep it neat and clean. In the Pine-Sol scented air, somewhere that's green.' (Another musical reference just to keep you on your toes, and this one is from *Little Shop of Horrors* by Alan Menken and Howard Ashman.)

Confronting Compensatory Strategies

If you have low self-esteem you may well compensate for it through your behaviour. Trying to hide your mistakes or distract attention from your shortcomings is very common, because you assume that they render you 'useless' or 'worthless'. You feel the pain of your low self-esteem so sharply that understandably you try to avoid triggering it off. Or perhaps you don't want other people to know how poorly you view yourself, in case they agree with your self-evaluation.

You can employ a variety of strategies to try to safeguard your fragile ego. Unfortunately lots of these strategies keep your negative beliefs about yourself at the forefront of your mind. Instead of giving you the chance to challenge your negative beliefs, compensatory strategies ensure that you continue to act as though they're true. This behaviour creates a vicious circle of low self-esteem thoughts and reinforcing actions, as illustrated in Figure 6-1.

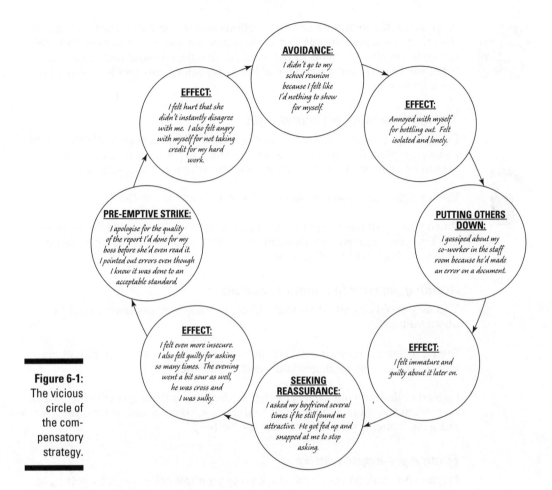

Figure 6-1:
The vicious
circle of
the com-
pensatory
strategy.

Getting honest about what you do to protect your ego

You may adopt any number of habits to try to cope with your low self-esteem. The next sections highlight some of the more common (but problematic) things people do to try to temporarily raise or protect their tenuous self-esteem.

As you read through the following sections and recognise yourself in some of the behaviours, give the suggested alternatives a trial run. You need time to notice the positive benefits of behavioural change, so allow yourself about three weeks to try out a new way of behaving before you decide whether or not it's working.

Trying too hard to 'get things right'

Doing things perfectly and acting perfectly at all times is impossible to achieve, so stop insisting that you must do everything right. Accept that you're a human being prone to making errors, bad decisions and misjudgements.

Every single person on the planet messes up from time to time.

When you try so hard to get things right, you lose a lot of the enjoyment of life. Enjoying yourself and allowing yourself to be imperfect is a crucial part of developing healthy self-esteem.

Avoiding potentially painful situations

You may avoid any situation that's likely to trigger off negative thoughts about yourself.

Trying to safeguard your self-esteem by avoiding certain places, situations and people just camouflages your negative self-beliefs.

Instead of driving your beliefs further underground through avoidance, work on challenging them and adopting better ones. (Have a look at Chapter 2 for more on changing your thinking for the better.)

Firing a pre-emptive strike

Maybe you think you can limit the pain of your low self-esteem by getting in the first punch. You may think that others are likely to be less critical of you when you do the criticising yourself. Apologising for the quality of your work as you present it or critically assessing your performance immediately after you've finished something are both examples of low self-esteem pre-emptive strikes.

Of course this behaviour just reinforces your negative thoughts and feelings, and so doesn't actually protect you at all. Instead of firing the first shot, keep your gun in the holster and give others a chance to respond to your work or performance.

Putting other people down

Your low self-esteem can lead you to compare yourself constantly with others. You may feel inferior so much of the time that giving others a right bashing can offer some respite. You may put other people down directly, in your mind or by complaining about them to others. You can try to escape your feelings of inferiority by trying to make yourself seem superior to others. But it's a short-lived solution.

Being so critical and judgemental of other people is exhausting and generally doesn't elicit warm responses from others. Instead of wavering between putting yourself down and character-assassinating others, stop doing both. Practise being accepting and non-judgemental towards yourself and those around you.

Over-emphasising a singular aspect of yourself

You may link all your sense of worth to one thing that you do well or have going for you. For example, you may devote all your time to study because you feel worthwhile when you get good marks. Or maybe you spend a lot of time and energy on your physical appearance because you get a sense of worth from being found attractive.

Making the most of your good points isn't a bad thing. But believing that your looks, intelligence or any other personal feature is the *only* thing that makes you worthwhile can cause problems. You may neglect other valuable aspects of yourself. You can also cause yourself a lot of anxiety because you fear losing that specific attribute and your self-esteem along with it.

Try to see yourself more holistically and put more emphasis on appreciating your whole self.

Seeking reassurance

If you rely on the approval of others to feel good about yourself, you can end up looking for reassurance. You may ask people directly to confirm that they like you or think you're doing a good job. Or you may be on the look out for hints, clues and evidence of what others feel about you.

Asking for reassurance is tiring for you and the people in your life. Plus, you probably never seem to get enough reassurance; the effects on your self-esteem don't last.

The solution is to provide yourself with reassurance when you really need some and to take your self-worth as a given the rest of the time. Your relationships are likely to benefit as well as your self-esteem. (In Chapter 12 we look closely at the effects of low self-esteem on personal relationships.)

Misusing alcohol or drugs

You may try to quell certain emotions because you think that they're a sign of weakness. For example, you may think that only weak people feel disappointment, anxiety, sadness or hurt.

Sometimes this refusal to allow yourself to feel certain ways can send you to the bottle. Although using alcohol or drugs may provide some temporary relief from painful emotions, it can lead to chemical dependency and lots of additional emotional problems in the long run. Also, the more you bottle up your feelings, the more risk you're at of developing psychological problems such as depression (see Chapter 2 for more details).

Experiencing strong negative emotions is a natural response to undesirable events; it's all part of the healing process. Try to think of your emotions as normal. Consider allowing yourself to experience feelings as a sign of psychological strength.

Convincing yourself that you're special

Trying to replace a belief that you're worthless with a belief that you're very special is fairly common. You may have the problematic idea that unless you're different and rare you don't count for much. Your beliefs about yourself may vacillate wildly between thinking you're insignificant or a 'nothing' and convincing yourself that you're a diamond in the rough, a prodigy waiting to happen.

You *are* special. But then again, so is everyone else. Challenge your idea that being special is the antidote to poor self-esteem. Read the earlier section 'Wearing the Skin You're In' and start to accept yourself as both average and worthwhile in equal measure.

Being a 'people pleaser'

Trying to like yourself by getting others to like you is a shortcut to social anxiety. Believing that you need to be liked and approved of by others in order to feel worthwhile leaves you in a state of desperation.

You may find yourself putting up with bad behaviour from others and allowing yourself to be taken advantage of in all manner of ways, none of which is terribly good for your self-esteem. *Wanting* to be liked by others but not *needing* always to be liked is consistent with healthy self-esteem. We talk more about this in the later 'Fending off the fear of negative evaluation' section.

Raising yourself above criticism

If like many people with self-esteem problems you believe that being criticised means you're a failure, no wonder you avoid it like the plague. You may go to extreme lengths to hide your mistakes or failures for fear of incurring criticism. Perhaps you put on a convincing façade of someone who's got everything figured out in order to appear flawless.

Hiding mistakes and difficulties can mean that you don't get any help when you need it. Small mistakes can grow into much bigger ones by keeping them under wraps.

Try exposing some of your mistakes and see what type of responses you actually get from others. You may be surprised how compassionate and helpful others can be. View criticism as a chance to discover some useful stuff. (You can find more information about how to make use of critical comments in Chapter 13.)

Blaming nature or your past for your problems

Refusing to take any responsibility for your low self-esteem beliefs can have the temporary advantage of minimising your sense of being 'useless', 'pathetic' or 'worthless'. But it also leaves you in a powerless position. Yes, your parents and your past may play a contributing role in the development of your self-esteem. Some of the problems you typically experience may also have some biological basis, but if you continue to play the blame game you never get off your victimised backside and make some useful changes.

Take some responsibility for your part in keeping old destructive messages from your past still playing today. Pay attention: You may be telling yourself the same old undermining things other people said to you earlier on in your life. Stop this low self-esteem-inducing repetition and create some new, more helpful self-directed messages. (Chapter 10 contains more on dealing with the past.)

Ferociously defending your self-worth

If you have confidence in your self-worth, you don't need to guard it like a Rottweiler. You respond defensively to any form of criticism because you believe that your self-esteem can be snatched away from you at any moment. You may be aggressive towards others if they disrespect you because your *self*-respect is negligible. Other people aren't the problem; your poor self-esteem is the issue.

You don't need to go around disabusing people of negative ideas they may hold about you. Instead you can let them have their opinions and form your own; you can choose to reject the ideas other people seem to have about you. When you have healthy self-esteem you're able to assert yourself when the situation genuinely calls for it. You don't need to confront every person who's rude or dismissive.

Coping with social anxiety

Feelings of low self-worth very often make social situations anxiety-provoking and hard work, which is a real shame because the desire for pleasurable social contact is hardwired into human beings. Humans want to feel part of a larger group and be in the company of others. Avoiding social contact can reinforce negative beliefs about yourself and lower your mood significantly.

Participating in painful post-mortems

If you battle with low self-esteem, you're likely to experience some degree of social anxiety. You probably worry very much about what others think of you based on your social conduct. You may also engage in the types of behaviours in the following list in an attempt to manage your fears and prevent social errors. Unfortunately these behaviours rarely benefit you and in fact do your self-esteem more damage in the long run. In the wake of a social event you may find yourself:

- **Reviewing the event over and over in your mind looking for any social errors you may have committed. Asking yourself questions like: 'Did I speak out of turn?', 'Did I say anything stupid or offensive?' and 'What kind of impression did I make?'**

    The more you search around in your memory for negative things, the more likely you are to find them or even make them up in your imagination. So you may end up taking a perfectly reasonable social interaction and turning it into a minefield of embarrassments and blunders in your memory. Needless to say, this behaviour does your mood and self-esteem no favours.

- **Replaying painful social moments over and over again.**

    You may focus on a single difficult moment – called a *cringe-making moment* because you tend to view it very negatively and inwardly (or physically) cringe when you focus on it – and ignore all the other positive and neutral aspects of the whole event.

    Dwelling on one awkward thing that you said or did in a social situation usually leads to blowing the severity of your social *faux-pas* completely out of proportion. You can make yourself feel very ashamed about something relatively minor in the grand scheme of things. Because you take your social gaffe out of context, you end up drawing all sorts of faulty conclusions about your overall social performance, such as: 'This just goes to show that I can't mix with others' or 'I always mess things up. No one will ever want me at a party again.' You may also believe that you'll never be able to recover from what's likely to have been only a minor social hiccup. Sometimes you can dwell on one small social incident for days or even weeks after the event.

✔ **Trying to re-script a social interaction in your head.**

If you're displeased with one aspect of your social performance (a cringe-making moment) you can sink deep into your imagination, trying to come up with ways you may have handled things differently. Thinking along the lines of 'If only I'd said *this* or done *that* instead' is a common habit among people lacking social confidence. You may think that you're going to discover something valuable by rewriting social events in your mind retrospectively. This is rarely the case; generally you simply make yourself feel more anxious and mortified about your actions.

Provoking a pre-mortem

You may try certain behaviours in anticipation of social interaction. These *pre-mortems* are very similar to post-mortems apart from the fact that you do them before rather than after an event.

Most people who engage in post-mortems also conduct mental pre-mortems, such as the following:

✔ Planning and preparing for an upcoming social event in your mind. You may invent fantasies about what's likely to happen in a future social situation, imagining all sorts of conversations, and try to prepare what you're going to say and do in an attempt to ensure that you 'get it right'. You may also put strict boundaries around your behaviour by insisting to yourself that you bite your tongue or do nothing to draw attention to yourself.

Planning can seem like a good idea but in fact you may just end up making yourself a bag of nerves. Also your predictions about what's going to unfold in a social setting are likely to be way off the mark. So your painstaking mental preparation is all for naught. Over-thinking how to handle conversations also squashes your spontaneity flat.

You can't predict the future and so you're better off just allowing it to happen and assume that you're going to handle things as and when they occur. You do your social confidence (and overall self-esteem) no good when you believe that you need to pre-plan your every social move.

✔ Doing an on-the-spot analysis. You may think really hard about what to say next during a conversation. Or, you start mentally analysing the effect of something you just said on the other person, searching her face and body language for clues about what she thinks about your last comment.

When you do this type of instant analysis, however, you often lose the thread of the conversation because you're so internally focused. Again your creativity and spontaneity get absolutely no airtime. You're so busy thinking about what to say or how to act that conversation becomes a labour-intensive procedure. Where's the enjoyment or naturalness in that? Instead of allowing conversation to flow naturally, you end up making every word you utter a test of your social capabilities.

You can't reasonably expect to find social interaction interesting and stimulating when excessive self-analysis is clogging up your mind.

Killing both pre- and post-mortem sessions

One of the most tragic things about participating in pre- and post-mortem styles of worry is that they actually impair your social performance. You may seem distracted and aloof during conversations. You may fail to join in on group discussions for fear of saying the wrong thing. You end up sitting in silence because you miss opportunities to interject due to your mental over-planning. Feelings of intense anxiety in social situations can lead you to stick to the walls and appear unapproachable. The post-mortem pain you put yourself through also tends to produce even more social anxiety and self-doubt. So you unwittingly bring about more of the types of experiences that you most want to avoid. Basically, none of this behaviour brings about desirable results.

You can start to overcome your fear of social *faux-pas* and awkwardness by taking on new attitudes and behaviours, such as the following:

✔ **Remember that what's done is done.** No amount of mental rewriting is going to change what has already happened. You can't travel back in time (if that were possible, where are the people from the future?). Try to accept whatever you said or did in a past social situation as history and *leave it alone*. Balance out your memories of social interaction by deliberately recalling the good stuff *and* the neutral aspects. Leave alone anything you're not happy with and mentally move on.

If you suffer from low self-esteem, you may find the pull of pre- and post-mortem social rumination difficult to resist. Worrying thoughts can feel very compelling. Try to catch yourself in the act and remind yourself that your negative thoughts and memories are more likely to be reflections of your low self-opinion rather than accurate representations of reality. Also try to use visual metaphors to interrupt rumination. For example, if you find yourself going over last night's party and cringing at memories of what you said or did, imagine crossing out the whole event with a thick black line. If the chatter in your mind becomes very loud, imagine hanging the phone up on yourself, slamming a book shut or forcefully closing a door against your negative thoughts.

✔ **Remind yourself that you're no mind reader.** You can guess what's in the mind of others until you're blue in the face but you never know for sure. Not unless they tell you, that is, and nine times out of ten, they don't. When you try to read other people's minds, your low self-esteem is likely to make all sorts of unpleasant and unhelpful guesses – the vast majority of them inaccurate.

You don't *need* to know exactly what others are thinking in order to interact socially. Give others permission to have their own thoughts and leave the mind reading to people like Derren Brown.

✔ **Recognise that smooth socialising is not your sole responsibility.** People with low self-esteem and poor social confidence often assume too much responsibility for the smooth running of social interactions. Remember that you're only ever one part of a conversation or group discussion. Other people play their part too. So when a lull or an uncomfortable moment occurs in a conversation, bear in mind that you don't have to be the one to fix it. Try to let the moment pass.

Remember that spates of awkwardness are a normal and inevitable part of human interactions. The world doesn't end if people run out of things to say or have differences of opinion.

✔ **Focus on the conversation and your external environment.** Rather than monitoring your every move and censoring your every word, look around you. Pay attention to what the other person is saying and let yourself respond without any preparation. Take in your environment instead of focusing on your own thoughts and feelings. (Harnessing your attention takes deliberate practice; you can find some useful tips in Chapter 5.)

✔ **Ask yourself whether people are *really* that fascinated by your social blunders.** Would you believe us if we told you that all the people who attended last night's party spent 1 hour the next day thinking about their own business and the other 23 thinking about your behaviour? We hope not. Although your social conduct may be very important to you, it's probably far less so to others.

When you're worrying about the impression you've made on others, put things into a more realistic perspective. Other people were not placed on this planet with the singular purpose of judging you.

✔ **Have faith in your social abilities.** The chances are good that you've got a lot more social skills than you may be giving yourself credit for. When you stop putting so much time and energy into pre- and post-mortems you have more space to unleash your social skills. Instead of worrying about what's best to say and do, try thinking: 'Whatever happens, I'll deal with it'. Have some faith in your ability to navigate conversations and to cope with any difficulties that happen to arise.

✔ **Be daring for a change.** Tear up the script and go improv: tell a joke, relate an anecdote, flirt ('In olden days a glimpse of stocking was looked on as something shocking but now, heaven knows, anything goes' . . . we did warn you about the musical references. This is a lyric from Cole Porter's *Anything Goes*). Offer your opinion, laugh like a hyena if you feel so inclined. Give your personality a chance to shine. If you truly want to feel more comfortable socially, you need to take some risks. Otherwise you're going to remain locked in a cycle of over-preparation and regret. The vast majority of people find that they enjoy social contact most when they're able to let themselves just be themselves. Try it out and see for yourself.

Fending off the fear of negative evaluation

If you honestly didn't care about whether or not people liked you and if you were completely uninterested in the opinions of others, that *would* be weird. In fact, it would be a little bit frightening. Having awareness of ourselves as social beings is part of what makes us human. Wanting to fit in socially and be accepted keeps us behaving responsibly.

Having said that, making sure that everybody you ever meet likes you is simply impossible. You just aren't going to be able to impress the socks off all the people you encounter.

Your own personality and tastes inevitably differ from those of others. Sometimes the mixture is a match made in heaven and other times not.

Even if you try to sacrifice your own personality in favour of pleasing others, you're going to fail. Your own unique traits and characteristics are stronger than you may think and you can't keep them suppressed forever. Subjugating your own views and individuality in an effort to fit in with the expectations of others makes for unhappiness and a poor sense of your own worth. That's why, in the interests of improving your self-esteem and getting the most out of life, holding a flexible attitude about the way other people evaluate you is of paramount importance.

By *flexible* we mean allowing room for the possibility of being both liked and disliked: keeping your preference to be liked and accepted but ditching your demand that you *must* be liked in order for you to think and feel positively about who you are.

Use the following suggestions of flexible thinking to combat your fear of negative evaluation:

✔ I want to be liked by others, but I can survive the disappointment of being disliked.

✔ I want but don't *need* to be approved of by people I admire.

✔ I value other people's opinions as important, but not more so than my own.

✔ I don't want anyone to disapprove of me, but although it's unfortunate and regrettable, such disapproval doesn't make me any less worthwhile.

✔ I don't enjoy the pain of being disliked, but it's not unbearable.

✔ I prefer to be likeable to others, but I accept that in reality I'm not going to be everyone's cup of tea.

Taking on board these flexible attitudes puts you in good stead for dealing with rejection. You're more readily able to process your negative feelings and recover. These attributes also make you more resilient to criticism and help you to make good relationship choices.

Overcoming your fears of being negatively evaluated by others allows you to flaunt your personality feathers and spread your wings of individuality. You can allow others to get to know the real you and let yourself find out all about them. ('Knowing me, knowing you . . . ah ha'. We felt we had to end the chapter with one more musical number and you guessed it! It's ABBA's *Knowing me, Knowing you*. Pretty easy to spot that one.)

Dropping Reservations about Liking Who You Are

Sometimes people have concerns about developing healthy self-esteem. This may sound preposterous, but people get used to feeling negatively about themselves and changing that seems scary. Perhaps you think that your low self-esteem protects you from taking risks that may end up in disappointment.

You may be well aware of the drawbacks associated with your poor self-opinion, and yet think that at least the feeling is familiar and in some ways comfortable. If you start acting as if you have a better opinion of yourself, no doubt you need to be doing new things. Throwing yourself into new experiences can be uncomfortable, strange and awkward. If you weigh up the pain of staying the same against the pain of change, however, you may find the scales tipping in favour of breaking out of your comfort zone.

People also sometimes worry that if their self-esteem improves they may become arrogant and egotistical. This outcome is unlikely, however, because as we hope we make clear throughout this book, healthy self-esteem is about appreciating yourself and putting your worth *on a par* with others. Healthy self-esteem is not equivalent to having a superiority complex.

Likewise, feelings of low self-esteem aren't the same as being modest or having humility. You can have very healthy self-esteem and still be modest. In fact most people who truly think well of themselves display appropriate levels of pride without boasting and bragging all the time. So you can put your mind at ease.

Chapter 7

Building a Better Body Image

*I*f you're totally honest with yourself, you probably care a great deal about how you look. Most people like to appear attractive to other people of both sexes. You're also likely to care a lot about being happy with how *you* think you look physically.

Wanting to look nice is normal. However, many people place too much emphasis on physical beauty and attach their self-worth to their looks, which can lead to low self-esteem.

Men and women alike have unrealistic expectations of how they *should* look and are perpetually dissatisfied with their appearance. Striving for the 'body beautiful' and thinking that you're less worthwhile if you don't look like a supermodel is probably one of the main causes of low self-esteem.

In this chapter we discuss ways in which you may be bringing yourself down on the basis of physical appearance and make suggestions on how to extract yourself from this common trap.

Looking in the Mirror (or Not!)

Mirror, mirror on the wall, who's the fairest of them all? You probably instantly recognise that quote from the fairy tale *Snow White*. And how do you respond to the question if you have good self-esteem? We don't want to encourage you to shout 'Me, I'm the fairest!', nor do we want you to mutter 'Certainly not me, I'm an ugly troll'. Both responses indicate far too much concern with physical beauty, and both are potentially self-destructive.

Beauty is only one aspect of your overall self. If you over-value appearance, at some point you're likely to put yourself down based on your looks. Your self-esteem is sure to suffer if you believe that good looks make you a 'good' person. Even if you like how you look and get lots of compliments about how handsome or pretty you are, basing your self-opinion on looks alone is problematic. If you decide that good looks make you a valued person (or even superior to others) what happens to your self-esteem when your looks alter or fade? What if someone fails to comment on your looks or doesn't seem to be that bowled over by your beauty? What happens when you meet someone that you assess as being even more attractive than you? Your self-esteem takes a nosedive. Equally if you're more of the 'I'm an ugly troll' opinion, you're calling yourself names and bullying yourself into perpetual low self-esteem.

So what's the best way to answer the 'Who's the fairest of them all' question? Well, ideally you don't ask the question at all. Instead, look into the mirror and say: 'That's me and I'm a worthwhile person just how I am'. Easier said than done, right? Well here's the good news, practice makes you better at it.

How you use mirrors indicates how much importance your place on physical appearance. A lot of people use mirrors too much and others avoid them like the plague. See if any of the more common mistakes people make when using mirrors apply to you:

✔ Avoiding mirrors altogether and turning away from your reflection in windows or shiny surfaces.

✔ Checking in mirrors frequently to make sure that you still look okay; for example, carrying a compact mirror and looking in it several times per hour or running off to the bathroom in the middle of meals or meetings to check yourself in the mirror. This *mirror checking* usually causes you to feel worse about your looks rather than better.

✔ Looking only in mirrors in which you think you look best; for example, mirrors that have a slimming effect or reflect only the top half of your body.

✔ Making faces at yourself in the mirror, not to amuse yourself but to belittle yourself because you think you're ugly.

✔ Making yourself late for work because you had to get your hair or make-up perfect.

✔ Pulling your face about in an effort to see whether you look better with different features; for example, changing the shape of your nose, lifting your eyelids, trying to smooth out your wrinkles and so on.

✔ Spending a lot of time at the mirror trying to look 'just right' or not leaving the mirror until you 'feel' okay about how you look. Everyone has his or her own routine for getting ready before leaving the house, but some take more time than others in front of the mirror.

✔ Standing in certain positions when looking in the mirror so that you see only specific parts of your body reflected or your face in profile.

✔ Using mirrors in rooms with low lighting.

Making these common mirror mistakes may help you to cope in the short term but you may well notice that you feel even worse about your appearance in the long term.

Both avoiding mirrors and using them excessively tend to reinforce insecurity about your looks.

Try to develop a different relationship with mirrors. Use the mirror only as long as is strictly necessary to style your hair or do your make-up. Resist the urge to keep checking how you look. Alternatively, if you're a mirror avoider, practise taking a passing glance at yourself in the mirror. Try to suspend judgement when you see your reflection. We offer you more techniques on making friends with your appearance in the following sections.

Discovering how to like what you see

Your body is your vehicle for experiencing the world and it deserves some respect and appreciation. If you can discover how to truly appreciate and cherish your physical self, you're well on the road to improving your overall self-esteem.

You probably have certain thinking habits associated with your appearance. Perhaps you think of yourself as unattractive and therefore that's what you expect to see in the mirror. If you have a habit of thinking of your appearance negatively, you can end up homing in on imperfections – real or imagined. Negative thoughts about your appearance and attention to flaws increase your dissatisfaction with how you look. Unfortunately, your poor opinion of your looks is also likely to lead you to the conclusion that everyone else in the world thinks you've been hit with the ugly stick too. In an attempt to get a better-balanced view of your attractiveness (and to divorce your self-worth from your physical appearance), consider the following points:

- ✔ **Attraction is more than a pretty face or a six-pack midriff.** The way you move, your facial expressions, the look in your eyes, your ideas, your gestures, your sense of humour, your likes and dislikes, your skills and your experiences – your whole personality is involved in how attractive you are to others. All these aspects of who you are (and more) can make you very attractive.

- ✔ **Beauty is in the eye of the beholder.** Some people prefer blondes, others brunettes. Tall or short, blue eyed or brown eyed, slim or curvy, muscular or lean – everyone has his or her own individual taste. If someone finds you attractive, that's up to them, not you!

- ✔ **Even models and movie stars don't like some aspects of their looks, so you're not alone in your dissatisfactions with your appearance.**

- ✔ **Imperfections that seem huge to you may be scarcely noticeable to others.** Even if others do notice imperfections in your looks, the chances are that they don't really care about them (certainly not as much as you do!).

- ✔ **Nature has given you what it has in the looks department,** and although you can make the most of that, basically you get what you're born with. So assuming that beautiful people have more worth than ordinary-looking people is plain crazy.

Have you ever known someone with a lot of physical appeal who fails to attract you in the personality department? What about people who are nothing special in terms of looks but knock your socks off when you get to know them? If you've answered 'yes' to these questions then it just goes to show that attractiveness is about more than just physical appearance. So if your low self-esteem tells you that you're unattractive, tell it to shut up. You don't have to be a knock-out physically to be attractive to others. We've all noticed that the more we get to like someone, the more attractive that person seems, and sometimes a person's physical 'flaw' becomes our favourite feature about him or her.

Healthy self-esteem involves being able to accept the way you look and being able to put the importance of looks into perspective.

Stop putting so much pressure on yourself to look a certain way. Try treating your body well and thinking about it in positive ways. Look into the mirror with a little love and gratitude for a change!

Ceasing counter-productive comparison

Looking at other people and measuring up your looks against theirs is common, and (surprise, surprise) you usually come out of the comparison feeling worse rather than better. See whether you engage in any of the following behaviours on a regular basis:

- ✔ Checking to see if other people are fatter, thinner, bigger- or smaller-busted, taller, shorter or more muscular than you.

- ✔ Comparing how types of clothing look on you against how they look on others.

- ✔ Concluding that other people look happier and more fun than you do (and therefore are more attractive because you look miserable and no fun by comparison).

- ✔ Focusing on facial features and deciding that another person has a prettier nose, stronger chin, more symmetrical face, bigger eyes and so on.

- ✔ Looking at people and deciding that they appear more confident and strong than you do.

When you play the comparison game, you're knocking yourself down. Instead of accepting yourself, you're searching for reassurance that you look okay, or that others look worse than you do, or both. Your attention is aimed squarely at physical appearance and so it becomes disproportionately important in your mind.

The truth is that in general the more accepting you are of your looks the more outwardly confident you appear, and self-respect and confidence are in themselves attractive features.

Instead of comparing, practise merely *observing* people around you. Stop making value judgments about your looks. If you see someone with great hair, allow yourself to acknowledge this fact but leave *your* hair out of it! If a pair of jeans flatter a woman's figure, great. Don't start musing on how much better they look on her than you think they would on you.

Being overly concerned with physical looks can obviously lead to low self-esteem. But your judgemental attitude may also mean that you harshly condemn others based on their looks. Try to notice when you pass negative comments on the way others look and make a deliberate effort to *observe* not *judge*. Train your brain to recognise that you're no better than anyone else just because you're good-looking. Nor are you to be any less valued than anyone else who's better looking than you: 'better looking' doesn't equal 'better person'.

People sometimes compare themselves to models in magazines – not a good idea. Models are perceived to be of above average good looks and that's why they end up modelling. In addition, the people appearing in advertisements and magazines have professionals doing their hair and make-up, skilled photographers taking their pictures and technicians polishing their image. Most people don't have make-up artists at their disposal.

The fact of the matter is that the majority of people in the world are relatively average-looking. Most people are attractive in their own unique ways but few are good-looking in the way that sells magazines. So resist comparing yourself to models or actors.

Seeing Yourself Holistically

When you're insecure about your looks, often you see only the bits you judge as bad or unattractive. You can easily think of your entire appearance as just a pair of big thighs or a set of crooked teeth. Not surprisingly, this kind of selective attention can lead to poor body image and ultimately poor self-esteem, especially if you link your self-worth to your appearance.

When you start to look at yourself holistically, you look at the whole picture. *Holistic* means looking at the entirety of something instead of just one or two select parts. Perhaps you've got a great infectious laugh, a sparkling wit, natural rhythm or a lovely voice. Don't underestimate how powerfully attractive these kinds of traits can be to others around you. Sometimes a person's face becomes suddenly beautiful when they laugh and you can see their personality shining through.

Being overly concerned with physical appearance can cause you to overlook or completely discount important aspects of your overall self that make you attractive. Figure 7-1 shows lots of common human attributes that contribute greatly to interpersonal attraction. See whether you're failing to take into account positive features of yourself when thinking about your overall attractiveness.

Finding out how to view yourself as a complex, multi-faceted human being is an important step in overcoming poor body image and poor self-esteem. Make the most of all your positive and intriguing features. Give yourself credit for the personal attraction that you hold beyond that of your face and body. Remember, you're not a flat, static photograph; you're a moving, living and vibrant creature, and that's part of your attraction.

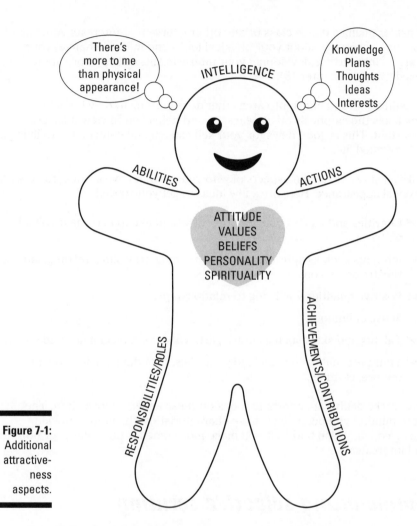

Figure 7-1:
Additional
attractive-
ness
aspects.

Accentuating aspects apart from appearance

In the spirit of putting the importance of looks into perspective, try focusing on making the most of some of the other aspects of yourself referred to in Figure 7-1.

Consider taking a dance class or any other course that interests you. Spend less time obsessing about your physical looks and instead channel your energies into further developing your interests and values (more about value-based living in Chapter 15).

Investing time and effort into areas that have nothing to do with how you look takes the emphasis off appearance and helps you to view it as less important. This is good news for your self-esteem and contributes to living a well-rounded life.

Make a list of at least ten aspects of who you are that have nothing to do with physical appearance. Here are a few ideas to get you started:

- ✔ Charities and causes you support (or would like to become involved with).
- ✔ Interests such as sports, animals, gardening, travelling, reading, cinema, theatre and so on.
- ✔ Positive qualities you bring to relationships.
- ✔ Sense of humour.
- ✔ Talents and skills such as music, art, woodwork, mechanics and so on.
- ✔ Your personal taste in all kinds of things, including music, food, architecture, clothing.

Now, make deliberate efforts to focus on these aspects more often. The more mindful you become of these characteristics, the more you value them. You may also find that you make more time for pursuing your hobbies and interests.

Surmounting selective scrutiny

When you look into the mirror you probably focus on the parts of yourself that you don't like. This selective scrutiny serves only to make your 'problem areas' seem more extreme than they are in reality. Focusing on the negative tends to lower your mood and further compound your poor body image. This body-focused negativity can easily cause you to a make a *global negative self-evaluation* (which in common parlance is low self-esteem).

In this section we take a little look at your *appearance demons* – the physical features that you really dislike about yourself. The usual areas of focus include:

✔ Body hair

✔ Body shape and weight

✔ Colour or texture of skin or hair

✔ Height

✔ Scars, moles, birthmarks, acne or other facial anomalies

✔ Shape of a physical feature; for example, nose, mouth and ears

✔ Size of a physical feature; for example, breasts, muscles, bum and tum, thighs, hands and feet

The list of possible areas of dissatisfaction is potentially endless; the effect, however, all depends on how you view yourself.

Use the space in Table 7-1 to identify your specific appearance demons, no matter how trivial or superficial your complaint may seem to others. What matters is the effect it has on *you*. So record your areas of focus even if they include something like the shape or length of your toes!

Table 7-1	My Appearance Scrutiny Summary
Physical Area	*My Appearance Demons*
Face/Head/Hair	
Upper Body	
Lower Body	
Other	

Getting specific about your appearance demons is important because it helps you discover what to stop focusing on so much.

Bearing down on your better points

People with a healthy body image don't necessarily think that they're utterly gorgeous. Instead they're able to take the rough with the smooth, as it were. They recognise that they have physical imperfections just like anyone else but they choose not to focus on them all the time. Instead, they focus their attention on what they like about the way they look.

When you have a healthy body image, you tend to make the best of your good points and view yourself as a whole package. And to do so, you need to get serious about identifying your good bits.

Use Table 7-2 to list the physical attributes you appreciate about yourself. Don't worry about how small your area of satisfaction seems, record it!

Table 7-2	My Best Features Fact File
Physical Area	*My Areas of Appreciation*
Face/Head/Hair	
Upper Body	
Lower Body	
Other	

Now review what you recorded in Tables 7-1 and 7-2. If you dislike many more attributes than you like, go back and see whether you can even things out. Remember compliments you may have had and check out whether you've recorded these features of your appearance. Also think about whether or not you're being fair to yourself. When you're used to thinking of your appearance very critically you may need to work hard to counteract this tendency.

The next step is to resist selectively focusing on your less good bits and instead to re-focus your attention onto your physical good points. Make deliberate attempts to look at yourself as a *whole person* rather than just dwelling on specific parts of your body or face. Pay a little extra attention to areas of appearance that you're satisfied with and give yourself one or two compliments every day.

Improving where you can

You may be able to exorcise a few of your appearance demons by making healthy and appropriate changes: work to shed extra weight or increase your muscle tone; have your hair dyed or your teeth whitened; get laser treatments to diminish or remove scarring or skin discoloration. (We strongly recommend that you postpone going for cosmetic surgery until you've been assessed for Body Dysmorphic Disorder (BDD). Often surgery is not the answer for BDD sufferers who simply transfer their negative focus to another area of the body or feel dissatisfied with the results of surgery. Check out Chapter 2 for more on BDD.)

Looking after your physical health and your emotional well-being is one of the simplest and most effective ways of making the most of your looks. Looking after yourself is good for your appearance.

Everyone tends to look their best when they're fit, happy and healthy. When you exercise regularly, make time to relax, eat well and get enough rest you can probably see the benefits in your appearance. Your eyes shine, your skin glows and your hair's glossy (well, we can't actually *guarantee* all that but we hope you get the general picture).

Making changes for the right reasons is vital. Any changes you make in your appearance must be aimed at improving your *personal* satisfaction with your looks. Making changes because you think they're going to make you more popular or likeable is potentially problematic. We re-emphasise here that your looks are only one aspect of your whole being. Double check that you aren't falling into the trap of believing that being better-looking makes you a better, more worthwhile person.

You're almost certainly going to dislike some aspects of your appearance that you can't change. However, you can decide to make them less important to you. See yourself more holistically and refuse to focus on individual flaws; in this way you can come to appreciate your appearance.

Getting help to counteract body-beautiful messages

You can't escape the fact that society and the media put a lot of emphasis on looks. Pressure to be slim and look young helps to sell a multitude of beauty products. The advertisers' message is that beauty really matters, and keeping a balanced perspective about appearance in the face of such strong external influences is difficult.

Some people find that their preoccupation with their looks causes them considerable emotional upset. If your dissatisfaction with your overall appearance (or one or two aspects of your appearance) is beginning to interfere with your ability to function, you may need some professional help.

Eating disorders and Body Dysmorphic Disorder (BDD) are two conditions that cause health problems as well as severe psychological distress. The symptoms of these disorders are outlined in more detail in Chapter 2. Don't hesitate to seek professional help when you think you can't overcome your body-image problems on your own or with the help of this book.

Cognitive behavioural therapy is the recommended treatment for both BDD and eating disorders. We recommend that you look for a therapist who has significant experience of dealing with body-image problems and eating disorders. Check the Appendix for a list of professional bodies where you can find qualified therapists.

Accepting That You Are Who You Are

Your ultimate goal in achieving healthy self-esteem is not only to accept yourself but also to truly appreciate your individuality.

Developing a more accurate and positive body image involves overcoming the fear of drawing attention to yourself. We're not suggesting that you go around dressed in a clown suit (unless you really want to) but we are suggesting that you resist hiding yourself away. You may be worried that if you draw attention to yourself others are going to pick holes in your appearance. Fear of what others may think of you can prevent you from exhibiting your own personal style, and then venturing outside of your comfort zone becomes pretty scary. But you can become more comfortable over time, especially if you hold a self-accepting attitude instead of being harshly self-critical.

Deciding to decorate yourself

Having a poor body image can often mean that you avoid going clothes shopping or indulging in accessories. You may think, 'What's the point? I'll only feel worse about my appearance if I make an effort with clothes.' Well, you may be wrong about that. Wearing the same comfortable 'safe' clothing all the time can get boring and reinforce negative views about your appearance. Taking the time to pick out clothing that you like, that fits you well and suits your figure can be very rewarding. Choosing colours that really go well with your colouring can give your wardrobe an exciting new dimension. You can also get yourself some nice accessories, such as jewellery, belts, watches, shoes, scarves, bags, cufflinks, glasses, ties, gloves or hair clips.

If you think of your body as the 'house' for all aspects of yourself, we're suggesting that you do some decorating. You probably have your home decorated according to your personal taste, and so why not apply the same principle to your appearance? Looking after your living environment has a positive impact on mood because you're implying that your home is worth looking after. Therefore, you must be worthwhile as well, by association. So if you want to feel better about your looks *and* be convinced of your intrinsic worth (whatever you happen to look like), try delving into decoration.

Developing deeper interests

Poor body image can get in the way of pursuing personal development goals. If you fear drawing attention to yourself (because you're insecure about your appearance and your general self-opinion is pretty low) you may not want to enter unfamiliar situations. Such avoidance can be a real shame because you can end up missing out on many fun and interesting things. You may also be doing your self-esteem further damage because you never give yourself the chance to acquire new skills or knowledge.

Take the risk and allow yourself to develop your personal interests. Doing so has many benefits, including helping you to take the focus off your appearance. Investigate classes, clubs or individual training in whatever subject takes your fancy. Don't allow your appearance demons to bully you into avoidance and inactivity. Remind yourself that by facing your fears you can overcome your fear of your face (or body for that matter)!

Chapter 8

Spotlighting Personal Development

*H*uman beings are goal-orientated. You feel best when you're actively engaged in pursuing goals and projects you find personally absorbing. Being goal-driven stimulates your mind and gives you a sense of purpose. Some goals are very concrete and practical, such as getting a new job, moving house, learning to drive and so on. Others are more to do with overcoming emotional problems, such as low self-esteem, and negative feelings such as guilt, anxiety or depression. Concrete, practical goals are mostly focused on personal development whilst other goals like developing healthy self-esteem are more focused on overcoming emotional problems.

In this chapter we offer you some basic guidelines for setting attainable goals, either practical or emotional. We also give you some tips on how to increase your motivation and inspiration to help you reach your personal goals.

Some of your goals may be directly related to improving your self-esteem, such as going out recreationally more often or joining a group of some kind. Others may focus on making positive changes to your lifestyle or circumstances (for example, eating well and exercising regularly), but indirectly have a positive impact on your feelings of self-worth. In general, goals are beneficial for you. They are part and parcel of personal development.

No hard and fast rules exist about what counts as a personal goal and what doesn't – unlimited goal-possibilities are available. In Chapters 14 and 15 of this book we discuss two related topics: ongoing personal commitments and value-based living. These terms refer to personal objectives that are persistent and more permanent lifestyle changes rather than goals that have a clear end point. You may find that reading those two chapters in conjunction with this one is useful.

Setting Sensible Goals

Your goals can be as diverse as pebbles on a beach. Whatever you want to achieve, follow the guidelines listed here via the acronym 'SPORT', to give yourself a 'sporting' chance of setting good goals and reaching them:

- **Specific:** Be clear about where, when, how (and with whom) you want to feel and act differently. For example, you may want to feel a bit nervous but not panicked about saying 'no' to a demanding friend when she asks you to build her website.

    Nervousness is a less extreme and uncomfortable feeling than panic. Nervousness allows you to be assertive when it's in your best interest to do so (liking saying 'no' to an unreasonable or inconvenient request). Panic on the other hand is likely to cause you to freeze up and you may end up agreeing to do things that you don't have time for or the desire to do.

- **Positive:** If possible, try to state your goals in positive terms that imply moving *towards* something or doing more of something. You give yourself more of a boost if you think of yourself striving *towards* rather than fighting *against* something. For example, express your goal as 'to be more socially active' rather than 'being less socially isolated'.

- **Observable:** Think of observable behavioural changes that signal progress towards your goal. For example, booking tickets to a concert and accepting dinner invitations are behaviours that are clearly in keeping with a goal of 'becoming more socially active'.

- **Realistic:** Choose goals that you can really see yourself achieving. Your goals need to be dependent on your own efforts and not on the actions of other people. Realistic goals can help to keep you focused and motivated. If your goals are too ambitious, you may get discouraged. For example, a goal 'to be invited out by friends every weekend' may be more often than is likely to happen and also implies that your friends are the ones who determine whether or not you achieve your goal.

✔ **Time bound:** Give yourself a realistic time frame in which to reach your specific goal. Having a time in mind fuels your motivation and increases the likelihood of you progressing with your goal-orientated behaviour.

Your time frame will vary depending on your goal. The basic rule of thumb is to give yourself ample time to reach your goal but not too much time so that you end up putting off taking action indefinitely. Concrete tasks like completing a course may be easier to set a time frame for than goals that involve overcoming emotional problems like depression or low self-esteem.

So set yourself a rough time by which you aim to see obvious improvement, but also be prepared to adjust your time frame if circumstances make it necessary to do so. Life sometimes gets in the way of your goals and it's better if you bear this in mind from the beginning. Doing so guards you against disappointment, discouragement and motivational crisis.

Some goals, such as overcoming low self-esteem, can take a long time to fulfil. Be wary of setting too rigid a time scale and making yourself vulnerable to depression or anger if success takes longer than you planned. Focus instead on having made improvement by a certain date and be flexible about how long developing and maintaining healthy self-esteem may take.

Getting to grips with goal-orientated behaviour

Goal-orientated behaviour is anything that you do that moves you closer to reaching your ultimate goal. If you bear your goal in mind and then think of the kind of actions that are consistent with that goal, you've got goal-orientated behaviour.

Whatever your goal is, practical or emotional, break it down into smaller steps or *sub-goals* (you can also call the steps leading to your ultimate goal *mini-goals*). You can use your mini- or sub-goals as markers for your progression towards your bigger overall goal.

Imagine yourself marching steadily towards your ultimate goal. Make a note of all the smaller achievements you're likely to realise along the way. These smaller achievements and new behaviours are the sub-goals that make reaching your big goal possible. Goal attainment is a journey, so it makes sense for you to chart your course by breaking it down into clear steps.

Trisha wants to get back to work now that her youngest child is school age. Her goal is 'to get back to part-time work as a receptionist'. Her list of goal-orientated behaviours is as follows:

✔ Doing an Information Technology (IT) course to improve her computer skills.

✔ Signing up with an employment agency.

✔ Drawing up her Curriculum Vitae (CV).

✔ Brushing up on her interview technique with a friend who works in human resources.

Harry has a more emotionally based goal. He wants to overcome his fear of offending other people. He states his goal as 'to become more able to speak my mind confidently despite the possibility of offending someone'. Some of his goal-orientated behaviours include:

✔ Offering his opinion on current affairs during social discussions.

✔ Voicing his dissatisfaction with specific procedures at work during the staff meeting and offering viable alternatives (like giving his opinion on improvement possibilities for the company's recycling programme).

✔ Asking his flatmates to turn down the TV when he's trying to get to sleep.

Setting target dates milestones

In order to maximise your goal-reaching potential, set target dates for your goal-orientated behaviours and choose a realistic time frame in which to reach your ultimate goal.

After you break your overall goal down into smaller bite-size chunks or steps, decide when you aim to chew the chunks and climb the steps. Build them into your daily life wherever possible and create a clear image of yourself reaching smaller targeted milestones on the way to arriving at your big goal. Every little goal-orientated action you take is grist to your ultimate goal mill.

Some goals are more concrete in nature, such as Trisha's goal to get back into employment. Other goals, such as Harry's, are more focused on changing your emotions and thinking. For this reason, Trisha can more easily estimate how long she's going to take to complete an IT course and find a job than Harry can judge when he'll be able to speak his mind confidently despite the possibility of offending others. However, both Trisha and Harry can look at their goal-orientated behaviours and allot certain times for carrying them out. For example, Harry can practise asking his flatmates to turn down the TV or do their share of the housework a minimum of twice per week. Similarly, Trisha can aim to have her CV done within a fortnight.

Weighing the Costs and Benefits

You may feel tempted to return to old unhelpful ways of behaving when you focus only on the short term and don't keep your ultimate goal in mind. For example, Harry may decide that keeping his mouth shut saves him a lot of anxiety in the present moment. However, on reflection Harry is often angry with himself for not acting more confidently in social situations. In the long term he knows that this behaviour is eroding his self-esteem.

Using a *cost-benefit analysis (CBA)* form (see Figure 8-1) can help rejuvenate your commitment to a specific goal. You can use CBA to examine the advantages and disadvantages of persisting with a number of different types of goals. You can use the form to examine the pros and cons of sticking with:

✔ Behavioural goals such as voicing your opinions or getting fit.

✔ Emotional goals such as overcoming depression or anxiety.

✔ Practical goals such as changing your job or completing a project.

✔ Thinking/belief goals such as aiming to think of yourself in positive and helpful ways.

When using the CBA form remember to think about costs and benefits:

✔ **In the short term:** Record what you stand to gain and lose in the present or near future by pursuing your goal.

✔ **In the long term:** Record potential gains and losses in the more distant future (like in six months, a year and longer) arising from pursuing your goal.

✔ **For yourself:** Write down the possible personal costs and benefits of reaching your goal.

✔ **For other people:** Consider and record the costs and benefits of achieving your goal to other important people in your life.

Complete the CBA form in pairs so that you actually end up assessing the costs and benefits of sticking with your goal as well as the results of abandoning it.

Figure 8-2 is the CBA form that Harry completed.

COSTS AND BENEFITS OF GOAL:	
COSTS:	**BENEFITS:**
1.	1.
2.	2.
3.	3.
4.	4.
5.	5.
COSTS AND BENEFITS OF RELINQUISHING GOAL:	
COSTS:	**BENEFITS:**
1.	1.
2.	2.
3.	3.
4.	4.
5.	5.

Figure 8-1:
Your cost-
benefit
analysis
form.

COSTS AND BENEFITS OF GOAL:
  Voicing my opinions and standing up for myself.

COSTS:	**BENEFITS:**
1. *I feel anxious that I might offend someone.*	1. *I feel better for voicing my opinions. Other people seem interested in what I have to say.*
2. *I could offend someone and lose a friend.*	2. *I get a good nights sleep when I ask for the TV to be turned down.*
3.	3. *I don't get depressed and hopeless when I do stand up for myself.*
4.	4.
5.	5.

COSTS AND BENEFITS OF RELINQUISHING GOAL:
  Staying quiet in social situations and not standing up for myself.

COSTS:	**BENEFITS:**
1. *I feel angry often about things other people do and it eats away at me.*	1. *I avoid anxiety and worry.*
2. *I rarely get what I want or need.*	2. *I'm unlikely to offend someone.*
3. *No one gets a chance to know what I think about issues. I feel left out of conversations.*	3. *People think I'm easy-going and easy to live with.*
4.	4.
5.	5.

Figure 8-2:
Harry's
cost-benefit
analysis
form.

After you've done your CBA, scrutinise any 'benefits' of abandoning your goal and the 'costs' of pursuing it. Are you being strictly accurate? Ask yourself how a good friend may respond to your arguments for giving up on your goal. The more you can convince yourself of the benefits of change, the more motivation you experience.

Part of successfully reaching a goal of any kind (such as taking on a new skill or overcoming social anxiety) involves tolerating short-term discomfort for long-term gain.

Keeping track of your progress

Being able to see progress helps you recover from setbacks and stay goal-orientated. You can congratulate yourself for your efforts and by charting your progress remind yourself that you're going to succeed in the end.

Figure 8-3 is a form you can use to keep a record of your progress towards your goal, including any obstacles and how you surmount them. We recommend that you use the form every two weeks to give yourself enough time to have made observable progress. Here's how to use it:

1. **Write down the specific goal you're working towards.**

   Include any information about problematic emotions and behaviours you may be experiencing as obstacles to reaching your goal.

   For example, Trisha identified her goal as 'getting back into work after having been a full-time carer for my children for the past seven years'. Harry recorded his emotional *problem* as 'feeling anxious about offending others and therefore keeping my opinions to myself and rarely standing up for myself' and his *goal* as 'being concerned about offending others but still acting in my best interest through assertion and open communication'.

2. **Record your progress.**

   Keep your goal positively stated and remain clear about what you want to achieve. Be specific about how you want to feel and act differently.

   Make note of even the smallest positive changes you make that bring you a little bit closer to your ultimate goal.

   Harry recorded talking in a staff meeting and telling his boss that certain deadlines for reports seemed unrealistic given his workload. Trisha recorded her progressive action of contacting a recruitment agency and seeing a career adviser.

3. **Rate how close you are to reaching your goal on a range from 0 to 10, where 0 means no progress at all and 10 means that you've achieved your goal.**

PROBLEM:		
GOAL RELATED TO PROBLEM:	DATE:	RATING:
	DATE:	RATING:
	DATE:	RATING:
	DATE:	RATING:

Figure 8-3:
Your
progress
chart.

Dealing with downfalls

On your journey towards your goal you may well stumble a few times and run into obstacles. When the going gets tough, your motivation can make a hasty exit, and if you start reneging on goal-orientated behaviour, your self-esteem may well follow suit.

When that happens, you need to get yourself back on track, firmly but kindly. Giving yourself a very hard time about setbacks may so demoralise you that you give up entirely. Remind yourself that Rome wasn't built in a day and that you're only human. Then pick yourself up, dust yourself down and try your hardest one more time.

Check your cost benefit analysis form again (refer to Figure 8-1) and add to it if you want.

Identifying Inspirational Role Models

Other people can be an enormous source of inspiration as you embark on your goal quest. Choosing a role model can help you to maintain your motivation to pursue an emotional or practical personal development goal. Ideally your chosen role model is someone who possesses the qualities and abilities that you want to acquire yourself.

You can find out a lot from observing and talking with someone you admire. You may discover helpful ways of thinking about yourself and valuable tips about goal attainment from the people who've already got what you want to attain or consistently act in the ways you want to act.

Finding a person to imitate

Your chosen role model can be anyone: a friend, family member or even someone famous (although choosing a role model with whom you can really identify is most helpful). Sometimes the people you see every day in ordinary situations are the richest sources of inspiration.

Look for qualities in your role model that you wish to adopt yourself because they'll serve you in achieving your personal goals. Also look for role models who seem to reflect your own values and priorities (see Chapter 15 for more about personal values).

Your low self-esteem may coerce you into comparing yourself negatively against those you admire. You may find yourself thinking: 'So and so is better than me'. Looking for inspirational role models is not about deciding that other people are 'better' than you, because they already represent your goal. They may well be able to do a specific thing better than you can. But don't let your low self-opinion fool you into thinking that your role model has more intrinsic worth than you have. Pursuing goals is about improving your life and enhancing your self-esteem, not about 'upping' your worth. Try to remember that your basic human worth is a given.

Pinpointing what you admire

Think about the person or people that you've chosen as role models. Be clear about what you admire about them. They may well represent your goals in action.

Use the following questions as prompts to help you identify specific attributes and actions that you admire in your chosen role model:

✔ **How does my role model interact with others?** Write down the ways your role model manages everyday social encounters and what you stand to gain by behaving similarly.

✔ **What has my role model achieved that I wish to achieve myself?** Perhaps your role model has attained your ultimate goal or some of your sub-goals. Record whatever it is that he or she inspires you to do yourself.

✔ **How does my role model deal successfully with negative situations?** Make note of the behaviours and attitudes your role model employs in the face of adversity. You may find that these serve you well too when it comes to managing difficulties and solving problems.

✔ **What values, personal standards and ideals does my role model embody?** Chances are you share many of these core values with your role model. You can behave more consistently with your own personal values by mimicking the actions of your chosen role model.

Harry admires a friend for her ability to be spontaneous during conversations and smoothly manage disagreements. Trisha may admire another mother from her child's school who has re-trained and obtained a decent paying job. Looking for inspiration among people who behave in ways you want to behave is sensible, spurring you on when you think: 'Well, so and so has done it, so there's every reason to assume that I can too'.

Remember to get really specific about what you admire in another individual. Harry pinpointed the following aspects he admires in his work colleague Melissa:

✔ She maintains good eye contact when listening and talking during work and social discussions.

✔ She laughs a lot and never takes teasing too seriously.

✔ When someone says something she disagrees with, Melissa firmly and respectfully puts her own point of view across.

✔ She seems to really have a lot of self-respect without being arrogant or defensive.

✔ She is clearly able to get her own needs met but she still cares about other people and is well liked.

Thinking about how they do it

When you've been specific about what you admire in other individuals, give some thought to *how* they may be achieving these desirable behaviours.

The following questions are devised to help you really get down to the nitty-gritty of what may make your chosen role models tick in the positive way you wish to tick too:

- ✔ How do my inspirational role models probably think that enables them to act in the way I admire?
- ✔ What beliefs do they seem likely to hold about themselves?
- ✔ What beliefs do they seem likely to hold about other people?
- ✔ What actions do they carry out that reflect my goal?
- ✔ How much effort do they seem prepared to put into achieving their aims?
- ✔ What may be their attitude towards mistakes and negative events?
- ✔ What else can I discover from observing my inspirational role model?

People who are confident, goal-orientated and genuinely content with themselves don't become like this by accident. Everyone's personal history is different (as we discuss more fully in Chapter 10). Some people have had more positive life experiences than others and therefore their self-esteem may not have been damaged as severely by the business of living.

Coming from a loving nurturing home certainly contributes greatly to the development of healthy self-opinion. Yet we see many people in our clinical practice who battle with low self-esteem despite having had stable childhoods.

No doubt your past plays a part in your current view of yourself. But the bulk of healthy self-esteem comes from deliberate effort to uphold helpful attitudes in the here and now, which is good news because it means that you can improve your sense of worth despite negative events that may have happened in your past.

Harry answered the preceding questions about his chosen role model, Melissa, like this:

- ✔ How do my inspirational role models probably *think* that enables them to act in the way I admire?

I imagine that Melissa thinks that her contributions to a discussion are significant. She probably also thinks that being wrong or disagreed with isn't the end of the world.

✔ What beliefs do they seem likely to hold about themselves?

Melissa seems to believe that she's a useful, likeable and worthwhile person. I don't think that she believes anyone else is any more worthwhile than she is, even if they're in a position of authority. Melissa seems to believe that she has something valuable to offer in her relationships.

✔ What beliefs do they seem likely to hold about other people?

I think Melissa believes that other people are on a par with her in terms of worth and significance. She seems to respect others and enjoy their company. Melissa seems to care about how others view her but she doesn't appear to worry too much about it.

✔ What actions do they carry out that reflect my goal?

Melissa speaks her mind appropriately, confidently and respectfully. She is comfortable and spontaneous in social conversations. She can laugh at herself and doesn't put herself down for making a social blunder. Melissa can also assert herself in a really skilled manner if she needs to.

✔ How much effort do they seem prepared to put into achieving their aims?

Melissa can be very determined about work projects. I get the impression that if she feels strongly about something she's prepared to put in a lot of work.

✔ What may be their attitude towards mistakes and negative events?

I think that Melissa has a healthy attitude towards her own mistakes and limitations. I think she has an attitude such as 'I'm allowed to make mistakes and I can survive any unwanted consequences'. I also think Melissa has a robust 'I can cope' attitude that serves her well when things go wrong.

✔ What else can I discover from observing my inspirational role model?

I respect Melissa a lot but I can also see that she's an ordinary person just like me. She's not a superhero or a genius although she's a really good communicator. So it stands to reason that if she can do the things I most admire then I can find out how to do them too.

You can also ask your inspirational role models directly about their beliefs and attitudes. Getting information 'straight from the horse's mouth' is very useful. Consider asking your role models to describe how they *think* about particular situations from which they seem to reap good results. Quiz them about the attitudes they hold that enable them to persist with their goals.

Copying shamelessly

Now we advise you to become a serious copycat. Imitate the positive behaviours that your role models exhibit and that you want to adopt. The more you practise behaving in goal-orientated ways the more second nature the behaviour becomes. Look for every possible opportunity to incorporate new behaviours into your daily life. Also try to adopt the healthy beliefs and attitudes that your role models seem to hold. Really practise thinking like them.

The combination of retraining yourself to think in helpful ways and behaving in accordance with new beliefs is very powerful. With continued practice you no longer just mimic thoughts and beliefs but they come to be your own.

You're trying to mimic and take on board the positive attitudes and actions of your inspirational role models. You're not trying to *become* just like them (that would deprive you of your own individuality). Recognise that you're unique. The point here is to discover new thinking and acting skills from other people who seem to have things down pat. Think of your aim as like asking a good cook to show you a few recipes or getting a coach to help you improve your tennis game.

Part III
Taking On New Techniques

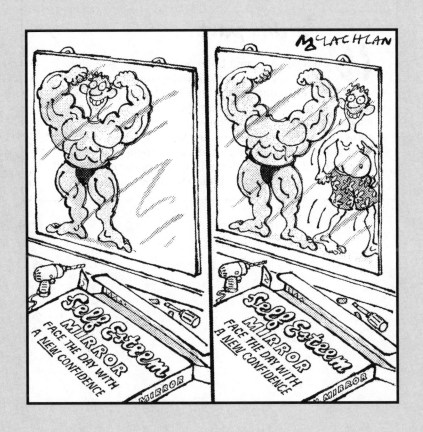

In this part . . .

We tell you all about building a better self-opinion through action and encourage you to ditch old low-self-esteem habits and get busy with new confidence-bolstering behaviours. You may think that your past determines how you feel about yourself in the present. But we show you ways to overcome the effects of yesterday's bad experiences and think more accurately about yourself today. You also discover techniques for nurturing yourself and testing out your predictions with scientific rigour.

Chapter 9

Speaking the Language of Love

*Y*ou may sometimes wonder why you have poor self-esteem. Although some obvious clues may reside in your past (as discussed in Chapter 10), you still want to know why you're full of self-loathing today.

Well, the fact is that you probably do lots of unhelpful things to yourself that you aren't even fully aware of – and unwittingly fail to do lots of helpful things.

Some of the thinking and behavioural habits that you develop over the years may be so second-nature that you give them very little attention or none at all. You just do them automatically. However, the ways in which you typically treat yourself have a lot to do with perpetuating and maintaining your low self-esteem.

In this chapter we help you to identify some of the seemingly automatic behaviours that keep you feeling bad about yourself. We also encourage you to put in place new ways of acting that build healthy self-esteem and improve your quality of life.

Being Your Own Best Friend

Low self-esteem puts you at war with yourself. After all, you're the person you spend the most time with (all your time, obviously), and so being on friendly terms with yourself just makes sense. So bury the hatchet and put some love in your cold heart.

Building healthy relations with yourself involves more than just thinking about yourself in accepting ways. Giving your self helpful and accurate messages is very important, but your self-image also takes cues from the way you treat yourself every day.

Imagine that you have lots of positive thoughts about another person, respect him, admire his uniqueness and like him enormously. If you don't tell him about your feelings or demonstrate them through action, how is he ever going to know that you really rate him? You probably don't tell your best friends how much you like and value them every day. Instead you make your affection for them obvious by how you speak to them and the ways you behave towards them. You demonstrate your positive regard for them through *action*. You probably do a really good job of it too. Your friends are probably in no doubt how you feel about them.

If you can do it for your friends, you can treat yourself with the same loving attitude. You may be surprised at the stark difference between the way you treat yourself and the way you treat the people you love. To develop healthy self-esteem you need to act as though you believe that you're someone worth looking after well.

To take a look at how you treat yourself compared with how you treat your friends, follow these steps:

1. **Outline a situation you're going through or an experience you've had and write down how you're feeling about it.**

   You can use something negative that happened recently or a memory of a long-ago event.

2. **Make a note of the way you're treating yourself in light of the situation and your feelings.**

   Pay attention to what actual behaviours you're engaging in and the way you're talking to yourself about it in your mind.

3. **Imagine that someone you care for is in identical circumstances to your own and that he shares the same feelings as those you're currently experiencing.**

4. **Imagine how you would try to make that loved one feel better about the situation.**

   Go into vivid detail. Think about what you would say to him and what you would do to try to lift his spirits. Be aware of the kind of language you would use to help your friend think and feel more positively about himself in light of the event.

5. **Become your own best friend and deliberately apply the same soothing behaviours that you offer your loved ones to yourself.**

   Use kind and compassionate language when talking to yourself about whatever has happened.

Gwen has a poor view of herself. She gives herself a very hard time over mistakes and dwells on her shortcomings all the time. (Sound familiar?) Recently Gwen had two bad experiences in quick succession. First, she got turned down for a promotion that she'd worked very diligently to get. Second, a few days later, while still smarting a lot from being refused the promotion, the man she'd been seeing for a few months told her that he didn't think they had a future together and broke off the relationship. Gwen was very upset because she thought things were going well between them.

Gwen decides to do some investigation into the difference between the way she treats herself when she has bad experiences and the way she treats her best friend Dania. Figure 9-1 shows the form she uses to conduct her investigations.

Gwen uses some pretty harsh words on herself. She also doesn't do anything to soothe herself but actually seems to *punish* herself. In sharp contrast, Gwen would treat Dania in a very caring way to encourage her convalescence. That's because Gwen holds Dania in much higher esteem than herself. In order to improve her self-esteem, Gwen needs to get appreciative of herself, just as she appreciates Dania.

Redress the imbalance in your own self-treatment by trying to treat yourself with the same care and consideration as you would your best friend. Figure 9-2 provides a blank form you can use to have a look at the discrepancies between your best-friend behaviour and the ways you treat yourself.

The event:

1. *Being turned down for the promotion at work.*

2. *Being rejected by my new boyfriend.*

What I told myself:

1. *You're useless and that's why you weren't promoted. Who the hell do you think you are going for a promotion anyway? You clearly don't deserve one. All that hard work you did just goes to show what an inadequate loser you really are, otherwise it would have paid off. Next time don't get ideas above your station.*

2. *He broke up with you because you're ugly, boring and you never say the right thing at the right time. It's a miracle that he stuck around as long as two months. The poor guy must have been tortured. You're going to end up all alone in your old age and it's all your own stupid fault.*

What I'd tell my best friend:

1. *Don't give up, Dania! You worked really hard for that promotion and I don't understand why you didn't get it but you can apply again. You deserve to be promoted and I'm sure it'll happen for you soon. All that effort will pay off for you.*

2. *Dania, that guy has no idea what he's missing out on. I'm really sorry that things didn't work out. You're a lovely person and you deserve to be in a relationship with someone else who really clicks with you. I guess he wasn't the right guy for you. You'll meet someone who really appreciates you one day soon.*

What I did to make myself feel better:

1. *I didn't make myself anything to eat. I went to bed without taking my usual bath or doing anything to relax. I deprived myself of talking to any friends about what happened because I felt too ashamed. I crushed the new suit I'd bought into a ball and hurled it into the bottom of my wardrobe.*

2. *I drank a whole bottle of wine and listened to really depressing songs. I ignored Dania's calls. I also refused to let my cat sit on my lap even though cuddling him often makes me feel good. I shut myself away for the weekend and didn't leave the house until I had to go to work on Monday.*

What I'd do to make my best friend feel better:

1. *I'd cook Dania a nice meal and put a candle on the table. I'd play some upbeat music and encourage her to tell me all about how she was feeling. I'd be affectionate and give her some hugs.*

2. *I'd try to make sure that Dania didn't drink too much. I'd foist her cat into her arms and let him give her lots of passionate head butts. I'd make sure that we went out and had some fun over the weekend. I'd give her time to talk about things but also try to distract her with interesting unrelated conversation.*

Figure 9-1:
Gwen's
'Being my
own best
friend' form.

<u>**The event:**</u> 1. 2.
<u>**What I told myself:**</u>
<u>**What I'd tell my best friend:**</u>
<u>**What I did to make myself feel better:**</u>
<u>**What I'd do to make my best friend feel better:**</u>

Figure 9-2:
Your 'Being my own best friend' form.

Supporting yourself emotionally

Strong and unpleasant emotions are a normal response to adversity. They tell you that something undesirable has happened and they can often be part of the healing process. Even very strong emotions pass if you allow them to and don't mask or attempt to deaden them artificially. Accepting your feelings (even though you don't enjoy having them) can help you to understand what has happened and begin to problem-solve.

Coping by covering up

Many people try to cope with strong negative emotions by drinking too much, hiding away from others and dissociating. *Dissociation* means psychologically cutting off from your feelings. The term is difficult to explain precisely because it refers to a mental state. When you dissociate you basically separate yourself from your emotions, refusing to acknowledge and process them.

All these strategies for dealing with unpleasant emotions are problematic because they prevent you from accepting how you feel and letting emotions run their natural course. Unexpressed feelings can build up and result in anger problems or mood disorders such as clinical depression (see Chapter 2). You may have strict personal rules about the types of emotions that you think are acceptable to experience. Some people believe that certain feelings such as hurt or sadness are a sign of weakness or inadequacy. Others believe that getting angry, jealous or envious is wrong, and that these types of emotions mean they have a spiteful character. Also, like many people, you may think that strong emotions are unbearable and that if you let yourself feel them they may overpower you so that you never recover. These attitudes, examples of which are in the following list, complicate your experience of negative emotions:

- ✔ 'I shouldn't be feeling this way.'
- ✔ 'I've got to pull myself together.'
- ✔ 'It's pathetic to be so upset over this.'
- ✔ 'I can't stand feeling like this; it will never end.'
- ✔ 'It's wrong to have these feelings.'

Rethinking your attitude

When your feelings are disproportionately strong in relation to the actual event, you can make corrections to your thinking and help yourself to feel a healthier and more appropriate level of negative emotion.

Low self-esteem can lead you to take an already painful situation and put an extra barb in its tail. You can make your emotional experiences more useful and easier to bear by checking out how your low self-esteem thoughts are affecting your interpretation of events.

Deciding to support yourself emotionally can make a big difference to your self-esteem. Follow these basic steps to get on the right track:

1. **Give yourself permission to feel whatever you're feeling.**

   Don't try to dampen down or run away from your emotions.

2. **Remember that strong negative emotions are natural responses to undesirable events. No matter how painful your emotions, you can survive them.**

3. **Look for errors in the meanings you assign to events.**

   Be vigilant. Spot low self-esteem skewing your interpretation of events.

4. **Reassess the actual events and assign accurate and fair meanings to them.**

5. **Treat yourself in the caring way you would a loved one.**

   Help yourself to process and recover fully from your painful emotions by doing things that help you feel better rather than worse.

6. **Use any information you gain from your experience to help you problem-solve and plan for the future.**

Gwen feels very depressed after being rejected for a promotion and because her boyfriend ended their relationship. Part of Gwen's profound depressed feelings are due to the meanings she gives to these negative events. After she does the 'best friend' exercise from the preceding section, Gwen realises that she's able to challenge these meanings and assign more accurate ones.

Gwen's low self-esteem led her to draw some pretty outlandish conclusions about the bad things that happened. Figure 9-3 shows the very simple technique that Gwen uses to challenge these original conclusions.

Through challenging her original conclusions, Gwen's able to feel very sad and disappointed but no longer depressed and hopeless.

Figure 9-4 provides a blank form to use to evaluate your own responses and assign more accurate meaning.

Event:

Being refused the promotion.

Low self-esteem meaning:

This means that I'm useless and inadequate. I'll never get promoted because I don't deserve to be.

Fair and accurate meaning:

This means that I didn't get promoted this time. There may be some useful feedback I can get from my boss to improve my chances next time.

Event:

My boyfriend broke up with me.

Low self-esteem meaning:

This means I'm unattractive in every imaginable way. I'll never have a good relationship and I'll die a lonely old lady.

Fair and accurate meaning:

This means that my boyfriend has his own reasons for ending the relationship. I guess this relationship wasn't meant to be. This means that I need to start dating again and give myself a chance to meet someone new.

Figure 9-3:
Gwen's
'more
accurate
meaning'
assessment.

Understanding self-harm

Self-harm has been the topic of many radio programmes and magazine articles in recent months, and the fact that it's being recognised and taken seriously is good. Common forms of self-harm include cutting, head banging, scratching and picking at the skin and inflicting burns on yourself. However, misconceptions still abound about the nature of self-harm and why people do it.

Many people assume that those who engage in self-harm are trying to seek attention. In the vast majority of cases this isn't the main reason people self-harm at all. Many people do it in secret and go to great lengths to hide it from others, and so the attention angle clearly isn't their motivation. Most people who engage in one form of self-harm or another do so as a means of coping with powerful and unpleasant emotions. Some people say that harming themselves is the only way they know to relieve the immense emotional tension that they feel.

If you've used dissociation as a method of avoiding and numbing the pain of traumatic experiences for a number of years, you may use self-harm as a means of expressing your emotions. You may be detached from your emotions to the extent that you rarely cry. People who self-harm often find that articulating what's going on inside them is difficult. You may be very adept at ignoring your feelings and bottling them up until they become too forceful and demand attention, and you feel driven to self-harm for relief. Another reason for self-harming is to punish yourself for having thoughts or feelings that you think are unacceptable. You may also be so guilty and angry about behaving in a way you don't like that you harm yourself. So the reasons why people resort to self-harm are much more complicated than attention-seeking.

Dangers are obviously associated with self-harm. You can give yourself a more serious injury than you intend by cutting too deeply. More rarely the effects of self-harm can be life-threatening. You can also end up with severe scarring that can be difficult to conceal.

If you self-harm you may find that the techniques and information offered in this chapter help you develop alternative ways of coping with your feelings. Self-harm is serious and if you can't manage to overcome it on your own, seek professional help (see the Appendix for resources). Don't feel ashamed of admitting your self-harm to a professional. They are there to help you and you don't need to worry that you're going to be judged. Self-harm is a destructive habit that's best nipped in the bud. So if you've self-harmed only a few times, get some help and make some changes right away before the behaviour becomes habitual. And even if you've been using self-harm as a coping mechanism for many years, it's never too late to get help.

Event:

Low self-esteem meaning:

Fair and accurate meaning:

Event:

Low self-esteem meaning:

Figure 9-4:
Your 'more accurate meaning' assessment.

Fair and accurate meaning:

Letting others help

Other people can be a great help when you're dealing with painful emotions. They can encourage you to look after yourself, offer advice and sympathy, help you out practically and distract you from your pain.

But if you want the benefits that come from others, you need to put yourself in their midst. Your low self-esteem may tell you that other people don't want to hear your problems. You may think that you're going to be a burden to them or that they don't really care about how you feel. Or perhaps you're too ashamed about what's happened (and your emotional response) to talk to others about it.

Give other people the chance to prove your assumptions wrong by opening up a little. The old adage that a problem aired is a problem shared (or a problem shared is a problem halved) contains a lot of truth; whichever way you look at it, you lessen your burden by speaking up.

You don't need to suffer in silence all on your own. Spill your guts and let the people in your life have a look at the contents. Okay, perhaps that's putting it a little too graphically, but we hope you get our point.

Seeking support from the right sources

Having just banged on in the preceding section about sharing your problem with others, we now want to put a few provisos on that suggestion. You may be reluctant to seek emotional support from others because you've had some bad past experiences when doing so. Maybe you spoke to someone about a problem and he heaped criticism on you, making you feel worse. Perhaps you approached someone for some practical help and he refused to give it. Or you shared a fairly minor problem with someone who overreacted and made it seem like a total catastrophe. These types of experiences can really put you off the idea of seeking emotional support from others.

Part of the art of finding out how to accept support from others is to go to the best possible sources. You can't get blood from a stone. For example, if you know that your father is critical and difficult to please, he's probably not the best person to go to for support about being made redundant at work. Likewise, a friend who is very self-absorbed and never lets you get a word in edgewise is unlikely to give you the time you need to express your feelings and difficulties.

Before you reach out to the wrong person, take a moment to consider the following:

✔ **What type of support do you need to help you through this difficult emotional time?**

Do you need a shoulder to cry on, someone to help you laugh it off or practical advice on how to work through some problem? Think carefully about what type of support would best help you.

✔ **Who of your friends and acquaintances is best suited and most able to provide the kind of help you need?**

Going to appropriate sources for emotional and practical support helps ensure that opening up to others is a positive experience.

Although the specific type of support you need may often come from the people you're closest to, this may not necessarily be the case all the time.

Figure 9-5 shows the list Gwen makes of the kinds of help she needs to get over her relationship break-up and promotion disappointment, and the people she thinks would be most ready, willing and able to supply that help.

Support needed:

I need help distracting myself from my ex-boyfriend. I need someone to pull me out the door and back into social situations.

Possible source:

Dania is the ideal source. She's single too and loves going out. She's also great fun to be with and is very out-going.

Support needed:

I need some practical advice about this promotion business. I want to talk to someone who understands how I'm feeling about it.

Possible source:

My co-worker also was denied a promotion last year but was successful a few months ago. I don't know her very well but I could ask her if she'd talk to me about how she coped with the first rejection. She could have some good tips.
I can also ask my boss for feedback on my application.

Support needed:

I could do with a little tea and sympathy. Having someone make a fuss over me would be nice for a few days.

Possible source:

My mother is likely to do this for me if I go visit her for the weekend.
My eldest sister is also a bit of a mother hen so I could give her a ring too.

Figure 9-5:
Gwen's
'suitable
sources of
support'
summary.

Try making your own list of support needs and potential sources. You don't need to write your list down; you can just as easily compile it in your head.

Outlawing Loathsome Language

When people with poor self-esteem give themselves a dressing down, the air can turn blue around them. We're not talking about a gentle reprimand here; we're talking about tearing a strip off yourself and going for the jugular.

The way you speak to yourself, the names you call yourself and the insults you hurl into the mirror are very damaging. Don't underestimate the effect that self-directed foul language has on your sense of personal worth: it can be extremely toxic.

You may abuse yourself out loud in small ways like saying: 'Oh gawd, I'm such an idiot'. That kind of thing can seem innocuous, but it isn't. Even the less profane names you call yourself chip away at your self-esteem. Would you label anyone else an idiot for making a small error? Very probably not. Nor would you apply some of the stronger, more offensive labels you give yourself to other people. The abusive things you call yourself in your mind are likely to be even more shockingly offensive than those you actually utter.

You may be so used to vicious self-evaluations that they seem to happen automatically. Abusive and offensive self-talk is tantamount to giving yourself a kicking when you're down, and it can have a subtle but profound under-mining effect on your self-opinion. Such talk is rude and unacceptable. In the interest of improving your self-esteem, try obeying these simple rules:

- ✔ Don't use *any* profanities when you refer to yourself out loud or in your own head.

- ✔ Don't say anything *to* or *about* yourself that you know would be unac-ceptable to say to someone else.

- ✔ Resist applying any labels to yourself whatsoever.

- ✔ Comment fairly and moderately on what you've *done* but resist making any comment about yourself. For example, say 'I parked the car poorly' instead of saying 'I'm a loser'.

- ✔ Apologise to yourself for being rude. If you catch yourself speaking nas-tily to yourself, stop and put it right. Have an internal dialogue along the lines of: 'Oops, that was offensive. Sorry, what I meant to say was. . .'.

Apologising to yourself may seem a bit daft or weird, but actually it's wholly appropriate given how rude you've been to yourself. Offering yourself an apology is no stranger than verbally or mentally beating yourself black and blue. An apology is in order, so say sorry to yourself.

In Chapter 4 we include some additional strategies for changing the way you talk to yourself.

You need to start communicating with yourself compassionately. Don't fall into the trap, however, of confusing healthy self-talk with positive thinking and trying to 'build yourself up'. In fact, saying over-the-top good things about yourself, such as 'I'm great' and 'I'm a winner', is every bit as inaccurate as saying negative things such as 'I'm worthless' and 'I'm a loser'. Remember that you're never 100 per cent good or bad. Instead, you're a basically worthwhile person who does a mixture of good, bad and neutral things.

Giving yourself grandiose positive messages may elevate your confidence temporarily but does little to correct your underlying negative beliefs. The way to correct beliefs about yourself as being inferior *isn't* to try to persuade yourself that you're superior. If you use superiority as a remedy to feeling inferior, life will almost certainly come back and bite you – reminding you that you can fail like anyone else. Then your superiority ideas go down the toilet, taking your self-esteem along for the ride.

Talking to yourself respectfully and fairly is the most effective way to counteract negative beliefs about yourself. Getting into the habit of being polite and complimentary towards yourself has the desirable effect of fortifying your self-esteem, as well as making you more resilient to setbacks and mishaps. You don't need to give yourself massive compliments, although you can when the situation merits it, of course. Just the steady drip, drip effect of giving yourself credit for little things often makes all the difference to how you think and feel about yourself. Here some examples of what we mean:

- ✔ When you've completed a task, regardless of how big or small, try saying to yourself: 'That's a job well done'.

- ✔ When you do something well or successfully, no matter how important or trivial it is, say something like: 'I did well there' or 'I performed well at that task'.

- ✔ When you get dressed in the morning or to go out in the evening, have something nice to say about your appearance. Try to make comments like: 'This dress looks nice on me' or 'The colour of this tie looks good on me'.

- ✔ When you behave well towards others, give yourself some recognition for it. Make internal comments, such as: 'That was thoughtful of me'.

The secret is all about weaving a little realistic and genuine positive attitude into your everyday communications with yourself, which is part and parcel of treating yourself with the same compassion and consideration as you treat other people. (You may want to look at Chapter 4 for more information about how to keep your self-esteem intact even when you make errors or behave poorly.)

Getting Your Hands Dirty

When you're aiming to improve your self-esteem you need to get actively involved in the process. Watching from the sidelines hoping to get a piece of the action isn't going to suffice.

Doing things that your low self-esteem normally prohibits is part of discovering how to act against your negative thoughts and feelings. Start ignoring and disobeying thoughts such as: 'Don't try that, you'll never be able to do it' or 'You'll make a fool of yourself, it's not worth the risk'.

Letting loose and enjoying yourself

Your fear of what others may think of you and your tendency to take yourself too seriously stop fun dead in its tracks. (We talk about managing your reaction to other people's opinions in Chapter 6.)

Enjoying yourself is hard when you're keeping such tight control over everything you say and do. Feelings of low self-worth can make you very self-conscious and wound up. You need to cut loose from the fetters a little . . . or perhaps a lot.

The idea that you're going to do something that makes you look silly and feel embarrassed is a common reason for not letting yourself go. Consider these points, however:

- ✔ Even if you do something 'foolish', it doesn't make you a fool.
- ✔ Even if you do feel embarrassed, you'll live.
- ✔ Far worse things can befall you than being laughed at.
- ✔ Others possibly thinking negative stuff about you is worth the risk in order to have a good time.

✔ You're your own worst critic; other people are generally far more accepting than you probably give them credit for.

✔ You may well be overestimating how much attention you actually draw to yourself; other people may take only a passing note of what you're doing.

Lighten up your attitude by realising that social embarrassments aren't so very serious. They happen to everybody and you don't need to give them as much weight and importance as your low self-esteem would have you believe. So you tell a joke and everyone groans, you sing off-key or you look like a piece of gum being chewed when you dance. Big deal. Welcome to the human race.

To help you get back into the fun run, ask yourself whether taking the chance of being noticed is worthwhile for the sake of enjoying yourself. We believe that the answer is a resounding, *Yes*.

The more accustomed you become to experiencing social embarrassment and living to fight another day, the more your social confidence is liable to increase. You begin to believe that you *can* tolerate awkward feelings in social situations and make a full recovery from blips.

Taking risks

The risks of social rejection when you let yourself behave spontaneously and naturally aren't as great as you think. If you link your basic worth to approval from others, your social performance, and what others think of your actions, you may assume that a real and present danger of rejection is lurking around every corner. Chances are that your low self-esteem is leading you to assume that others are more judgemental and unforgiving than may actually be the case.

When you divorce your sense of overall worth from your individual actions, the risks seem smaller. The world looks less frightening and other people less threatening when you start to truly believe that you're just as worthwhile as anyone else. Even falling flat on your face, doing something silly or failing at something, doesn't mean that you're not worthwhile.

You may be pleasantly surprised by how readily people accept (and forget) your social awkwardness or embarrassing moments. Give others the benefit of the doubt and try flexing your social muscles more freely. Even if you get a funny look or receive a condemning comment, you can choose to let it bounce off you. As long as you remind yourself that you *want* but don't *need* to be approved of by everyone you meet socially, you can survive the odd reproach.

Get some paper and make a list of things that you'd like to try but haven't mustered up the courage to do yet. They don't all need to be big things. Include smaller things too like dancing at a party or instigating conversation with a stranger. Write down anything that you avoid doing because your low self-esteem tells you that it's much too dangerous. Next, work your way through your list and remember to bear the listed points from the previous section in mind.

Take a look at Chapter 11 for some behavioural experiments that can help challenge your low self-esteem restrictions.

Nurturing Yourself

A well-tended garden tends to grow and thrive. Your self-opinion needs a lot of nurturing and tending too.

In order to get some sense of your own value and worth, you need to treat yourself like a prized possession. Many people with low self-esteem habitually overlook this important point.

You may look after your car, for example, more carefully than you do yourself. Or perhaps you treat your pets better than you do yourself. Fido gets a juicy bone and a belly rub but you may come home from a hard day's work and not even give yourself a good meal. In addition to the points we discuss earlier in this chapter, consider making some efforts in the following areas as well.

Limiting loneliness

Maintaining a regular social life is very good for your mood. Try to schedule in definite times to see your friends so that you don't end up putting it off. When you have clear plans to meet up with people, letting your social life slip off the map is harder. That's not to say that your social life can't occasionally take a back seat due to work pressures or family commitments, but try to get back into the social scene as soon as possible.

If your social life needs a boost, join a club or a class of some kind. Being in a book club or an art class (or anything that fits with your interests) helps you meet like-minded people and make new friends.

Surrounding yourself with smells and bells

Put some effort into your surroundings. Your home should be somewhere that's pleasant to spend time in.

Often your mood is reflected by the state of your living environment. For example, because you love your pet hamster ('Hamlet'), you keep his cage clean. He gets fresh water, clean bedding and perhaps a little running wheel to keep him amused when you're away. Hamlet's home is nice-smelling and comfortable because only the best will do for little Hammy. Take a little care with your own metaphorical cage too.

If you want to feel better, make your surroundings uplifting. Here are some helpful hints:

- ✔ Keep your bed linen clean and fresh.
- ✔ Make sure that you have comfortable furniture to relax in.
- ✔ Tidy away clutter and make it easier to find your possessions.
- ✔ Keep rooms smelling nice with air fresheners or scented candles.
- ✔ Hang photos, prints or other art you like to look at on the walls.
- ✔ Light your rooms adequately and choose atmospheric options occasionally – candlelight can be soothing even when you're by yourself.

If you're strapped for time or cleaning just isn't your bag and you can afford it, hire a cleaner. You're giving someone a job and it may transform your living environment.

Practising self-soothing behaviours

Soothing yourself when you're emotionally upset or tired is a real skill. When you suffer from low self-esteem, you may be more familiar with neglecting yourself than soothing yourself. (Have a look at the example of Gwen in the 'Being Your Own Best Friend' section earlier in this chapter).

Self-soothing behaviours are things that make you feel a bit better in the present but also don't carry any medium- or long-term negative consequences. Eating three tubs of Häagen-Dazs ice cream, downing a bottle of whisky or spending this month's wage on a pair Jimmy Choo stilettos is *not* behaviour likely to make you feel good in the longer term. Instead, when the going gets tough, look for things that you can do easily and cheaply to comfort yourself:

- ✔ Watch a favourite DVD or television programme
- ✔ Go out for a meal with a friend
- ✔ Take a long soak in the bath
- ✔ Put on some nice music
- ✔ Go for a walk or a bike ride

Keeping yourself fit and well fed

The official guidelines for keeping physically fit are five sessions of twenty minutes of cardiovascular exercise per week. If you're like much of the population, you fall short of this mark.

Regular exercise is good for your body and your mind. You can increase the exercise you get by making small changes to your routine, such as walking instead of driving and taking the stairs rather than the lift. These things can help but you may also want to consider joining a gym or signing up for a regular exercise class. Try to pick physical activities that you enjoy so that you're more likely to stick with them.

What you eat also has significant implications for your physical health and emotional well-being. Fast food and junk foods contain a lot of additives and other nasty stuff, as well as having high fat and calorie content, which all makes you feel physically poor, limits your energy and even lowers your mood. We also highly recommend that you get your 'five-a-day' quota of fruit and vegetables and ensure that all the major food groups are represented in your daily diet.

If you're vegan or vegetarian you may need to make more effort to get enough low-fat protein. If your diet is restricted due to other health issues you may also need to be more creative with menu planning to ensure that you get all your essential vitamins and minerals.

When you're trying to lose weight, exercising more and eating sensibly is better for you, and generally more effective, than embarking on a fad diet. The best thing to do is to speak to your GP or see a dietician and develop a plan based on professional advice.

You can find some useful information about healthy eating and exercise from the World Health Organisation (www.who.int) and British Heart Foundation (www.bhf.org.uk).

Reaping the rewards of relaxation

Relaxation is essential for recharging your batteries. Any activity that helps you to de-stress and shrug off the day's pressures is a valid form of relaxation, whether it's kickboxing, sitting down to read a good book, tai chi or yoga. Ideally your relaxation activities are a combination of invigorating things like exercise and chilling out on the sofa.

Relaxation is something that you need to make time for or it can get marginalised by daily commitments. Build relaxation time into your weekly schedule and be specific about the activities you plan to do.

You can also think about giving yourself an occasional relaxation treat such as having a professional massage. Or book yourself in for a spa day and have lots of different treatments such as mudpacks and the like, if you enjoy that sort of pampering. You can investigate loads of different alternative therapies, such as acupuncture, reflexology and aromatherapy, and build them into your relaxation routine.

If you decide to give aromatherapy, reflexology, acupuncture or any other alternative therapy a whirl, make sure that you see a qualified practitioner who's recognised by an accrediting organisation.

Chapter 10

Rewriting Your Own History

● ●

In This Chapter

▶ Taking the past into consideration

▶ Giving new meanings to old events

▶ Understanding and identifying your core beliefs

▶ Building and strengthening new healthy ways of thinking

● ●

*Y*our past, to some extent, shapes and influences your current self-view. Events that happened a long time ago often continue to affect the way you think and behave in the present, whether you know it or not.

You may be very aware of the hold that particular experiences you've been through still have over your understanding of yourself, or you may not realise that ideas about yourself formed by childhood (or early adulthood) experiences are still operational today.

In this chapter we urge you to examine how aspects of your past lead you to develop beliefs that may be causing you trouble in the here and now. We also offer some suggestions on how you can begin to confront and challenge long-held, problematic beliefs in the interest of building healthier self-esteem.

If you're feeling very depressed at the moment, now is not the time to do the exercises in this chapter because they have you delving into unpleasant memories. Wait until your mood is better.

We advise you to do the exercises during the day when you're feeling pretty upbeat so that you can go off and do something enjoyable or absorbing afterwards. Otherwise you may feel quite emotionally stirred up or depressed from trolling through your past. If you're seeing a therapist, you may want to suggest that you do the exercises together during a session so that you have some support if the process becomes painful or overwhelming.

Travelling through Time to Find Early Influences

Everyone has an individual background. Many different living circumstances and family dynamics lead to a multitude of experiences.

Although everybody's personal histories are different, many people's experiences share common themes. Certain types of themes (usually the negative and undesirable ones, we're sorry to say) tend to stick with you and inform your view of yourself, your opinion of others and of the world in which you live.

Common themes that we hear reported from people battling with low self-esteem often include:

- **Abandonment:** This theme can include being left by a parent or parental figure through death, divorce or a wilful action on his or her part.

- **Abuse:** This theme can be sexual, physical and/or emotional abuse.

- **Continued and sustained belittling and undermining treatment:** This theme refers to a type of abuse that's less obvious than other types. Being constantly subjected to harsh criticism over a long period of time is an example of emotional or mental abuse. Bullying falls into this category, whether within the family home or in a school environment.

- **Loss:** This theme can include the loss of a familiar environment (such as a home, community or country), prized possessions (often things that offer comfort in childhood, such as stuffed toys and blankets), family members, friends and even pets.

- **Neglect:** This theme involves not being protected and cared for or offered affection by parents and parental figures.

- **Painful experiences and traumatic incidents:** This theme can include illness, accidents, witnessing attacks on others or the death of others through assault or accident, rape and other violent assaults, or any other type of life-threatening event.

Human beings are social animals and therefore highly susceptible to the messages they receive from those around them.

Witnessing trauma is traumatic

Seeing bad things happen to other people can traumatise not only children but also adults. *Witness trauma* is a well-recognised condition and its negative effects aren't to be underestimated. For example, many people involved in war efforts or who live in a war zone suffer trauma related to events that they witness even though they've escaped such experiences themselves.

Observing the abuse of another family member is a common and pernicious form of witness trauma. Evidence also suggests that being told graphic details about traumatic events can (especially if they've happened to a loved one such as a parent) can vicariously traumatise children and adults.

If you think that you're experiencing severe symptoms such as flashbacks and nightmares arising from a personal or witness trauma, you may benefit from getting some professional therapy for *post traumatic stress disorder* (PTSD). We recommend that you ask your GP to refer you to a cognitive behavioural therapist (CBT), or look for one yourself via some of the organisations included in the Appendix of this book.

Extreme and intensely negative life experiences can make deep imprints on the way you think about yourself and your present life. However, even when your past hasn't been obviously punctuated with traumas or extraordinarily bad events, you may still have low self-esteem and other associated emotional problems (see Chapter 2 for more about the types of psychological disorders and emotional problems associated with poor self-esteem).

Your past doesn't need to be extremely negative for you to develop problems with your self-esteem; the problems are common among people from all sorts of backgrounds. We see many people in our clinical practice with poor self-image who come from stable homes and relatively 'normal' backgrounds. So don't make the mistake of thinking that the information in this chapter doesn't apply to you because you had a relatively 'normal' upbringing.

Get a piece of paper or a notebook and be ready to write down life experiences that you suspect play a part in the development of the ideas you currently hold about yourself. No event is too minor to merit recording. Bear in mind that all sorts of experiences – even seemingly innocuous ones – can have a significant effect on your thinking and emotions. Reading through the next sections helps you to recall significant events in your life.

Reflecting on family influences

Giving some careful thought to your early influences may help to unearth possible original sources of your negative self-belief. In the preceding section we outline common themes that may have a profound and lasting effect on how you think of yourself; if you experienced any of those problems, include them when you record your own memorable events and influences.

Use this list to call up other events that had an impact on you:

- ✔ Cultural, religious or community rules and expectations.

- ✔ Family mottos or rules.

- ✔ How your parents interacted with one another.

- ✔ How you were consistently treated by the other members of your family.

- ✔ Messages you picked up about yourself from parents, teachers and other caregivers.

- ✔ Mistreatment or rejection by siblings or members of your peer group.

- ✔ Parental expectations about your behaviour and achievements.

Here are three examples of recorded histories, past events and family influences. Although your own history may vary greatly from these examples, focus on any similarities rather than on the differences. Looking for attitudes and experiences that resonate with your own situation helps you to get the most benefit.

- ✔ **Lauren** comes from a family that strongly values academic achievement. Both her parents are professors and all three of her sisters attended red-brick universities. Lauren is the youngest and she remembers always feeling under enormous pressure to live up to her sisters' academic achievements. Teachers often mentioned her sisters and told Lauren that they expected 'great things' from her too. But Lauren wasn't as successful at schoolwork as the other members of her family. She preferred being outdoors and making things to sitting inside studying books. Although she was an average student she always felt stupid in comparison with her sisters. Lauren's parents told her that they just wanted her to be happy but she always sensed that they were disappointed with her.

  As an adult, Lauren has her own flower-arranging business that she greatly enjoys, and yet she still basically believes that she's not good enough. Lauren's sisters somewhat affectionately refer to her as 'the manual labourer of the family'. Lauren can't help feeling hurt by her sisters' teasing.

✔ **Seamus** grew up in a rural community. His father was an alcoholic and often came home drunk and aggressive. His mother was beaten badly by her husband and on more than one occasion had to be hospitalised.

Seamus remembers his mother telling the doctors that she had been in a car accident. He was confused and frightened by his mother's secrecy about what had actually happened. She told Seamus that it was no one else's business and said, 'When you've made your bed, you sleep in it. Nobody wants to hear about your sob story.' Seamus was sworn to keep his father's abuse a secret.

Whenever Seamus was beaten by his father, his mother comforted him but also made clear that it was a family affair. Seamus grew up feeling powerless, weak and ashamed about the abuse. He still feels guilty today about not being able to protect his mother and thinks of himself as weak.

✔ **Pippa's** mother died shortly after she was born due to complications during the labour. Her father tried to look after her but ended up sending her to stay with her aunt most of the time. Pippa's aunt seemed to resent her for her sister's death and often told her: 'Your mother would still be alive if it weren't for you'.

Pippa's father eventually remarried and started a new family. Pippa's aunt sent her to a respectable boarding school around the same time, when she was 11 years old. She made a lot of friends at school and did well but her teachers, who were very fond of her, found her problematic when it came to holidays. Pippa's aunt was often reluctant to have her and her father rarely offered because he said he had no room for her. Pippa remembers feeling like an intruder on the rare occasions when she spent holidays with her aunt or her father's new family. She ended up spending the majority of holidays at the school with a few other children in similar positions.

Pippa felt unwanted, unloved and rootless. Although she now has a loving family of her own, Pippa still feels unlovable and worries a lot about being an inconvenience and a burden to others.

Lauren, Seamus and Pippa all bear emotional problems and negative beliefs from their childhood experiences. You can easily see how their negative ideas about themselves, other people and the world may have taken root due to personally significant events in their lives.

In the following sections of this chapter, we take a closer look at how the meanings you assign to certain events in your past can lead you to form enduring beliefs that you carry with you into your present and future.

Peering into peer group propaganda

Your peer group has a lot of influence on you when you're growing up. At certain stages in your development, especially during adolescence, your friends can be more influential than your family. You may pay more attention to your peer groups' values and opinions than to those of your parents. Forming strong relationships with people your own age is part of normal development.

If your home life was difficult, your friends may have become a real lifeline. In Pippa's example, the friends she made at boarding school were the only semblance of family that she had.

However, children and adolescents can also be very unkind to one another. Bullying is a common occurrence for lots of people when growing up. Being the 'new kid' or different in some way can often make children a target for bullying. Seamus, for example, was quiet and withdrawn at school because he felt so upset about what was happening at home. Other children thought that he was weird and unfriendly. He had a few friends but bigger boys often pushed him around. This treatment reinforced his beliefs about being weak and powerless.

Your beliefs about yourself today may have been shaped in part by how your peers viewed and treated you in the past. Therefore, when you're recording past events that may have contributed to how you think and feel today, be sure to include anything relevant that went on at school.

Assigning Meaning Then and Now

People like to understand what's going on around them and why certain things happen to them. The trouble with negative childhood experiences is that you were probably very confused by them and came up with faulty explanations for why they happened. Not understanding the reason for painful experiences is quite frightening for adults – for children it can be even more so.

Generally you try to give a meaning to an event even if you have little evidence to go on. You then forget to update your understanding of a past event as you gain more information or wisdom through age.

It's possible that some of the low self-esteem ideas you battle with today took root in your early life. If you struggled with schoolwork, for example, you may have drawn the conclusion that you're stupid. People in your life – parents, siblings, peers or teachers – may have reinforced the message that the reason for your lack of academic success was that you were simply unintelligent. If you don't look back on the event and assess the validity of your original conclusion, you may continue to think of yourself as stupid in the present.

Undoing the damage of low-self-esteem beliefs formed in your early years involves deliberately assigning new fairer meanings to old events.

Working out what an experience meant then

When something is happening to you or around you, you naturally try to make sense of it. You gave events in your past specific meanings so that you were able to understand them, but many of those meanings were deduced when you were a child and had only a child's ability to reason.

In order to dig out your own personal meaning for things you experienced in your past, try following these steps:

1. **Write down an important event that you still think about sometimes and that had a big impact on you.**

   It can be from any time in your life. Even if the details are sketchy, record what you remember.

2. **Try to capture the meaning that event holds for you in one or two sentences.**

   Try to boil the personal meaning you give the event down to its essence. You can even fill in the blanks:

   • This event means that I am _____.

   • This event means that other people are _____.

   • This event means that the world is _____.

3. **Ask yourself if you still believe that meaning is true today.**

   After you isolate the meanings attached to personal past events, you may notice that those meanings are pretty negative.

If you still believe the negative meanings given to past events today, chances are your self-esteem is suffering as a result. Although you may not realise it, you may still be operating under unhelpful ideas and beliefs that you formed at an early age. You haven't updated the meaning as you've grown and gained more insight and understanding.

Early beliefs are formed not only out of what is actually happening but also through some of the assumptions you make that seem to explain things. For example:

✔ Lauren forms the belief 'I'm not good enough' based on her inability to meet her family's academic expectations for her. She makes the following assumptions:

- My sisters do better at schoolwork than I do, so they're better than I am.

- My parents are very proud of my sisters, so I must be a disappointment.

- Being good at school must be more important than anything else.

✔ Seamus develops the belief about himself 'I'm powerless and weak'. At the time when his father was being abusive to himself and his mother, Seamus made these assumptions:

- I'm too little to fight back; he's doing this to us because we're weak.

- Mother won't let me tell anyone about it so it must be something shameful.

- I can't do anything to help mother or myself; people like my father are just too powerful.

✔ Pippa believes that she's 'unwanted and unlovable'. As she was growing up she made the following sort of assumptions about the way others treated her:

- Daddy sent me to live with my aunt because he doesn't want me around.

- My aunt is mean to me because I'm not a very nice little girl.

- Daddy is starting a new family because he doesn't love me.

- My teachers are kind to me because they pity me. They all know that nobody wants me.

Working out a more accurate meaning now

Now that you're older and have more strings to your reasoning bow, you can review past events and assign more accurate and realistic meanings to the events you experienced earlier on in your life.

You can't take a bad event and turn it into a good one, but you can try to understand it in a way that makes more sense and is more helpful to you.

Figure 10-1 is a worksheet we created to help you keep focused when re-interpreting a past event from a more compassionate and astute perspective.

Event	Old Meaning	New Meaning

Figure 10-1:
Your old
meaning
and new
meaning
worksheet.

To use the form in Figure 10-1, follow these steps:

1. **In the first column, briefly record the facts of the event.**

2. **In the second column, write down the meaning you gave to the event at the time.**

   Record what your reaction to the event caused you to think about yourself and what you think the event means about you as a person.

3. **Use the third column to record a healthier and more accurate interpretation of what the event actually meant.**

   This healthier understanding of yourself is a self-image that you want to strengthen.

Table 10-1 shows a few examples from Pippa's worksheet.

Table 10-1	Pippa's Old Meaning–New Meaning Worksheet	
Event	**Old Meaning**	**New Meaning**
Dad sent me to live with my aunt.	He doesn't want me or love me anymore.	Dad didn't know how to look after me and thought my aunt would do a better job.
Dad got remarried.	I'm not lovable.	Dad got married again for his own reasons. He did neglect me but not because I'm unlovable. Dad didn't cope very well after mum's death.
Aunt was unkind to me.	I'm not nice. No one can love me.	My aunt behaved badly. She was wrong to say those things to a child.

Confronting Core Beliefs

Core beliefs are long-held and enduring beliefs about yourself, others and the world. They're *core* because they typically lie at the very centre of your thinking or your personal philosophy.

Although core beliefs usually start to form during childhood they can develop later on in life. Generally, the seeds of core beliefs are sown very early on and then subsequent life events reinforce these burgeoning ideas. After the seeds are sown, life can throw up additional events that germinate the seeds and lay fertile ground for them to flourish into strong invasive weeds.

Your early experiences give rise to beliefs and ideas about who you are and what your worth is, but they also lead to additional beliefs about other people and the world in general.

Core beliefs aren't always negative and unhelpful. Good life experiences and positive relationships with others frequently contribute to the development of healthy ideas about your own worth, the value of others and life in all its infinite glory. We're dealing with negative and unhelpful core beliefs here because these are the ones that cause you emotional distress and feed low self-esteem.

A useful method of really getting to know your personal beliefs is to simply fill in the blanks in the following list. Give yourself a few minutes to let your mind wander over what you typically tend to think about yourself and those you meet. Now stretch your thinking to include a wider perspective on the world and 'life'. Fill in the blanks with whatever phrases seem most accurately to reflect your thinking. Don't worry about getting 'the right answer', because there isn't one. This exercise is about finding out what *you* believe. Also, no one else is going to see what you write unless you decide to share it with them.

- ✔ I am _____.
- ✔ Other people are _____.
- ✔ The world is _____.

Do this exercise a few times until you can really put your finger on phrases that concisely describe your beliefs. Think of the process as doing several drafts and then eventually settling on a final version.

Here's how Lauren, Seamus and Pippa from the preceding section filled in the blanks.

- ✔ Lauren's filled in her blanks like this, based on her experience of being unable to meet her family's academic expectations:
  - I am <u>not good enough</u>.
  - Other people are <u>more worthwhile and useful than I am</u>.
  - The world is <u>a place that favours the gifted and exceptional</u>.
- ✔ Seamus had a physically abusive father. Here are his filled blanks:
  - I am <u>weak and useless</u>.
  - Other people are <u>powerful and potentially dangerous</u>.
  - The world is <u>uninterested in the suffering of others</u>.
- ✔ Pippa's father sent her to live with her aunt after her own mother died. Here's how Pippa filled in the blanks:
  - I am <u>unwanted and unlovable</u>.
  - Other people are <u>more important than I am</u>.
  - The world is <u>a 'members only' club that I'm not invited to join</u>.

Identifying your core beliefs can help you to understand why you continue to have the same kinds of emotional problems and how your self-esteem remains poor. Negative core beliefs about yourself often seem to fall into two predictable categories:

> ✔ **Worthless and bad:** With these core beliefs, you see yourself as useless, inadequate, bad, evil, a failure, unlovable, defective, insignificant and so on.
>
> ✔ **Helpless and powerless:** With these core beliefs, you see yourself as weak, incapable, ineffective, anonymous, futile, pathetic and so on.

Not very nice stuff, is it? Don't be discouraged though; in later sections we outline ways of challenging unhelpful core beliefs.

Inspecting how beliefs interact

Your core beliefs about yourself, others and the world interact with and reinforce one another and they have the potential to erode your self-esteem.

If you believe that you're weak and everyone else is strong, then your self-esteem is being hit from two different angles. Add to that a belief that the world favours the strong and disregards the weak, and your self-esteem takes another hit.

Negative and extreme beliefs about other people and the world undermine your sense of personal worth almost as much as the beliefs you hold about yourself. It's a bit like imagining that you're a worm and that the sky is constantly swarming with hungry birds.

Figure 10-2 shows how Seamus's core beliefs about himself, others and the world make a pungent low-self-esteem cocktail.

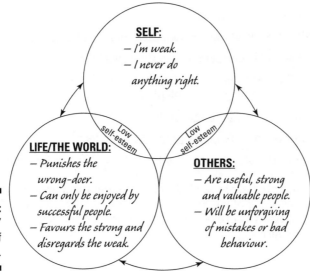

Figure 10-2:
Seamus'
core belief
interaction.

SELF:
– I'm weak.
– I never do anything right.

LIFE/THE WORLD:
– Punishes the wrong-doer.
– Can only be enjoyed by successful people.
– Favours the strong and disregards the weak.

OTHERS:
– Are useful, strong and valuable people.
– Will be unforgiving of mistakes or bad behaviour.

Aiming at your own belief dartboard

As a visual way of understanding how your core beliefs inform your actions and thinking, look at the problem as a dartboard, like the one shown in Figure 10-3.

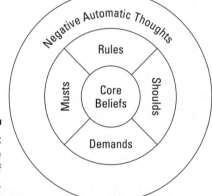

Figure 10-3:
The core
belief
dartboard.

Your core beliefs are at the centre of the dartboard. On the inner circle are your:

- **Demands:** Unrelenting pressures you put yourself under in an attempt to diminish or rectify your core beliefs.

- **Musts:** The rules about what you must do or must avoid doing in order to cope with your core beliefs.

- **Rules:** The rigid principles that you believe you must follow in order to make up for or prevent your core beliefs from being exposed or triggered.

- **Shoulds:** Strong impulses that you follow in order to stop yourself experiencing painful emotions arising from your negative core beliefs.

On the outer circle are your *negative automatic thoughts*. These thoughts are ones that pop into your head in certain situations seemingly without any warning or invitation. In fact, they're the results of your core beliefs and the thoughts that are at the forefront of your consciousness. You may not immediately recognise them as 'core' but they carry the essence of your fundamentally held beliefs within them.

To make this point clearer, have a look at Seamus's dartboard, shown in Figure 10-4.

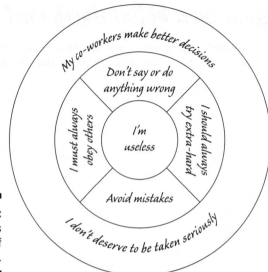

Figure 10-4:
Seamus's
core belief
dartboard.

Figure 10-5 is a blank dartboard for you to fill with your own beliefs. The first step in overcoming your problematic beliefs is to know what they are.

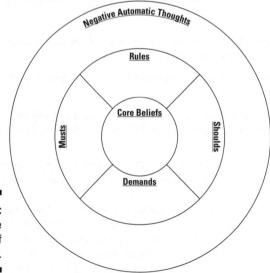

Figure 10-5:
Your core
belief
dartboard.

Curtailing negative views of yourself

Your negative core beliefs about yourself lie at the root of your low self-esteem. They work like a filter through which all your experiences pass.

Low self-esteem is tantamount to having a prejudice against yourself. If you have low self-esteem you probably take in negative information that fits with your unhealthy self-view and ignore, reject or dismiss positive information that doesn't fit with your negative beliefs.

Sometimes you may even take positive information and events and transform them into negative ones. For example, if your core belief about yourself is 'I'm a failure' and your boss compliments your performance, you may conclude: 'She's only saying that because she feels sorry for me' or 'That was just a lucky break – a lobotomised monkey could have done as good a job as I did'. And in this way a positive becomes a negative.

You're most likely carrying out this behaviour unwittingly, as an automatic response that you've developed over time, and aren't even noticing when it happens. Now is the time to start taking notice and giving that damaging filter the heave-ho.

Figure 10-6 shows how low self-esteem rejects and mangles positive information and readily accepts negative stuff. Low self-esteem is reinforced and perpetuated because only information consistent with your poor sense of personal worth makes it through the filter.

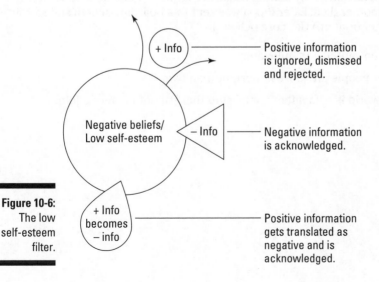

Figure 10-6:
The low self-esteem filter.

Negative beliefs/ Low self-esteem

+ Info — Positive information is ignored, dismissed and rejected.

– Info — Negative information is acknowledged.

+ Info becomes – info — Positive information gets translated as negative and is acknowledged.

Pinning down your positive points persistently

Keep a positive data log in which you record anything that spits in the eye of your negative core beliefs. Write down your counter-experiences every day for about three weeks. All you need to do is jot down information that contradicts or doesn't wholly fit with your negative view of yourself. You can also use the positive data log to gather evidence against your negative core beliefs about others and the world.

Keeping a positive data log has two potential functions:

✔ It forces you to look for and acknowledge information that contradicts your negative core beliefs, and this can help you to reinforce better ways of thinking.

✔ You can review it when you find yourself tempted to give into your old negative core beliefs. The log may give you a fresher perspective and help you to see things more realistically.

As you deliberately and regularly collect information and evidence that negates your damaging views of yourself, the world and other people, your self-esteem gets a chance to grow. Your general outlook on life is likely to improve and you may begin to trust others more too.

Figure 10-7 shows an excerpt from Pippa's positive data log. (Pippa was sent to live with an unfriendly aunt because her father felt unable to look after her after her mother died. Later Pippa was sent to a boarding school and saw little of her father or aunt.) Her core beliefs are:

✔ I am unwanted and unlovable.

✔ Other people are more important than I am.

✔ The world is a 'members only' club that I'm not invited to join.

Monday the 26th of September:

Core belief about self: *I am unwanted and unlovable.*

Evidence against:

-My husband gave me a big kiss before leaving for work.

-My toddler told me he wants to marry me one day.

-I got a postcard from my friend who's on holiday in Brazil saying that she misses me.

Core belief about others: *Other people are more important than I am.*

Evidence against:

- An acquaintance at the gym asked me for advice about breastfeeding her new baby.

- A man held the door open for me at the supermarket.

- My book club rescheduled our evening discussion for a time when I could attend, even though I was the only member who couldn't make the original proposed date.

Core beliefs about life: *The world is a 'members-only' club to which I'm not invited to join.*

Evidence against:

- A lot of shopkeepers and people I passed on the street smiled at me today.

- I'm a valued member of my book club (see above).

- My mother-in-law rang to ask me if I'd like to go shopping with her over the weekend.

Figure 10-7:
Pippa's
positive
data log.

Finding your belief formulation

Building a comprehensive formulation of your personal beliefs can be useful in your quest to improve your self-esteem. Really laying the issue out in black and white can help you to understand your behaviour better and make you more mindful of what you need to change in order to improve your self-esteem and overall satisfaction with your life.

Figure 10-8 is a blank form you can fill in with your own accumulation of core beliefs. Follow these basic guidelines when filling in each box of your formulation form:

- ✔ **Box 1:** Record any early or significant events that you think have contributed to the development of your negative core beliefs.

- ✔ **Box 2:** Jot down your specific negative beliefs about yourself, others and the world.

- ✔ **Box 3:** Write down the demands, musts, rules and shoulds that you typically place upon yourself, others and the world. (Refer to 'Aiming at your own belief dartboard' earlier in this chapter for help with recognising these negative core beliefs.)

  You can put these in the form of *assumptions*, or *if-then statements*, such as '*if* I make a mistake *then* it proves that I'm useless' or '*if* I avoid any errors *then* others may think I'm capable'.

- ✔ **Box 4:** Record what you do to cope with your negative beliefs.

- ✔ **Box 5:** Write down anything positive you can think of about yourself that defies your negative beliefs. Really go for it with both pistols blazing.

Once your formulation is complete you can make an effort to challenge your negative beliefs, change the way you behave and maximise your personal skills and strengths.

Figure 10-9 shows the formulation form that Seamus filled out.

FORMULATION OF MY BELIEFS AND RULES

RELEVANT EARLY/PAST EXPERIENCES

CORE UNHELPFUL BELIEFS
I am...., The world is...., Other people....

RULES/ASSUMPTIONS
If....then...., Demands about self, the world, others.

AVOIDANCE AND COMPENSATORY BEHAVIOURS
Situations you tend to avoid or things you do excessively
as a consequence of your beliefs/rules

WHAT I'VE GOT GOING FOR ME
List your personal strengths and assets

Figure 10-8:
Fill in this
form with
your own
accumula-
tion of core
beliefs.

RELEVANT EARLY/PAST EXPERIENCES

– *Being physically abused by my father and seeing him beat my mother.*
– *Being told that the abuse was a family affair to be kept secret.*

CORE NEGATIVE BELIEFS

– *I'm weak and useless (self).*
– *Others are powerful and potentially dangerous.*
– *The world is uninterested in the suffering of others.*

RULES/ASSUMPTIONS

– *I must not displease others.*
– *If I trust others they will hurt me.*
– *I should try very hard to always get things right.*

COMPENSATORY BEHAVIOURS

– *I let other people have their own way all the time.*
– *I try to hide my mistakes.*
– *I only do things I'm sure I can do successfully.*
– *I avoid turning to others for support.*

WHAT I'VE GOT GOING FOR ME

Figure 10-9:
Seamus's
belief for-
mulation
form.

– *I'm hardworking and reliable.*
– *I've got a good sense of humour.*
– *I have good organisational skills.*
– *I'm athletic and good at team sports.*

Circumnavigating your negative views of the world

Life is neither fair nor balanced, that's true. The world is also full of random events, some good and others bad. If you can accept that the world is a complicated place and no rhyme or reason exists as to why some people seem to have an easier time than others, you may be able to appreciate its richness.

Perhaps you're so accustomed to looking for the bad stuff that you just keep expecting the world to kick you in the teeth when you're down. You may not even register some of the good things the world has to offer you.

Give the world a second chance. If you want to improve your self-esteem, you need to revamp your beliefs about the world in which you live. Otherwise you're going to be fighting a steep uphill battle and may end up having thoughts such as: 'Things always go wrong for me, it's just typical because the world is against me'.

Make a determined effort to notice even the smallest most commonplace things that go right for you. If you want to feel better about yourself, try to stop seeing the world as your enemy. The world is not a wholly bad or good place; it's a mixture of the two. Nor is it accurate to say that the world is against anyone. The world just . . . *is*.

Capsizing your negative view of others

Not only does your self-view take a battering through life experiences, but the way you think about others is also affected.

You may be distrustful of others or even fearful of them because of certain events in your past. Your negative ideas about people may prevent you from forming satisfying relationships. Without meaning to, you may be cheating yourself of the joy that can come from appreciating others.

Chronic low self-esteem can often be a double-edged sword: one edge cuts because you assume that everyone else is fundamentally better than you, and the other edge cuts when you're as unreasonably critical of others as you are of yourself.

Your low self-esteem may prompt you to adopt some unhelpful and critical attitudes and ideas about other people:

- ✔ Your self-esteem is temporarily inflated by criticising others. You get to feel superior for a little while.

- ✔ You resent other people's failings because they remind you of your own faults.

- ✔ You deflect attention from your own perceived weaknesses by criticising others.

- ✔ You're so angry with yourself all the time that berating someone else feels good for a change.

- ✔ You blame other people for your feelings of unworthiness, and so belittling them in turn is 'just desserts'.

- ✔ Your feelings of low worth lead you to conclude that something must be fundamentally 'wrong' with anyone who appears to care for you.

- ✔ You're so convinced that you're worthless that taking down the rest of the world with you seems right.

- ✔ You've been treated badly by others in the past and now you want to exact some form of revenge.

- ✔ You don't see why you should value anybody when no one seems to value you.

Being critical and mistrusting of others serves only to keep you locked in a cycle of low self-esteem. Negativity breeds negativity.

Try treating others in the way that you would like to be treated yourself.

Instead of being blinkered by your beliefs, take an objective standpoint and look for new information that may help you think more positively and fairly about others. Give people the benefit of the doubt and don't allow your negative core beliefs to stop you finding out what other people are *actually* like.

Charting new territory

The past, though a powerful influencer, need not determine how you think, feel or live in the present and in the future. You can fight back against your unhelpful beliefs.

Your negative core beliefs are so ingrained that you may never get rid of them completely. In fact your best line of defence is to weaken them and develop healthy alternative attitudes that can effectively do battle with them.

Although your old ways of thinking may still be present, your new beliefs can steer you into more constructive directions. Instead of going over and over the same territory led by the compass of self-doubt, you can branch out into new pastures using healthy self-esteem as your very own satellite navigation system.

We don't pretend that changing the way you think is easy. If it were, therapists and books like this one would be a lot less in demand. But you can win through and keep hold of a constructive, helpful attitude most of the time.

Adopting Updated Attitudes

After you know what your unhealthy and unhelpful beliefs are, you can begin to build new and better ones.

Use these tips for constructing your own new adaptive beliefs:

- ✔ **Include a self-, other- and world-accepting statement**. Give yourself and others permission to be human and sometimes get things wrong or do things poorly. Include a proviso like 'Doing a bad deed does not make a person bad'. Allow a margin for error and deviation from ideal behaviour.

    Also cut the world some slack. Indeed life is often unfair and can be difficult, but include in your new belief recognition that life is full of good things too.

- ✔ **Make your new belief sound believable to you.** Use language that really makes sense to you. Don't worry about grammar or fancy vocabulary. What's most important is that your new belief sums up the way you want to think about yourself, others and the world. Actually keeping it simple makes it easier to remember.

- ✔ **Add a coping statement to your new belief.** Building confidence in your ability to survive undesirable events is a big part of healthy self-esteem. In your new belief include a reminder that even if things don't go as you ideally want them to you, you can cope and recover.

Make sure that your updated healthy beliefs are comprehensive like the following examples.

A few examples of how to construct new attitudes follow:

- ✔ Lauren's old belief is 'I'm not good enough'. Her new healthy belief goes like this: 'I'm a worthwhile person just like everyone else on the planet. Even if I'm not as academically capable as members of my family, I'm still no less worthwhile than they are. I have my own unique skills and talents that are worth as much as anyone else's.'

- ✔ Seamus thinks of himself as 'weak' and 'useless'. Here's his new attitude: 'I'm useful and capable in many ways. I prefer not to make mistakes but I also accept that there's no reason why I shouldn't make any. Even if I fail at something I'm still a worthwhile person who has made a mistake.'

- ✔ Pippa has always believed that she is unwanted and unlovable. She came up with this new way of thinking about herself: 'I'm a worthwhile person who's capable of being loved and wanted by others. I don't need everyone to like me in order to like myself. I can survive rejection from others even if it's painful.'

Write your new belief on a small piece of paper that you can easily carry with you. This paper is your new attitude flashcard. Read it regularly and remind yourself of how you want to think even in difficult situations.

Structuring a suitable 'soundbite'

Even with the aid of a flashcard carrying your new, healthy attitude, you may have trouble remembering your new belief precisely in certain situations. You may not be able to get your flashcard out or you may experience a strong emotion that clouds your thinking.

Condense your full healthy belief into a brief phrase or *soundbite* that captures the essence of your updated attitude. Ideally, make your soundbite underline the main point of your longer healthy belief statement. It's like using a highlighter pen to identify the main point in a paragraph of text.

You can use your soundbite as a reminder of the rest of the useful information contained in your full healthy belief statement.

Making a soundbite is useful because it's brief enough to recall even in times of stress. You can write down your brief soundbite version of your belief at the top of your flashcard, so it's there for you to refer to as well.

Soundbites for Lauren, Seamus and Pippa follow:

- ✔ Lauren's soundbite: 'My worth is on a par with everyone else.'

- ✔ Seamus's soundbite: 'If I make a mistake that just means I'm human.'

- ✔ Pippa's soundbite: 'I want people to like me but if they don't, I'll survive.'

Moving meaning from head to heart

At first, although you understand that your new attitudes are sensible and helpful, you may still have trouble believing that they're true and applicable. You can *know* intellectually that your new beliefs are correct but not *feel* emotionally convinced by them. We call this the *head-heart conundrum*.

Like many people, you may find that you start thinking in better ways but still feel emotionally disturbed. Your feelings take a while to catch up with your thinking. Emotions are like the slow horse in a race: they make it to the finish line but probably not before the belief and behaviour fillies have collected the ribbons. So you need to exercise a little faith and patience.

Practise what you preach

You can use a couple of techniques to help you feel more convinced by your new beliefs:

- ✔ Ask yourself what you want a friend, or someone you love, to really believe. You can often see the truth of your beliefs when you apply them to people you care about more clearly than when you apply them to yourself.

- ✔ Think about what you would encourage children to believe about themselves. For example, Seamus realises that he'd be horrified if his three-year-old son ever came to think of himself as useless. Instead, he wants his son to believe that he's a useful and worthwhile little person. Similarly, Pippa would never encourage her children to believe that they were unlovable, no matter what happens in their lives. She wants her children to know that they're lovable and to believe that they have many qualities for others to appreciate and love.

If your new ways of thinking make sense for others and you'd recommend them to those you love, they hold true for you too. What's good for the goslings is good for the goose and the gander.

Assemble an arsenal of arguments

Making a new belief statement is probably not enough to get you to really change the way you think. But coming up with lots of strong arguments to support your new belief can help resolve the head-heart issue. You may need to do this process several times and come up with more compelling arguments over time before you begin to feel the benefits.

Write the belief you want to strengthen at the top of a page in your notebook. Next put your belief through its paces using the following questions: Seamus's answers are shown in Figure 10-10.

Belief I want to strengthen:

'I am a useful and worthwhile person who is capable of both success and failure'.

* Is this belief true and sensible?

Yes. I have lots of evidence of times when I have successfully completed a project and done things to a high standard. So this is proof that I am useful or else I would never succeed at anything. All humans make errors and fail at their endeavours sometimes and this has no impact on their overall worth and usefulness. I'm no different to other people in this respect. I'm basically capable and worthy even if I fail at something important to me.

* Is this belief flexible?

Yes. This belief acknowledges that I'm complex and that I have worth whether I fail or succeed at specific tasks. It takes into account that even though I have basic worth and usefulness, not everything that I do will be useful or successful. It's true that I'm both useful and that I sometimes do less useful things.

* How does this belief allow for mistakes and bad events?

This belief allows me to continue to think positively and fairly about myself even if I make a mistake or something undesirable happens in my life. It helps me to understand mistakes as part of being a human rather than deciding that making errors means that I am useless or lesser than others.

* How is this belief helpful?

It helps me to feel disappointed but not depressed when I do fail or make mistakes. It also spurs me into problem-solving action if things go wrong. When I hold this belief I'm more willing to take risks and push myself to try new things. Believing that I have basic worth and usefulness- no matter what- prevents me from fearing failure and being anxious about the possibility of making errors.

Figure 10-10:
Seamus's
belief-
supporting
arguments.

✔ Is this belief true and sensible? Record ways in which your belief fits with reality and makes logical sense. For example, it's both true and sensible to say that all humans make errors, since you see it happen in reality all the time.

✔ Is this belief flexible? Your belief is flexible if it outlines your *preferences* for your own and others' behaviour and world conditions. Flexibility means that your belief withstands the test of time. You can still believe it to be true even when it isn't met fully because it highlights your desires and ideals but doesn't insist on a specific outcome.

✔ How does this belief allow for mistakes and bad events? A healthy helpful belief leaves a margin for error. In other words, your belief acknowledges that nothing in life is perfect, including you.

✔ How is this belief helpful? Your belief needs to make your life easier and not harder. A healthy belief leads you into effective problem solving when you're unable to meet it fully or life throws you something odd or unexpected.

You can use this technique to strengthen new beliefs about yourself, others and the world.

Live alongside a new belief

Starting to hold onto a new belief includes acting in ways that reinforce the belief and make it grow stronger over time.

People tend to act in ways that reflect the types of beliefs they hold. Therefore, you need to alter your behaviour deliberately to fit with the ways you want to think and believe.

For example, Seamus wants to make decisions and work hard, and yet not kill himself in the process. These two desires are in accordance with his new self-belief of 'I'm a useful and capable person'.

Take your new beliefs into every situation you encounter. Ask yourself, 'If I truly believed in my heart of hearts that my new beliefs were true, how would I behave in this situation?' Then make a concerted effort to act in the manner you identify.

If all this effort sounds like a lot of hard work, that's because it is; like digging out the foundations of a building on your own, by hand, and then laying down a new one. However, we urge you to consider the potential benefits to your self-esteem, appreciation of others and enjoyment of life. Besides, the whole process is likely to become easier with time and practice.

Negative core beliefs are formidable opponents and so you need to hit them hard and refuse to give up. You can weaken them and maybe even destroy them over time.

Your new healthy beliefs grow and strengthen if you continue to represent them through action:

- ✔ Act in ways that reflect your new beliefs. For example, ask yourself: 'If I truly believed that I'm likeable and worthwhile, how would I act in social situations? What might I do differently at work? How would I behave in my romantic relationships?'

  Be specific about how you would hold yourself physically and the types of things you would say and do.

- ✔ Troubleshoot for any obstacles to your new belief. Think about how you can keep your new belief strong even if things go badly sometimes. Imagine yourself coping with a social glitch or recovering from mistakes with your healthy new belief still intact.

- ✔ Watch what other people do. Is there anyone else around you who seems to be operating under the type of beliefs you want to hold and strengthen? How do they deal with criticism? What do they do in awkward social situations? What's their body language like? Watch them closely and mimic their behaviour.

If you pay close attention to how you're behaving, you may well get an insight into whether or not your old negative core beliefs are making an unsolicited comeback. Breaking the habit of a lifetime is difficult. So don't be surprised or disheartened if you do find yourself acting on an old belief despite your resolve to do just the opposite. Catch yourself with your hand in the poisonous cookie jar as quickly as you can, and then go to the oven and bake up a fresh new batch of beneficial behavioural biscuits.

Being selective about the company you keep

When you're giving your all to adopt a healthier view of yourself, you may be best off avoiding the company of people who can sabotage it.

Take note of any people who have given (or continue to give) you negative messages about yourself, others and the world. Even if they're members of your family, you benefit from keeping them at arms length until your new beliefs are solid enough to resist their influence.

We're not suggesting that you cut people who are important to you out of your life forever. But limiting the contact you have with those who bring out the negative in you is a good idea for a brief period of time.

Make an effort to spend time with people you feel good around. Be on the look out for people who seem to exemplify the new beliefs you want to strengthen. You can choose the people to associate with despite the contrary information that your negative core beliefs sometimes send you. Remember that you deserve to be in the company of people who:

- ✔ Accept and respect you.
- ✔ Hold a realistic but optimistic view of the world.
- ✔ Restore your faith in the kindness and compassion of others.
- ✔ Stimulate and interest you.
- ✔ Treat you with genuine interest and care.

Chapter 11

Proving Your Worth to Yourself

*D*ust off your white coat and clipboard because this chapter is your chance to get in touch with your inner scientist. (And if you're already a scientist, here's your chance to use your talents at putting theories to the test to improve your self-esteem.)

This chapter draws from the proven principles of *Cognitive Behavioural Therapy (CBT)*, which emphasises treating your thoughts about yourself, other people and the world around you as hunches. Like many people suffering with poor self-esteem, you probably think that your feelings and thoughts are facts, when actually many of the thoughts you treat as facts are mere hunches that may or may not accurately reflect reality. Your hunches can be true or false, partly right or partly wrong. The idea is to conduct experiments to test your hunches, guesses and predictions.

In this chapter we guide you through the steps involved in becoming better at rigorously testing your predictions.

Devising Experiments to Improve Your Self-Esteem

As your own personal scientist, you can elicit your negative predictions and put them to the test. The more you discover that the predictions stemming from your low self-esteem aren't 100 per cent true, and certainly not true 100 per cent of the time, the more able you are to take with a big pinch of salt your negative thoughts about yourself, what others think of you and your future. This section is your guide to designing behavioural experiments.

Give yourself the chance to prove yourself wrong and prove yourself worthwhile. Have fun donning your white coat.

Looking at experiment basics

The key to designing a good behavioural experiment is to take time to put your experiment, and the data it yields, down on paper. Writing down not only helps you formulate a clear prediction and test, but also gives you the opportunity to reflect on your experiment. Like any good scientist, you can then move on to another experiment.

The basic procedure for any scientific test is to firstly develop a *hypothesis,* (or in everyday English, a *guess*) about something. Generally your hypothesis is an attempt to explain a phenomenon. So, staying with low self-esteem issues, your hypothesis may be that the cause of your social anxiety is your fundamental inability to be likeable to others. Doing a behavioural experiment gives you the chance to consider an alternative hypothesis and see which one best fits the facts. For example:

> Hypothesis A: I feel anxious in social situations because I'm unlikeable and will be rejected by others.

> Hypothesis B: I feel anxious in social situations because I fear the possibility of being disliked and rejected by others.

Scientific tests also test out the validity of *predictions,* which typically take an 'if-then' format. For example, *if* you toss a burning match onto a pile of newspaper *then* the paper is likely to ignite. You can easily test out such a prediction by doing a practical experiment and monitoring the ensuing result (no real surprise results arising from that example!).

Returning to low self-esteem, however, your predictions may be more based on conjecture than on physics. Your negative predictions are frequently generated by low-self-esteem ideas and beliefs. These unhelpful beliefs about yourself give rise to equally negative assumptions about the kinds of results you'll get in certain situations. You may assume that you'll get rejected if you risk engaging with others, for example. Your assumption that you'll be rejected leads you to predict: '*If* I ask my co-worker out for lunch *then* he will flatly refuse.' Your low self-esteem may tell you that this negatively biased prediction is a cold hard fact and lead you to avoid extending a luncheon invitation.

Setting up your own experiment

In the interest of developing healthy self-esteem, it pays to test out your assumptions and predictions to see if they are accurate all the time.

To design an experiment to test your negative assumptions about yourself, follow these steps:

1. **Specify the fundamental low self-esteem belief or assumption that you want to test out for validity.**

   For example:

   - If I can't learn something quickly it means that I'm stupid.
   - If I don't please people they're going to abandon me.
   - If I make a mistake it proves I'm not good enough.
   - I'm a failure.
   - I'm unlikeable.
   - I'm unlovable.
   - I'm useless.
   - I'm worthless.

2. **Identify a specific negative prediction to put to the test and rate the likelihood of it being accurate.**

   Remember to use an 'if-then' format. Pinpoint a future situation that you're making a negative prediction about – going to a party, applying for a job or trying out a new sport. Your prediction is based on your general assumptions about yourself and can be about any kind of situation or event. Your low self-esteem is likely to produce lots of the kinds of negative beliefs and assumptions listed in step one. Here are some examples of low self-esteem predictions:

   - *If* I go to the party *then* nobody will talk to me and I'll have a miserable time.
   - *If* I apply for a job *then* I'll screw up the interview.
   - *If* I take up tennis *then* I'll be terrible at it and never improve.

   Be as specific as you can in your prediction. You may well already know intellectually that your fear isn't likely to come true, but behavioural experiments are all about *showing* your mind something in reality rather than simply persuading it of something in the absence of concrete action.

Rate the likelihood of your prediction being accurate on a scale of 0 to 10, where a 10 rating means that you believe your prediction is wholly true 100 per cent of the time and 0 means that you believe your prediction is wholly untrue 100 per cent of the time.

The benefits of rating how deeply you believe your negative prediction are twofold:

- You may realise straight away that your rating is way too high and that evidence exists to suggest that it doesn't *always* come true or at least not entirely. You may decide to lower your rating, thereby reducing the risk of a negative outcome in your mind *before* you start your experiment. (Assigning a more mid-range rating can bolster your motivation to actually bite the bullet and put your prediction to the test!)

- Even if your pre-experiment rating remains very high, after you've done a few experiments you may be surprised to find that your original rating was a gross overestimation of the likelihood of a negative outcome. You can then lower your rating in light of being pleasantly proved wrong. As you continue to conduct experiments and gather evidence that contradicts your negative predictions your ratings will lower and become more realistic.

3. **Identify an alternative prediction based on healthy self-esteem.**

Consider alternative outcomes; imagine the prediction you would make if you already had better self-esteem.

Try this exercise: Imagine that you have a clone, the same as you in every way except with good self-esteem; what predictions would your clone make? What predictions or assumptions do you think someone you know with healthier self-esteem would make? For example, a healthy alternative prediction may be: '*If* I take up tennis *then* I'll probably be poor at it to start with but will improve with practice.'

If you can't identify an alternative prediction before you do your first behavioural experiment, don't worry – just focus on putting your negative prediction to the test. You may find it easier to develop a healthier more accurate alternative prediction after you've done a few experiments.

4. **Specify how to assess evidence for and against the accuracy of your predictions.**

Consider how you're going to know whether your prediction is true or not. For example, if you predict that your co-worker will reject you if you approach him, what would you look for as evidence of this?

Often your low self-esteem fools you into taking even minor negative results as compelling evidence that your negative prediction is entirely true. Be clear about what concrete results prove and disprove your prediction. So if you test your prediction out by asking your co-worker to lunch and he says 'Yes', that disproves your prediction. Even if he says 'No, not today but maybe tomorrow', your prediction is not completely proved.

Even in the unlikely event of your co-worker saying 'No, I won't have lunch with you. Not today and not ever', you can still test out your assumption that *everyone* will reject you via more specific tests. Your co-worker's refusal proves the prediction that he would say 'No' correct, but it doesn't prove anything about your assumption that you'll always be rejected when you approach people.

The next section, 'Putting Your Predictions to the Test', offers a variety of sample predictions and testing methods.

5. Plan and carry out your experiment.

Write down what you intend to do in order to put your prediction(s) to the test.

To test your predictions properly, you need to change your behaviour – you need to experiment with new ways of thinking about situations, otherwise you won't be likely to notice any differences. You may choose to face up to a situation you normally avoid to see whether your fears come true or not. Like seeing if you can learn to play tennis or if you actually do completely screw up an interview as predicted. To conduct a proper test, you need to concentrate on learning the tennis moves instead of focusing on your thoughts about being clumsy and useless. Or you need to concentrate on the questions asked in the interview and focus less on your nervousness. Both these examples involve overriding your low self-esteem and behaving in ways that give you a better chance of disproving your negative predictions.

Do several tests for a given prediction and don't give up too easily. It can be difficult to resist the pull of low self-esteem. Thinking about situations more positively and acting in ways that reflect healthy self-esteem take time to adopt, so be patient with yourself.

There are no hard and fast rules about how many experiments you should conduct to test out the accuracy of a specific prediction. However, doing more rather than less is a good idea because it gives you more information. In general aim to carry out a *minimum* of three tests for each prediction. Carry on until you find that your conviction in the validity of a negative prediction drops significantly on your 0 to 10 rating scale (see Step 3). You don't need to devote the rest of your life to relentless testing of one prediction. Once you have the procedure down pat, you can move on to testing other predictions as and when you deem it necessary.

Low self-esteem can bring about self-fulfilling prophecies. In other words, low self-esteem assumptions can set you up to fail because they lead you to act in unhelpful ways. Keep focused on gathering evidence or facts and disregard your biased thoughts when conducting behavioural experiments.

6. **Record your results.**

Get your notebook out and write down the actual outcome of your experiment. Record all the factual results. Be as fair and accurate as possible about recording evidence that supports or contradicts your initial prediction. Then review your outcome information and decide what it tells you about the accuracy and truth of your negative prediction.

Consider the evidence that supports your prediction(s) and how strong it seems. Look at whether the results of your experiment best fit with your negative prediction or have you discovered something unexpected instead? Perhaps your primary poisonous prediction isn't as sturdy as you first thought and you can develop a more positive probable prediction to take its place.

Many experiments leave you with tentative conclusions, so come up with an idea for what your next experiment may be so that you can gather more information. You can repeat the same experiment, modify it or try something completely different.

Putting Your Predictions to the Test

In the following sections, we offer you some examples of the behavioural experiments you can use in your ongoing quest to improve your self-esteem and enjoyment of life. (You can find more information about the kinds of thoughts and habits associated with low self-esteem in Chapter 6.)

Treating your problem 'as if' it's something different

In this kind of experiment, you try out a different perspective on a problem to see how well it works: for example, treating your view of yourself as worthless 'as if' it's a product of overly critical thinking, rather than a product of lack of love or success. In this way you can try out a new strategy and see what you think of the results. If you're not happy with the results, try a new strategy, or even go back to your old one.

Julie has a problem with feeling frequently hurt and angry towards her husband, because she tends to blame him for her view of herself as unlovable. However, in her calmer moments she realises that she felt this way before she ever met him. Figure 11-1 shows her experiment in treating her problem differently.

Step 1. Specify the self-esteem belief that you want to change.

I'm unlovable.

Step 2. Identify the thought or prediction you want to put to the test.

That I'm unlovable is something that I'm inevitably going to see as a FACT if I can't get my partner to pay me more attention.

Step 3. Identify an alternative prediction.

That it might work better to treat my problem as a BELIEF that I'm unlovable that's the product of my mind rather than a fact.

Step 4. Specify the experiment you plan to test your prediction.

I'm going to spend the next three months trying to suspend judgement about whether it's true or not that I'm unlovable and steadily work through the exercises in 'Boosting Self-Esteem For Dummies'.

Step 5. Record your results.

In general I feel far better. Although I have had some 'moments' of becoming hurt and angry over the past three months I certainly feel like they are happening less often and last less time.

Step 6. Write down your conclusions from the results of your experiment.

I can see now that 'I'm unlovable' is a BELIEF that I sometimes feel is true, but certainly isn't 100% true. It definitely has worked better to tackle this as a thinking problem than constantly feeling angry and resentful towards my partner.

Figure 11-1:
Julie's changing perspective on a problem worksheet .

Freeing up your feelings

You may fear that other people are going to think badly of you if you show emotion, or that your emotions are going to overwhelm you and run out of control if you allow yourself to experience them. All human beings, however, have a system of emotions – it's part of how we're built.

Feelings exist to be felt, and trying too hard to control or avoid them can often cause problems such depression and anxiety. In other words, as far as controlling your emotions is concerned, the cure can be worse than the disease. Therefore, your experiments in this area can target your predictions about your emotions.

Conan lost his mother, to whom he was very close, six months ago. He tends to avoid his emotions and was beginning to notice that he was easily tearful and his mood was down much of the time. He devised the experiment in Figure 11-2 to help him work through his emotions.

Step 1. Specify the self-esteem belief that you want to change.

I'm weak.

Step 2. Identify the thought or prediction you want to put to the test.

If I allow myself to get upset about my mother's death I'll end up falling apart and won't be able to cope with any of the rest of my life.

Step 3. Identify an alternative prediction.

It's true that I might get upset and shed some tears, but after a while I will very probably be able to pull myself back together.

Step 4. Specify the experiment you plan to test your prediction.

I'm going to write out a letter to my Mum to say some of the things I meant to say to her when she was around but never managed to say.

Step 5. Record your results.

This was strangely liberating. I did get choked up a couple of times, but didn't fall apart.

Step 6. Write down your conclusions from the results of your experiment.

I might be able to cope with my grief better than I thought, and I might be tougher than I think. I need to see how I cope with visiting Mum's grave next.

Figure 11-2:
Conan's experiencing emotions worksheet.

Running the risk of falling flat on your face

One coping strategy commonly used by people who have low self-esteem is to avoid tasks or situations in which they fear they may fail, perform poorly or appear foolish. This tendency is partly driven by the idea that these experiences somehow 'confirm' their negative view of themselves, and of course the view they're afraid other people may take of them.

You can experiment with the following predictions:

- ✔ You're going to fall flat on your face.

- ✔ You're sure to be humiliated.

- ✔ People are going to think less of you.

- ✔ Your self-esteem is going to suffer a terrible blow.

In fact, even falling flat on your face can be an excellent opportunity to deepen your acceptance of yourself as a fallible human being who defies 'rating' or 'measuring' as worthless, useless or stupid.

James has long-standing low self-esteem, which he can trace back to being severely criticised by his father when he was young. He tends to cope with his self-esteem problems by avoiding doing anything unless he's sure that he's going to succeed. His experiment is shown in Figure 11-3.

Step 1. Specify the self-esteem belief that you want to change.

I'm a loser.

Step 2. Identify the thought or prediction you want to put to the test.

If I join a drama group, which is something I've wanted to do for years but have never had the courage to do, I'll be the only one who can't follow what's going on and I'll stick out like a sore thumb.

Step 3. Identify an alternative prediction.

If I don't take it all too seriously, keep my attention on what's going on around me, and avoid being too self-conscious I might enjoy it.

Step 4. Specify the experiment you plan to test your prediction.

Go along to the drama group that I've seen advertised outside the local school.

Step 5. Record your results.

I was so nervous before I went I nearly pulled out, but apart from one rather odd woman, the people were really welcoming. The group do some really daft warm-up exercises and everyone looked pretty silly. It wasn't just me and I actually quite got into it by the time the evening was over.

Step 6. Write down your conclusions from the results of your experiment.

This does help me to see that I can have more fun if I risk being foolish. I really need to make sure I do more of this though, otherwise I know I'll slip back into avoidance.

Figure 11-3:
James's fear of falling on his face form.

Setting down social situation safety behaviours

Safety behaviours are the things people do in situations that they find anxiety-provoking, in order to prevent the things they're afraid of from happening. Safety behaviours include carefully monitoring how you think you're coming across, planning what you're going to say and trying desperately not to seem anxious.

A crucial problem with this behaviour in any kind of social or performance situation is that you feel more self-conscious and make things feel much more awkward and difficult. Don't take our word for it, though – test your behaviour out! These experiments can make a colossal difference if you suffer from shyness, social anxiety or performance anxiety.

Justin has social anxiety, which leaves him feeling very shy, nervous and uncomfortable in social situations. Like many people with social anxiety, he tries too hard to avoid seeming weird by using safety behaviours that ultimately make him feel even more self-conscious. Figure 11-4 shows how he experiments with dropping his safety behaviours and moves along the road to recovery.

Step 1. Specify the self-esteem belief that you want to change.

I'm weird and unlikable.

Step 2. Identify the thought or prediction you want to put to the test.

If I don't plan topics of conversation, and how I'm going to address them before I go out for an evening I'll end up doing or saying something weird and my friends won't like me.

Step 3. Identify an alternative prediction.

I can allow myself to focus upon the conversation when I'm in the situation. I don't need to try so hard and the evening will flow OK.

Step 4. Specify the experiment you plan to test your prediction.

I'm going to go along for a night out this evening without preparing what I'm going to say. Instead I'm going to keep my attention focussed on the people, sounds, the situation around me and simply respond to the conversations as they come up.

Step 5. Record your results.

This was far, far, far easier. I did feel self-conscious from time to time, but on the whole I was much more relaxed and the conversation and evening flew past compared to normal.

Step 6. Write down your conclusions from the results of your experiment.

If anything I think I seemed more normal when I just relaxed and went with the flow. I need to keep practicing keeping the focus of my attention off me and onto the world around me. NO MORE PREPARING!

Figure 11-4: Justin's stopping safety-seeking strategies worksheet.

Daring to self-disclose

Revealing aspects of yourself of which you're ashamed can be enormously liberating. A revelatory action may involve expressing an opinion if you normally keep yours close to your chest, or something bigger such as telling people close to you that you're gay.

The point is that shame really saps self-esteem. This kind of experiment is particularly helpful when you harbour thoughts such as: 'If they found out what I'm really like. . .'. You can test out your predictions of how horrified people would be and for how long by telling them something about yourself that you tend to keep hidden. People's reactions may not as bad as you think, and you may find that you can cope with other people's disapproval better than you predict.

Sheila suffers from depression and feels shameful about it. She fears that people are going to think less of her if they know her secret. However, she also hates the ignorance and stigma around mental health problems and so experiments with 'coming out' about her depression; her experiment is shown in Figure 11-5.

Step 1. Specify the self-esteem belief that you want to change.

I'm inadequate.

Step 2. Identify the thought or prediction you want to put to the test.

If the new friends I've made at work find out that I suffer from depression they won't want to have anything to do with me.

Step 3. Identify an alternative prediction.

They might be more understanding than I think.

Step 4. Specify the experiment you plan to test your prediction.

I'll try out talking to Sue and Jean, as they seem like the best people to start with.

Step 5. Record your results.

Well, I have no idea what I was worried about. Apparently Jean has been on anti-depressants for years, and Sue has known all about it. They were both really supportive and we ended up having a good laugh about how nutty we all are.

Step 6. Write down your conclusions from the results of your experiment.

I need to 'come out' as a 'depressive' more. Even if some people don't understand, I think there's a pretty good chance that plenty of people will.

Figure 11-5: Sheila's sharing a shameful secret worksheet.

Flaunting your flaws

If you have a body image problem, you can test out your predictions concerning people's reaction to you revealing the imperfections in your appearance. This experiment may involve a trip to the pool, letting your partner see more skin, wearing less make-up or changing the way you use clothing from dressing for camouflage to dressing for comfort. (See Chapter 7 for more advice on dealing with body-image issues.)

Georgina suffers from relatively mild body dysmorphic disorder (BDD). She spends three to four hours a day preoccupied with the quality of her skin, checking for imperfections and covering up with very carefully applied make-up. Her experiment is illustrated in Figure 11-6.

Step 1. Specify the self-esteem belief that you want to change.

I'm not good enough.

Step 2. Identify the thought or prediction you want to put to the test.

If my housemates see me without make-up they'll be shocked at how bad my skin is.

Step 3. Identify an alternative prediction.

They may not even really notice.

Step 4. Specify the experiment you plan to test your prediction.

On Monday morning I'm going to go down and have breakfast before college without wearing any foundation, and try to have a conversation with any of my housemates who are around.

Step 5. Record your results.

It took me a while to pluck up the courage but I faced everyone. I wore mascara but no foundation. I found myself thinking that they must be noticing but no one seemed to be treating me any differently.

Step 6. Write down your conclusions from the results of your experiment.

I can't be sure what people are thinking of my skin, but I very much doubt it's as important to them as it's become to me. I need to keep practicing this until it gets easier.

Figure 11-6:
Georgina's flaw flaunting form.

Making mistakes

This type of experiment is the one for you if you try to boost your self-esteem by putting yourself beyond criticism through perfectionism. It demonstrates that being human means you have an inherent (and inescapable) capacity for making mistakes.

Truly happy and successful people tend to be pretty good at bouncing back from mistakes and failures, seeing those situations as opportunities to discover things rather than disasters. Being a perfectionist can also slow down your productivity, and this rather defensive way of approaching the world ultimately makes you harder to get along with.

All Michael's friends and colleagues regard him as a perfectionist. Part of the problem is that Michael secretly quite likes this reputation (although other people dearly want him to take life a little less seriously!). However, even he has begun to face up to the fact that he didn't really choose his perfectionist ways; he felt compelled to be this way because of his underlying low self-esteem and fear of being 'found out'. Figure 11-7 shows how he starts to break out of the perfectionism trap.

Step 1. Specify the self-esteem belief that you want to change.

I'm inferior.

Step 2. Identify the thought or prediction you want to put to the test.

If I don't double check my emails at work to make sure there are no mistakes I might send one out with an error and everyone will think I'm no good at what I do.

Step 3. Identify an alternative prediction.

If I don't check I might not make any major mistakes, and even if I do make one people will probably just be glad to see that I'm only human.

Step 4. Specify the experiment you plan to test your prediction.

To send off my emails without checking them, unless it's really important for head office, for the next two weeks.

Step 5. Record your results.

It meant living with a bit of discomfort and uncertainty but I certainly wasted less time. No one has said a thing about my emails.

Step 6. Write down your conclusions from the results of your experiment.

Maybe people are right when they tell me I don't need to be such a perfectionist.

Figure 11-7:
Michael's prevailing over perfectionism plan.

Exercising more effort

One of the consequences of low self-esteem, especially if your mood has become low, can be that you fall into the habit of thinking: 'What's the point'. These thoughts can mean that you put less effort into your home, your work or studies, your interests, your relationships and even caring for yourself. Try carrying out some experiments in making more effort in one or more of these areas and measure the effects on your self-esteem.

Gus suffers from long-standing low mood and low self-esteem. Over the past few years, he's slipped into progressively taking less care of his diet, clothing and the cleanliness of his home. This behaviour in turn makes his life less pleasant, and further lowers his mood. Figure 11-8 shows his experiment to change things.

Step 1. Specify the self-esteem belief that you want to change.

I'm worthless.

Step 2. Identify the thought or prediction you want to put to the test.

There's no point in taking better care of myself, nothing will make me feel better about who I am.

Step 3. Identify an alternative prediction.

Possibly I might feel better if I take better care of myself and my home, I don't suppose I've got that much to lose if I try.

Step 4. Specify the experiment you plan to test your prediction.

I'm going to set aside 20 minutes a day for the next week to spend on housework, and make myself three meals each day.

Step 5. Record your results.

I do feel better than last week.

Figure 11-8:
Gus's exerting effort exercise.

Step 6. Write down your conclusions from the results of your experiment.

I'm going to need to treat myself and my home better if ever I'm going to lift my mood and feel better about myself.

Assessing assertiveness

Treating yourself as if you're worthwhile and deserve a degree of respect can help you become more confident about your own self-worth. If you think you need help with becoming more assertive, you can devise some experiments to target the thoughts that get in the way. Openly communicating your feelings, making a request or refusing a request can all become experiments to test your predictions and fears.

Sally has difficulty keeping her own needs as a high enough priority in her life. She finds saying 'No' hard, and tends to see herself as less important than other people. Figure 11-9 shows one experiment that helps her to improve her assertiveness.

Step 1. Specify the self-esteem belief that you want to change.

I'm unimportant.

Step 2. Identify the thought or prediction you want to put to the test.

If I say no to my daughter's friend's mother who often seems to be asking me for favours she'll take great offence and be rude to me.

Step 3. Identify an alternative prediction.

She may be understanding, or she may just be a little disappointed.

Step 4. Specify the experiment you plan to test your prediction.

Next time she asks if I can look after her daughter and it's not convenient for me I'm going to say no and explain why.

Step 5. Record your results.

I did it! I said no! She seemed a little surprised but I expect that's just because she's got used to me saying yes.

Step 6. Write down your conclusions from the results of your experiment.

I CAN say no without it needing to be a big confrontation. I need to practice more assertion to feel more comfortable with it.

Figure 11-9:
Sally's assertive action experiment.

Making things as easy as 'ABA'

Nope, not a spelling mistake, nor have we forgotten our alphabet – 'ABA' is a kind of research design. Before you nod off, bear with us, because ABA experiments can be enormously helpful in discovering whether a particular strategy you use is part of the solution or part of the problem.

You may know intellectually that a particular strategy isn't good for you and yet still find yourself drawn to it. Our experience is that when people do an ABA experiment on a behaviour we suggest is unhealthy, they come back and tell us: 'I knew this behaviour was problematic before, but now I really see what you mean.'

The key is to start off with your usual level of behaviour that you're targeting (phase A) and record information about how you feel on that day. The next phase is to boost (double) the behaviour you're targeting (phase B) and record how you feel. Now return back to your normal level (phase A).

Mary has had a narrow view of what makes her worthwhile ever since she was a young child. She tends to try to lift her personal sense of value by making herself valuable to other people. This behaviour has in turn started to make her feel rather hollow and resentful. Figure 11-10 shows how she uses an ABA design to help herself see that her solution to her self-esteem has actually become a problem.

Step 1. Specify the self-esteem belief that you want to change.

I'm not good enough.

Step 2. Identify the thought or prediction you want to put to the test.

Trying to offer everyone around me help and support is the best way to boost my self-esteem because then people will like me, value me and that will make me feel good about myself.

Step 3. Identify an alternative prediction.

This strategy actually worsens my self-esteem as I just end up feeling used.

Step 4. Specify the experiment you plan to test your prediction.

Spend two days 'as usual' and two days being extra helpful to everyone at work and in my social life, then go back to 'usual'. On each day record how strongly I believe I'm not good enough 0–100%, and rate my overall mood before I go to bed.

Step 5. Record your results.

Doing more for other people really did leave me feeling undervalued and worn out.

Figure 11-10: Mary's ABA test.

Step 6. Write down your conclusions from the results of your experiment.

I need to keep more of my energy back for myself.

Seeking data with a survey

Surveys are especially helpful when you tend to regard something about yourself as abnormal. You can design your own questionnaire and have a dozen or so people fill it out. This process helps you normalise your own thoughts, feelings and experiences by finding out that you're not alone. You may imagine that 'it's just me', but using a survey allows you to check that idea out.

Here are some ways in which you may think that you're unusual, but actually you're far from alone:

- ✔ Being rejected
- ✔ Having an emotional problem
- ✔ Having been teased or bullied
- ✔ Having failed
- ✔ Having self-doubts

You may partly know that you're normal in an important respect, but perhaps not really believe it strongly enough. Carrying out a survey can help you see this situation for yourself.

Wayne worries that his experience of being bullied as a child reflects the fact that he's inherently defective. Figure 11-11 shows how he used a survey as part of changing the meaning of his experience at the hand of bullies.

Step 1. Specify the self-esteem belief that you want to change.

I'm pathetic.

Step 2. Identify the thought or prediction you want to put to the test.

Nobody had as much teasing at school as I got. It must have happened because the bullies could sense how defective I am.

Step 3. Identify an alternative prediction.

Maybe some people will have had similar experiences of bullying.

Step 4. Specify the experiment you plan to test your prediction.

I'm going to do a survey of 20 colleagues and friends on their experiences of teasing and bullying at school.

Step 5. Record your results.

Everyone had some experience of being bullied or teased at school at some point. Most didn't sound as bad as mine but a couple sounded as bad. In fact one was clearly much worse and you'd never know.

Step 6. Write down your conclusions from the results of your experiment.

Bullying and teasing are common experiences, and it doesn't need to define who I am.

Figure 11-11:
Wayne's
sweeping
survey.

Part IV
Looking at the Ripple Effects of Low Self-Esteem

'Marjorie's decided to come to your party after all, despite her issues with self-esteem.'

Part V

Looking at the
Knock-on Effect of
Low Self-Esteem

In this part . . .

*L*ow self-esteem can really knock your personal and
professional relationships for six. These chapters are
geared to get your friendships and romantic life cooking
again. We give you an insight into how you can deal with
conflicts and come out unscathed as well as tips on how
to overcome jealousy, improve communication and put
trust in others. You also find advice on how to take your
healthy self-esteem into work with you everyday.

Chapter 12

Romancing and Relationships

*R*elationships are important. Human beings thrive on social contact and very few people can be truly content without friendships. If you've been battling with low self-esteem for a long time, however, your social circle may be limited and you can find certain aspects of relationships tricky. Your feelings of low self-worth prevent you from fully engaging with others or from being able to relax and enjoy your relationships.

In this chapter we discuss some of the most common ways in which low self-esteem affects how you interact with other people. We also explore some alternative ways of thinking and behaving that enhance relationships and promote healthy self-esteem.

Evaluating the Effects of Low Self-Esteem on Your Relationships

Low self-esteem inevitably has an effect on how you get along with others. Some of the things you do to compensate for negative feelings about yourself can produce the very results that you want to avoid. For example, although you may really want to be part of a social group, your low self-esteem may lead you to stay on the fringes and limit your involvement.

Getting to recognise and understand how you behave around others can help you begin to make positive changes. Have a look at the following list of typical low-self-esteem-driven behaviours and their potential effects on relationships. See if any of them resonate with you:

- You avoid giving away too much personal information about yourself, including how you feel and think. You fear being rejected and therefore don't give people much of a chance to really get to know you.

- You avoid other people and group activities, giving people the impression that you're uninterested in forming friendships with them. Even though you really crave connection with others, low self-esteem sometimes makes you appear you aloof.

- You mistrust others because you expect to be betrayed, rejected or abandoned. You then feel jealous and suspicious in your romantic relationships.

- You're very sensitive to criticism. You may react defensively to even minor criticism from your friends and family. Other people in your life may feel like they're 'walking on eggshells' around you.

- You misinterpret other people's motives. Low self-esteem sometimes leads you to expect the worst from others. You see malice, lack of caring or rejection in what others do even when their motives are pure.

- You make poor relationship choices. You may choose to form alliances with people who are quite self-focused because they don't really ask you much about yourself. Although this kind of friendship spares you the discomfort of risking sharing your thoughts and feelings, it also leaves you unsupported emotionally.

- You may be so fearful of losing a friendship or love relationship that you put up with unacceptable behaviour from others without complaint.

- You blow hot and cold with the people in your life. When your mood is up, and you're able to think more positively about yourself, you may be more socially engaged and perhaps more demonstrative with your feelings. When your self-esteem takes a tumble, however, and your mood drops, you may suddenly withdraw from others.

  This mood-dictated behaviour is a common offshoot of poor self-opinion. It can confuse the people in your life because one minute you seem really to be interested in them and the next you seem to be avoiding them.

Take note of what you think you do in an attempt to protect your self-esteem during interaction with others (you may also benefit from the additional information in Chapter 6). Next, give some thought to the actual effect this behaviour can have on others in your life and on the overall quality of your relationships.

Try your best to act *against* what your low self-esteem dictates. Now, we realise that this is a darn sight easier said than done. But focusing on the results you want to achieve can encourage you to try out new ways of interacting with others.

Making loved ones pay the toll

Feelings of low self-worth obviously have an undesirable effect on you. But do you ever consider that your poor self-view may also upset the people who care about you?

Think about this for a moment: The people who like or love you genuinely disagree with your negative self-beliefs. From where they're standing you're clearly a worthwhile, valuable person. You're someone that they really like (or love for that matter).

Hearing you speak ill of yourself is painful for your loved ones. They don't want to see someone they love suffer. How do you want your friends and family to think of themselves? How do you feel when the people you love behave self-critically? You're likely to do your utmost to convince them of their worth and encourage them to see all their good points as clearly as you do. Above all, you're most likely to want them to be happy.

Poor self-esteem and happiness aren't good bedfellows. Your friends and loved ones realise this as keenly as you do: no wonder that your pain causes them pain too.

We're not suggesting that you make yourself feel guilty about the effect your low self-esteem has on others. That's not going to help anyone, and you probably have enough guilt and other negative emotions going on already. But we encourage you to put yourself in the footwear of your loved ones and think about how they want you to view yourself. Becoming more self-accepting may be the best gift you can give.

Your refusal to see yourself in the positive way your loved ones do can be very disempowering for them. They may feel powerless to impress upon you how strongly they feel about you. No matter what they say or do, your low self-esteem quashes their efforts and bats back compliments like a highly skilled squash player. Put down the racquet and give other people the chance to influence the way you think and feel about yourself.

Making love not war

Low self-esteem can wreak havoc on your sex life. People with self-image problems often have difficulty being uninhibited during intimacy. You can run into all sorts of interpersonal trouble by believing (wrongly) that you must have a beautiful body to gain or retain someone's affection. Low self-esteem can also fool you into thinking that you've got nothing to offer in terms of conversation, humour and overall personality.

Broaching body-image issues

You may feel uncomfortable or dissatisfied with your own body and reluctant to get up close and personal. Even when you've been with your partner for years, negative thoughts about your physical appearance may make you self-conscious despite your familiarity.

If you're single and entering into a new romantic relationship, you may be quietly terrified about being rejected when things get serious and the clothing comes off.

Low self-esteem can tell you all sorts of garbage about your attractiveness to others. You may believe that you look passable fully clothed and groomed but that your new love will run screaming from the bedroom when confronted with your naked body. It's unlikely.

Most of us look pretty much as expected in our birthday suits, so it's pretty improbable that your naked form is going to take your significant other by surprise.

So give your 'low self-esteem sexual relations saboteur' a firm slap and let the person getting close to you be the judge of how attractive you are. No matter how much you believe the contrary, physical looks are *not* the be all and end all of attraction. There's much more to you than meets the eye.

You may have had a better relationship with your body at a previous stage in your life but now have difficulty accepting and adjusting to changes due to the natural process of ageing and factors such as childbirth, illness and other kinds of experiences. Try not to assume that your partner has the same difficulties. Your partner may seriously disagree with your opinion of how you look. Changes in your physicality that seem huge to you may be hardly noticed by the person you share your bed with.

Another thing to consider is how much your looks really matter to your partner. You may be greatly bothered about gaining weight, but perhaps your partner doesn't place as much importance on it as you do.

Talking openly with your partner about how you're feeling can help you to get over sexual reluctance and avoidance. Sometimes greater problems arise when intimacy difficulties aren't openly discussed. Your partner may mis-understand your behaviour and draw faulty conclusions about your feelings towards him or her. For more information on how to address body image problems, take a look at Chapter 7.

Incidentally, body concerns are relevant to both men and women. It's not only women who worry about physical issues like their figures and showing signs of ageing.

Broadening beyond body image

Some emotional and psychological problems associated with low self-esteem (we say more on this aspect in Chapter 2) can put a halt to bedroom activities.

Depression and other emotional problems often reduce your sex drive. You may be so absorbed with worries and distressing feelings that romance is the last thing on your mind.

Putting the zip back

Sometimes couples get into the habit of not having regular sex and find talking about it difficult. When physical intimacy goes off the boil, you may wonder how to get it back on track. You may be surprised by how many men and women come to our offices expressing confusion and distress about inti-macy problems in their relationships.

These few simple tips may help you to put love-making back on the agenda:

- ✔ **Reintroduce non-sexual physical contact such as cuddling, hugging and holding hands.** Touch is a very effective form of communica-tion. You can demonstrate care and interest to your partner by small gestures such as giving him or her a kiss goodbye in the morning. Affectionate non-sexual contact can help you to feel physically comfort-able with one another again.

- ✔ **Create opportunities for resuming intimacy.** Sometimes couples get into habits such as going to bed at different times or spending evenings and weekends doing separate things. Often these habits develop as a result of busy work schedules and juggling parental responsibilities. Or maybe you like to stay up later than your partner does and you pursue different interests in your free time. Although spending some time apart and having individual interests is healthy for couples, it can limit opportunities for intimacy. Your separate routines may leave little time for sex. Perhaps your partner is asleep by the time you get to bed or maybe you typically watch TV in the evenings while your partner catches up with some work on the computer.

Being in the same room as one another (and in the same bed) helps when renewing sexual contact. Ideally you're both awake too! Have a look at your routine, and make sure that you schedule in times to spend together so that sex becomes more of a possibility again.

✔ **Do caring things for one another.** Sometimes couples can start to take one another for granted without noticing or meaning to. Cooking a nice meal, running a bath or doing a chore you know your partner dislikes are all considerate actions to try out. Doing considerate things for one another (small or big) can restore warmth between you. And with warmth comes the potential for things to get steamy.

✔ **Make time to talk about your sex life: it's good to talk.** Sometimes impasses in your sex life can be resolved without any direct discussion but other times you may need to work things out together. If you think some open communication is required, arrange a time that suits you both. Try to ensure that you're both in an objective frame of mind instead of in the aftermath of an argument, for example, when strong emotions may complicate matters.

✔ **Have fun together.** Book a day out doing something you both enjoy. Choose an activity that's exciting and stimulating. You may find that doing something out of the ordinary reminds you how much you enjoy each other's company.

Many couples find that their sex lives improve when they're on holiday away from the stress and routine of daily life. Adding a little spice to your usual routine can help get things cooking in the bedroom.

Seek help when you need it

If you're having quite severe or long-term sexual problems that are impacting on your relationship, you may benefit from professional help. Many therapists are familiar with such issues and can deal with them sensitively.

You may feel embarrassed or even ashamed of your difficulties with sex. Remember that your problems are not uncommon and that you deserve to get whatever help you need. Therapy for couples can also be very helpful in opening up lines of communication with your partner.

You can seek out therapists experienced in dealing with relationship problems via the organisations listed in the Appendix.

Managing conflict

Dealing with disagreements, arguments or conflict can be difficult for anyone. For the person with low self-esteem, coping with these situations can be especially tough.

Even with the best of intentions, you may find that you frequently wind up doing and saying things that escalate or prolong conflicts.

Instead of instigating useful discussion, your low self-esteem can produce unhelpful behaviours such as:

- Assuming that the other person acted with more deliberate malice than is actually the case.

- Being slow to accept an apology.

- Jumping to the conclusion that the entire relationship is a farce because of one thoughtless action or misdeed.

- Nursing hurt feelings and holding grudges.

- Sulking and making the other person guess what's upset you.

The irony is that like many people, you probably don't relish conflict and ideally prefer to resolve an unpleasant situation sooner rather than later. However, low self-esteem can be a serious obstacle to effective communication and communicating is pretty much an essential part of conflict resolution.

Remember that other people are only human too. People sometimes behave poorly towards you and that's just part of the rich experience of personal relationships; clearly that experience isn't fun, but it is normal.

Relationships can weather arguments and disagreements. You can even have a major blowout with someone and still have your relationship recover.

The following points can help you to accept disagreement and ruptures in your relationships without catastrophically concluding that it's all over between you.

- Be prepared to give others a second chance even if your low self-esteem leads you to distrust people's motives.

- Let the other person apologise and try to accept sincere expressions of regret for misdeeds. Holding grudges serves only to keep you feeling angry and hurt.

- Let the other person know precisely what you're upset about. Using statements such as 'When you did x, I felt y' can make this easier.

Your self-esteem improves as you become more confident in your ability to negotiate conflicts within your relationships. Being able to offer and accept apologies can be very liberating. It means that you don't have to be anxious about the possibility of arguments developing because you know that your relationships can survive them.

Helping loved ones heal

Saying 'I'm sorry' can be difficult when you have low self-esteem. You may feel awkward about owning up to mistakes or misdeeds because you worry that the other party is going to be unwilling to forgive and forget. Your low self-esteem may lead you to believe that you're not allowed to offend others. You're probably very unforgiving of yourself when you do something wrong and assume that others feel the same way. You may believe that you deserve harsh judgement and perhaps even punishment for your wrongdoings – no wonder you find apologising for genuine offences difficult.

The first step is to re-align your thinking about upsetting other people. People with low self-esteem often hold the following beliefs about conflicts with their friends, colleagues and partners:

- ✔ If I upset people, I can't stand the discomfort; it's too much to bear.
- ✔ If I upset people, it means that I'm a bad friend/partner.
- ✔ If I upset people, those relationships are never going to recover.
- ✔ If I upset people, their opinion of me is going to be altered for the worse – forever.
- ✔ If I upset people, they'll never forgive me.

Accepting that all relationships (especially long ones) suffer some fractures along the way can make conflict resolution more straightforward. You may unintentionally offend or hurt someone that you care about. Other times you may act thoughtlessly or consciously behave in an inconsiderate fashion towards another person. You're only human after all and expecting that you're *always* going to get things right is just not realistic.

Instead of holding a rigid rule for yourself, such as: 'I must never behave badly towards anyone in my life or it means that I'm bad and unforgivable', try embracing a more flexible *guideline* such as: 'I really prefer not to behave badly towards (or offend) others but I also accept that I'm capable of doing so. Upsetting another person means that I've done a *bad thing*, but it doesn't make me a *bad person*.'

Try to remember these types of helpful attitudes about conflict within your relationships:

- Although upsetting someone is undesirable, it isn't truly awful.

- Even the most exemplary friends and partners occasionally do things that upset, anger or hurt their loved ones.

- Most relationships recover from ruptures; conflict is a natural and largely unavoidable aspect of relationships of every kind.

- Other people's opinion of me may change for a while, but most likely they'll think well of me again when the conflict is resolved.

- Unpleasant and uncomfortable though conflict is with another person, I can bear it. I can stand the negative feelings I may have about offending another person.

When you're able to truly and unconditionally accept yourself, even when you behave poorly, you're more able to square up to your misdeeds and say 'sorry'.

Making an appropriate apology

When you apologise to someone, follow these hints to make the process easier and more effective:

- Be specific about what you're apologising for. Avoid overdoing things by apologising for just being alive. Saying things like 'Oh gawd, I'm so sorry, I'm such a terrible person' isn't necessary or true and doesn't do much to help other people feel better when they're cross or upset about a particular incident. Instead, name the deed. Saying 'I'm really sorry that I didn't invite you to come to the cinema, and I can see how that made you feel left out' demonstrates that you acknowledge what you've done wrong and that you understand how the other person is feeling.

- Don't beg for forgiveness, just ask. Simply say that you're sorry for causing offence and leave your apology at that. When you beg for forgiveness in a 'Please, please forgive me, I feel so bad. . .' style, you may reduce the impact of your apology. Begging for forgiveness shifts the focus from the injured party onto how badly you're feeling and may give the impression that you're more concerned with making yourself feel better than with soothing the other person's feelings.

- Make amends. Apologies are often best demonstrated through action. So if your partner is cross because you came home late without calling to let her know, make sure that you call next time. If your friend is hurt because you haven't been very supportive about her divorce, make a special effort to spend an evening with her. Showing that you're truly sorry through reparative action often speaks louder than words.

Stop apologising needlessly

Ironically, your low self-esteem can lead you to do a lot of apologising for things that aren't your fault or even remotely connected to your actions. Do you ever find yourself apologising to someone who has bumped into *you*? Or maybe you say sorry when a friend is in a bad mood even though you know the mood is nothing to do with you.

Over-apologising can maintain low self-esteem. Monitor how often you say sorry unnecessarily, and then stop yourself before you say you're sorry for something you aren't responsible for. Reserve apologies for when they're actually appropriate.

Fostering Friendships

Friendships require a bit of maintenance. All types of relationships involve a significant degree of give and take. When you think well of yourself and treat yourself respectfully, your self-esteem blossoms and so do your relationships. In these sections we explore some key ways you can do your self-esteem and your friendships some good.

Taking a compliment gracefully

Compliments are wonderful things. They're little verbal gifts (or sometimes quite substantial ones). A sincere compliment can give your self-esteem a real boost if you let it.

The problem is that low self-esteem often prevents you from accepting compliments properly, which is a real shame. Don't let yourself miss out on the pleasure of receiving compliments any longer.

You can discover how to accept compliments by following these simple steps:

1. **Maintain good eye contact.**

   Look the compliment-giver in the eye. Don't let your eyes dart about out of nervousness or embarrassment.

2. **Listen attentively to what the other person is saying.**

   Allow the compliment-giver to finish. You may feel embarrassed and be tempted to cut the person short or wave the compliment away before it's even been fully stated. That behaviour takes the wind out of the

other person's sails and can even appear a little rude. Ignore what your
low self-esteem says and listen to the more positive message you're
being given instead.

3. **Acknowledge the compliment.**

   You may tend to dismiss, minimise and disagree with compliments due
   to your low self-esteem. When someone makes the effort to pay you a
   compliment, the polite thing to do is accept it gracefully and with poise.
   Take the compliment for what it is – a nice and valuable thing.

4. **Say 'Thank you'.**

   'Thank you very much.' 'That's really nice of you to say.' 'Thanks for
   that, I really appreciate hearing it.' 'Oh, thanks a lot.' Any similar phrase
   does very nicely when accepting a compliment. Try one.

Compliments are worth collecting when you're on a quest to improve your
overall self-opinion. Keep them in mind and draw upon them when you feel
low self-esteem encroaching. We recommend that you record them in a notebook so you can review them. Try to record them as 'word for word' as possible to avoid your low self-esteem trying to distort them in your memory.

Getting and giving gifts

The same rules that apply to receiving compliments also work for the giving
and getting of gifts. If you give someone a gift, do so in a straightforward
manner. Don't minimise your gift or apologise for it as your low self-esteem
may persuade you to do. Let the recipient thank you and simply say something like 'You're welcome' or 'I'm glad you like it'. Avoid saying things such
as 'Oh, it's just a little thing' or 'I'm sorry it's not much'.

When someone gives you a gift, act as if you truly believe that you're worthy
of receiving something nice (even if your low self-esteem typically tells you
otherwise). Look the other person in the eye and offer your thanks verbally
and with a hug or a kiss if appropriate. Be wary of saying too many 'Oh you
shouldn't have'-type statements. Of course, they should have! If people want
to give you gifts, that's up to them and not you. Your job is simply to show
your appreciation.

Terminating Testing

If you don't think that you have much to offer other people, you may question why they want to be your friend or partner. You may not believe that
they're going to stay in a relationship with you for very long because you

don't understand what they see in you. This type of insecurity born out of poor self-opinion can hold true in all types of relationships. Instead of being able to relax and enjoy your relationships, you feel fraught with anxiety about them abruptly ending.

You may set up tests designed to show you some sort of proof or guarantee that your friends and partners aren't about to dump you. You try to see how much people actually care about you.

The trouble with this strategy is that frequently the other person has no idea what you're up to and may not act in the way you've decided is appropriate. This situation can leave you feeling hurt and resentful or increase unwarranted feelings of jealousy.

Patricia has been living with her partner Julian for three years. Despite the length of the relationship, Julian's attentive behaviour and his assertion that he loves her, Patricia still feels insecure. She gets very jealous if Julian mentions another woman from work or talks to females at social functions. Patricia also tests Julian. She decides that unless he kisses her as soon as he gets in the door, he's gone off her. If he doesn't call or text her at least once during the day, Patricia jumps to the conclusion that he's about to end their relationship. Patricia realises that her testing behaviour serves only to increase her insecurity and low self-worth. Julian also finds Patricia's jealousy very wearing and has told her that he's offended by her accusations.

The painful irony is that in your attempts to get some certainty that your relationship is secure, you end up feeling more and more anxious. When you resort to testing, you can also put strain on your relationship that otherwise doesn't exist. So setting up tests is a bit like shooting yourself in the foot.

Patricia decides to stop making up little tests for Julian to pass in order to prove his commitment to her. Instead, she looks for alternative reasons for why he may not kiss her instantly or contact her during the day. She also challenges her jealous thoughts about his contact with other women. Here's what she came up with:

- ✔ 'Julian may be tired and distracted when he gets home from work. I can always go up and kiss him first. I usually wait for him to kiss me first because I'm testing him. But if he doesn't think that *I* don't love *him* when I don't instantly kiss him, it doesn't make much sense for me to draw that conclusion either.'

- ✔ 'If Julian doesn't give me a call or text during the day, he's probably busy. Also, he may not have much to say or he prefers to talk to me in person at the end of the day.'

> ✔ 'I have no reason to feel jealous in my relationship with Julian. He's always very complimentary about my looks and rarely flirts with other women. Even if he does find another woman attractive it doesn't mean that he prefers her to me. Noticing members of the opposite sex and finding them attractive is normal and doesn't mean our relationship is in jeopardy.'

As much as you may want to have a cast-iron guarantee that your relationship is secure and that your partner loves you forever, you just can't get one. The best you can do is foster good relations by being yourself. Put your efforts into enjoying your relationship rather than exhausting yourself with pointless testing. The same also holds true for your friendships.

Taking others at their word

Trust can be difficult when you're riddled with insecurity. You may have difficulty believing what others tell you, particularly as regards how they feel about you.

Not taking others at their word can be damaging to your self-esteem and to your relationships. Your partner and friends may stop bothering to say how much they care about you because you never seem to believe them. Every time you doubt the sincere words of a loved one you chip another notch out of your sense of self-worth.

The best idea in relationships is to work on the assumption that no smoke means no fire. You probably wouldn't like it if your friends or partner never seemed to trust that you were telling them the truth. Put yourself in their shoes for a minute and try to trust them as you'd like to be trusted yourself.

Try assuming that what others tell you is true for a change. Resist doing things that increase your suspicion and undermine your trust, such as rifling through pockets or searching around for clues pointing to infidelity or betrayal.

Julian tells Patricia that he loves her all the time but she wonders: 'What if he's just saying that because he thinks he should?' He assures Patricia that he has eyes only for her but still she doubts him. Sometimes she even goes through his pockets and his phone looking for evidence that he's having an affair. Julian starts to feel powerless about impressing his true feelings for Patricia upon her. He also gets hurt and resentful about Patricia's suspicion because he knows it's unfounded.

Ceasing seeking reassurance

Another not-so-very-helpful strategy to alleviate insecurity is seeking reassurance. You may constantly be looking for verbal or behavioural reassurance that your partner still loves you or that your friends still like you.

This behaviour can take the form of testing as discussed in the preceding section and also can mean that you often ask questions such as: 'Are you sure you still love me?', 'Do you find that person more attractive than me?' and 'Are you sure you really want to see me?' Of course you probably get the answer you're looking for, but the reassurance you feel is likely to be short-lived, otherwise you wouldn't feel the need to keep on asking the same sorts of questions.

Seeking reassurance traps you in a vicious circle that maintains insecurity and poor self-esteem. You get a bit of temporary relief from your anxiety but then the doubts start again. So you ask for reassurance once more and the cycle continues. You never come to a point where you can just relax and accept that others want you in their lives.

Quite frankly, constantly asking others for reassurance can also become tedious for them. People generally prefer to offer declarations of devotion when the mood takes them rather than on demand.

Resist asking others to tell you desirable things because your low self-esteem drives you to do so. Think of it as feeding a monster: you keep stuffing the warm sentiments into those gaping jaws but its belly never becomes full. Instead, try to offer some words of love yourself *because you want to say how you feel* but not to try and elicit a similar response in return.

Allow others to express themselves of their own accord. You're likely to find the things they say more valuable when they come naturally and you haven't gone fishing for them.

Letting the future unfurl

Although being able to see into the future would be useful in some ways, the truth is that you can't, and therefore living in the present makes much more sense. People with low self-esteem often waste a lot of time trying to predict the future of their relationships. You may worry about your partner one day leaving you or friendships ending for one reason or another. You may think that worrying about the future somehow prepares you for the painful feelings that arise from rejection and loss.

The fact of the matter is that worry tends to lead to yet more worry and nothing useful comes from it.

Living in the present means taking things as they come and trusting in your ability to cope with whatever happens in your relationships. Instead of fretting about what may or may not happen in the future, try to enjoy your current relationships. Every time you find your mind wandering off into 'what if' territory, re-focus on the here and now, using these steps:

1. **Take note of what you think you do in an attempt to protect your self-esteem during interaction with others.**

   You may benefit from the additional information in Chapter 6.

2. **Give some thought to the actual effects your actions may have on others in your life and on the overall quality of your relationships.**

3. **Make a resolution to act *against* what your low self-esteem dictates.**

   Instead, focus on the results you want to achieve. This can encourage you to try out new ways of interacting with others.

4. **Make a list of social behaviours that are consistent with healthy self-esteem and incorporate them into your daily life.**

   Think about how you would act in social situations if you truly believed that you're a worthwhile person with a lot to offer.

Chapter 13

Working with Others

*I*n your quest to develop healthy self-esteem, practising as much as you possibly can is vital. For many people, work takes up the majority of their waking hours between Monday and Friday, therefore an excellent idea is to practise healthy self-esteem habits in the workplace.

In this chapter we look at how to make a good impression at work and offer ideas on how to act like someone with truly solid self-esteem when dealing with bosses and co-workers. We discuss how to deal with and make use of positive and negative feedback, and talk about assertion in the workplace, outlining some key points about becoming healthily assertive in general.

Taking Self-Esteem to Work

So, you've been working on upping your self-esteem and things are going pretty smoothly. But perhaps you find that keeping your opinion of yourself positive and fair is difficult when you encounter problems at work. Don't be discouraged.

The workplace is a common 'trouble spot' for people wrestling with self-esteem issues. Why? Well, if you think about it, the workplace typically involves dealing with authority figures, performance appraisals and achievement expectations. Keeping your self-esteem intact is particularly difficult when you're faced with multiple duties or tasks and the onus is on you to get things done correctly and on time. Couple these conditions with regular input, monitoring and possible criticism from bosses or managers and the stakes become even higher.

Work also can be a real hotbed of potential self-denigration because it tends to be very important to your self-image. After all, we're talking about your livelihood here, aren't we? You've got to support yourself and maybe a family through your efforts at work. No wonder that doing well at work can be very close to your heart.

The more important that succeeding at something is to you, the more vulnerable you become to denigrating your whole self if you fail to do well in that area. (Take a look at Chapters 3 and 4 for more discussion on not judging the whole of yourself on the basis of individual behaviour or performance in just one area of your life.)

The good news is that you can work towards upholding a positive overall view of yourself *even* when things go wrong in areas of great importance to you. The secret is to hold a flexible, realistic attitude towards your performance rather than a rigid, unrealistic one. Table 13-1 offers a few examples of helpful versus hurtful attitudes.

Table 13-1	Sample Attitudes towards Work
Rigid, Unrealistic Attitude	*Flexible, Realistic Attitude*
I've got to be a success at work or I'm going to let everyone down and prove what a total idiot I really am.	I want to be a success at work but no hard and fast rule says I absolutely have to be. I can survive not doing as well as I'd like to and find other ways of making ends meet.
I must never make a serious error at work or it'll be a disaster and my team will never trust me again.	I try to avoid making serious errors at work but I'm only human. If I do make a big blunder, people will get over it and so will I.
Being successful at work makes me a worthwhile person and failing at work makes me an utter failure.	Being successful at work is a good thing but success doesn't make me a better person. Failing at work is a bad thing but I'm still a worthwhile person even if do fail.
Mistakes are a sign of weakness.	Mistakes are pretty much inevitable for human beings all over the world.

More often than not, holding rigid and inflexible attitudes leads you to feel anxious and worried about your work obligations. When you make a mistake you're prone to feeling depressed or even hopeless. Instead of being in a mindset that helps you to problem-solve and make necessary adjustments to how you work, you feel more like hiding away and giving up.

In contrast, flexible and realistic attitudes about your performance at work help you to bounce back from mistakes without feeling depressed or ashamed. They also encourage you to think creatively about solving problems and improving the way you work.

No matter how many demands you put on yourself to succeed at work, you can never remove the possibility that you may not. You're just a regular human being and therefore you can never be immune from mistakes or failures. Your demands to do well serve only to heap more stress and anxiety on your shoulders. Accepting the stark reality that mistakes and failures are possible for everyone, including you, can relieve a lot of unnecessary stress and worry. You can focus on going about your business instead of being preoccupied by worries about possible future errors.

Keep your high standards and the desire to do well; but boot out your exacting demands. Give yourself permission to make mistakes even while you work hard to avoid making them. Working hard to reach your personal standards is within your control but a guarantee of perpetual success isn't possible.

Presenting yourself positively

When you enter a new job (or at your existing job) make efforts to act like someone with good self-esteem. If you're still working on improving your sense of self-worth, 'acting the part' can be a real boost. Observe friends and colleagues who you think exhibit the characteristics of someone with a positive self-opinion and adopt similar behaviours.

Try out the following tips for presenting yourself positively:

- Keep your head up and walk with a straight back.
- Avoid over-apologising: say 'sorry' only when the situation genuinely warrants it.
- Make eye contact.
- Speak clearly and take your time.

✔ Ask for guidance and support when you need it.

✔ Sit centrally during meetings rather than hiding away in the corner.

✔ Offer your opinions and ideas.

✔ Listen respectfully to what others have to say.

You can build on these tips with the advice in the next section.

Talking and walking like a professional

Being taken seriously at work is a boon to most people's self-esteem. If you want to be seen as professional you need to make your behaviour reflect that aim. Behaving in a professional manner increases your confidence at work and in turn impacts positively on your self-esteem.

You don't need to be the most outgoing or innovative thinker in the team. Professional conduct speaks volumes and is frequently highly valued by employers.

Make sure that you can tick the following basic boxes:

✔ **Be punctual:** Arrive in good time to start your working day. Do your best to limit lateness and unauthorised absences.

✔ **Be prepared:** Come to work ready to work. Be organised, have everything you need (your tools of the trade so to speak) and be in a fit state to carry out your duties.

✔ **Observe social niceties:** Be polite to your co-workers. Take time to say hello and exchange pleasantries. You don't need to be bosom buddies with everyone you work with but a little consistent politeness goes a long way toward fostering good working relationships.

✔ **Dress the part:** Wear appropriate clothing. Many work places are more casual than formal these days so you may not be expected to wear formal business attire. Whatever the dress code of your workplace, make efforts to be well groomed and wear suitable clothing.

✔ **Keep work and home life separate:** Your manager and co-workers expect you to do a specific job. Avoid coming into work and offloading about how difficult your relationship is at the moment, how the children are acting up or that you're overwhelmed with housework. Organise your personal life so that you can concentrate on work during the hours that you're being paid to do it.

✔ **Practise good assertion skills:** When at work, be straightforward and clear about any complaints, questions or conflicts. Check out 'Accessing Your Assertiveness' a bit later in this chapter.

Ticking all the basic professional presentation boxes sets you up to give a good impression in the workplace. Your confidence is likely to benefit when you're assured that you've got the fundamentals covered. Improved confidence at work often translates into increased ability to perform, which ultimately is good news for your overall self-esteem.

Overcoming Defensive Anger

Ego-defensive anger describes the anger you experience when you think that your personality or character is under attack. Basically the term refers to becoming angry in an attempt to defend your self-esteem.

When you have low self-esteem, you can misconstrue any type of criticism as an assault on your ego. You may be highly sensitive to any negative comments partly because you deeply fear other people finding fault with you. You may, like many people with low self-esteem, assume that you need other people to *always* approve of your behaviour in order to believe that you have worth. Unfortunately, this way of thinking leaves you vulnerable to becoming angry and depressed when criticised, and also means that you allow your opinion of yourself to be dictated by the reaction you get from others.

Although caring about what other people think of you and your behaviour is normal, you place your self-esteem in peril when you hold the opinion of others as paramount. Instead, try to maintain your own self-opinion even while listening to and judging the validity of external criticism.

Approval from others is beneficial but not absolutely necessary for you to think well of yourself.

By all means continue to care about and be interested in what other people have to say about your behaviour. Take on board any valid points and amend your behaviour when you think necessary. But don't let your self-esteem be shaken to the very foundations whenever someone expresses disapproval. Realising that your self-esteem barometer is internal allows you to hear criticism more easily without becoming unduly angry or upset. You're then in the desirable position of being able to make use of helpful comments and to calmly reject unhelpful ones.

Giving others the right to be wrong

Human beings make mistakes; that's the nature of the beast. Sometimes people in your life (such as partners and bosses) say things about you that are incorrect or unfair.

You don't have to agree with what other people say about your behaviour or performance, but you also don't need to become ego-defensive. Give other people the right to be wrong about you. Remind yourself that other people form their own opinions and that's just the way things are. You can't control what others think of you any more than they can control how you choose to think about them.

Accepting the fact that you're not in control of other people's thoughts and opinions can spare you a lot of needless anxiety, anger and depression.

Giving yourself the right to be wrong

You can get things wrong as well. You may criticise someone in your social or work life unfairly or make a judgement about him that you later realise is incorrect.

Allow yourself to make mistakes and misjudgements. If you insist that you always have to 'get it right', you're liable to feel guilty if your conclusions about others prove faulty. Instead of giving yourself a hard time, simply apologise if appropriate and see your foible as part of being human.

Cutting others some slack

People's behaviour is affected by lots of different factors. Your boss may be more short-tempered than usual, fly off the handle and 'bite your head off' in a moment of high stress. That doesn't make the behaviour acceptable, but does make it more understandable.

When someone criticises you harshly, disrespectfully or unfairly, you naturally feel offended and annoyed. But if that person later apologises and provides an explanation, try to be open-minded and hear him out.

Low self-esteem can lead to hurt feelings and 'grudge holding'. You can assertively express your displeasure about another person's behaviour and still accept an apology. (We talk about being assertive in the upcoming

'Accessing Your Assertiveness' section.) Talking things through with a willing party and reaching a resolution is far better for your self-esteem than being quietly resentful, and also leads to better working relationships.

Feeding Off Feedback

Being able to recognise constructive criticism is an integral part of maintaining healthy self-esteem at work. Criticism isn't automatically bad. If you're never told where you're going wrong how can you expect to improve and grow? You need the important information contained in constructive criticism to assess your performance accurately.

Your low self-esteem may be preventing you from making good use of appraisals. You can draw extremely negative and faulty conclusions about your work (and yourself) when your low self-esteem tells you that negative feedback means: 'I'm useless and my boss thinks so too'. Fight back against the tyrannical messages generated by low self-esteem. Polish your skills at accepting all kinds of feedback by discovering how to recognise different types of input.

Here are a few components of constructive criticism:

✔ The person giving the feedback delivers it in an appropriate place and at an appropriate time; for example, in a private office (where nobody else is likely to overhear) and during an agreed meeting.

✔ The person giving the feedback speaks to you respectfully.

✔ The feedback given is clear and specific. Any complaints or compliments are supported (ideally) with concrete examples.

✔ The feedback given is potentially useful. You can build on positive feedback or take away useful lessons from negative feedback.

The three main types of constructive feedback are as follows:

✔ **Positive feedback or praise (the good stuff):** Positive feedback includes praise for your performance within your overall role. It may also include recognition and praise for your efforts on a specific task or project.

Example: 'You've done really well keeping within the budget. You came up with some really clever ways of reducing our overheads.'

✔ **Negative or corrective feedback (the not-so good stuff):** Negative feedback involves pointing out where you've gone wrong or can improve. Corrective feedback involves giving you clear guidance about how to make improvements.

Example: 'You've been an hour late for your shift every day this week. I need you to arrive at work on time. Your lateness affects your co-workers, who end up staying late to cover for you.'

✔ **Instructional feedback (the neutral stuff):** Instructional feedback gives you information about a change in your existing role or information about a new project or task. Instructional feedback is informative but isn't an assessment of your work performance.

Example: 'The office is undergoing a refurbishment next month. I'd like you to oversee the reallocation of work spaces for your team while the refurbishment is being done.'

Graciously accept and enjoy the positive feedback you receive. Be wary of your low self-esteem leading you to ignore or dismiss the good stuff you hear. Take action on useful information contained in negative feedback and refuse to beat yourself up about it.

Dismissing unproductive feedback

Having your work performance criticised may not be a strictly pleasant experience, but if the feedback is delivered in a constructive manner (as outlined in the preceding section), it can be highly useful.

Unfortunately, not everyone you meet is able or willing to give feedback in a constructive way. Some people, even those in well-respected professional positions, are pretty poorly skilled at giving feedback to their employees. Others just don't seem to be bothered about the effect their method of giving criticism may have on the receiver.

So, in the interests of preserving your self-esteem, you have to become more resilient to all kinds of feedback, including the unproductive kind.

Here's how to spot unproductive feedback:

✔ The feedback comes unexpectedly or in an inappropriate place such as in a busy staff canteen. The timing may also be inappropriate – for example, during your lunch break or just as you're leaving to go home.

✔ The person giving the feedback may not speak to you in a respectful and professional manner. He may use profane, insulting or patronising language.

✔ The feedback may be vague and unclear. You may end up feeling confused about what exactly you've done wrong or failed to do.

✔ The feedback leaves you feeling bad but without much idea of how to make improvements. You may be given unreasonable deadlines or threatened with unreasonable repercussions.

You may not be able to stop people being harshly or unfairly critical towards you, but you can decide to deal with it in a mature and professional way.

For example, Georgia's boss comes up to her in the middle of an open-plan office and speaks to her loudly and angrily. He proceeds to tell Georgia: 'I'm totally dissatisfied with your work on this project! It's simply not good enough, what have you been doing? You're incompetent! I'd better see something impressive by the end of day or heads are going to roll.' Georgia feels rather shaken by her boss's outburst but holds her ground by saying: 'It seems obvious that we need to have a proper discussion about this in private.' Georgia and her boss go to a private office to talk.

Instead of accepting her boss's comments without protest, Georgia asks the following questions to compel him to clarify and substantiate his points:

'In what specific ways is my performance lacking?'

'Can you give me an example of what you mean?'

'What exactly would you like to see accomplished by the end of the day?'

'What exactly do you want me to do differently in future?'

'Can you make suggestions on how I can improve my performance?'

'I'd like to arrange a time to sit down with you and review my work performance in more detail.'

'I disagree with some of your comments for the following reasons. . .'.

When you ask for specific details, examples and clarification of unconstructive feedback, you shift some responsibility back onto the person giving the criticism. In addition, the feedback is more useful to you.

Sometimes you're able to refute directly feedback that you think is inaccurate or unfair, but at other times you can't. You don't need to disagree openly with another person's comments about you when the situation doesn't permit it. The most important thing is to remember that you can choose to reject unhelpful feedback.

Try exercising a little faith in your own knowledge and judgement of yourself. Low self-esteem can put you in the habit of assuming that other people must be right to criticise you, even if what they say is abusive or outrageous. Unskilled feedback often comes as an attack on your personality and character instead of being strictly focused on your performance. Remember to stubbornly refuse to let your self-esteem be knocked by personal criticisms that you know in your heart are unfounded.

Allocating responsibility using a pie chart

If you find that dismissing unproductive feedback is difficult, you can use the pie-chart method. Instead of taking the whole responsibility for things going wrong, give yourself a fairer slice of the pie, following these steps:

1. **Use the blank pie chart form in Figure 13-1 or draw a big circle on a piece of paper.**

2. **Write down the negative situation or event at the top of the page.**

3. **Make a list of all the factors that contributed to the situation or negative event.**

   Try to look at the situation as if you're an outsider and your emotions aren't involved. Be fair. Don't just record your own part in things; really think about other aspects of the event that have little or nothing to do with you.

4. **Use a ruler to slice up the pie giving an appropriately sized slice to each of the factors contributing to the negative situation or event.**

   Remember to leave yourself until the last (otherwise you may give yourself far too hefty a chunk).

5. **Take a second look at the pie after you've carved it up.**

   Chances are you've given yourself a smaller portion of the pie (a more accurate share of the responsibility for what's happened) than you did initially.

Georgia was having trouble rejecting her boss's accusation that she was incompetent. So she made a note of all the other possible factors that may have contributed to the work project failing to meet with her boss's approval. Figure 13-1 shows you how to slice up your own pie chart.

Using the pie-chart method helps you to view yourself and your performance more fairly.

Factors outside of George's control that
contributed to the project going poorly.

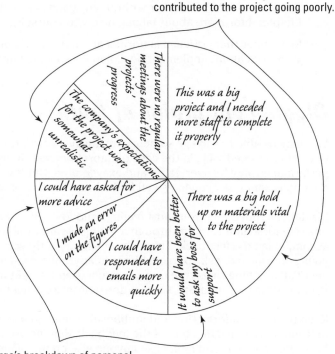

There were no regular
meetings about the
projects' progress

The company's expectations
for the project were
somewhat unrealistic

This was a big
project and I needed
more staff to complete
it properly

I could have asked for
more advice

I made an error
on the figures

I could have
responded to
emails more
quickly

It would have been better
to ask my boss for
support

There was a big hold
up on materials vital
to the project

Figure 13-1:
Your
responsibil-
ity pie chart.

George's breakdown of personal
responsibility for the project going poorly.

Incorporating Constructive Criticism

Low self-esteem can stop you making use of constructive input at work. You
may be very sensitive to even slight criticism, become depressed and feel
like just giving up altogether. Or you may fail to hear the good stuff and focus
only on the less-good comments.

You can do a few things to help yourself out of this low-self-esteem trap:

✔ Record positive feedback in a notebook and review your entries often.
Give yourself credit for good work and individual skills.

✔ Think creatively about how you can make more use of your strengths at
work and write down some clear plans.

✓ Record negative feedback as well but be careful to only record the facts. Try to be objective and fair without engaging in self-abusive talk (see Chapter 4 for more about talking nicely to yourself).

✓ Remember that criticism is normal and not the end of the world. Talk to your boss about implementing a plan for specific improvements.

Digging out grains of truth

You may be able to salvage some useful nuggets of information even from unproductive feedback. In the case of unproductive criticism, flaws in your performance may be overstated and exaggerated. But if you can shift through the unpleasant chaff you may well find a kernel or two of wheat.

It's difficult, but shove your hurt feelings and low self-esteem thoughts to one side for a minute. Shift through any unpleasant or abusive messages that accompanied the feedback. Think about what exactly was said about you or your performance. Ask yourself: 'What (if anything) can I learn from this feedback?'. If anything rings true or gives you a useful insight into how to improve your performance in future, write it down or make a mental note of it.

Keep the useful information and stubbornly refuse to accept the abusive, judgemental or insulting bits of the feedback. Remind yourself that you may have shortcomings and faults like anyone else on the planet and it's useful to have these brought to your attention from time to time. But also remind yourself that poorly delivered feedback is a negative reflection on the person who's giving it, not on you.

For example, Georgia rejected her boss's assessment of her as 'incompetent' but accepted that it would be better if she checked her emails every morning rather than leaving them until later in the day.

Changing for the better

Getting more robust about feedback is ultimately good news for your self-esteem. After all, you simply can't avoid being criticised at some point in your professional or personal life.

Your self-esteem doesn't need to sit on a knife's edge depending on what others tell you about your performance and behaviour. Instead, you can think of yourself as a worthwhile person with good and bad points and make your own mind up about what to accept or refuse from feedback.

Everyone needs feedback in order to improve after making mistakes. When your self-esteem is robust enough to weather criticism, you can actively seek out negative feedback in the interests of promoting your personal development.

Accessing Your Assertiveness

People with poor self-esteem are very commonly slow to assert themselves. Unfortunately, failing to assert yourself when necessary can further diminish your self-esteem, leading to problems at work and preventing you from getting ahead in your career. Have a look at the following questions and tick those to which you answer 'Yes':

❑ Do you tend to let other people have their own way at work or in other areas of your life?

❑ Are you slow to put forth your preferences or opinions for fear of being disagreed with?

❑ Even if you think you have a good idea or are right about an issue, do you tend to defer to what other people say?

❑ If someone offends you, do you normally just brush it under the carpet rather than talking about it with them?

❑ Do you avoid asking for things such as pay rises, promotions or improved working conditions because you're not sure that you deserve them?

❑ Do you avoid asking for instruction or help at work because you think you should be able to do things on your own?

❑ Do you go out of your way to quell any disagreement between your friends or colleagues out of fear of it developing into a row?

❑ Do you worry that if you disagree with others they may stop liking you?

❑ Do you avoid confrontation at all costs because you don't believe that you've got what it takes to cope with how others may behave towards you?

If you answered 'Yes' to more than two of these questions, you may well be avoiding conflict situations to your own cost. Perhaps you've never really discovered how to be healthily assertive. Maybe your family fought a lot among themselves and you developed a fear of arguments. Or perhaps you worry so much about hurting other people's feelings that you avoid any form of confrontation.

People dislike confrontation for many different reasons. For one thing, confrontation and conflict aren't much fun. Tempers may be raised and sometimes one party or the other comes away feeling bad. Most people don't like to be involved in or even witness disharmony and arguments. However, sometimes you need to deal with conflict and sort out disagreements with others.

Conflict doesn't have to culminate in a fight situation or involve aggression, violence or other types of abuse.

Although you can't control how other people behave during a confrontation, you can at least be in control of your own responses and conduct. You may not like the process of asserting yourself but you can feel better in the long run for having done so.

You're likely to encounter two types of situation that need assertion:

- ✔ **Planned assertion:** This type of assertion means that you have time to think about what you want to say to someone. For example, you may have arranged a meeting and told the person involved what you want to discuss. You can plan to have an assertive conversation with your boss, colleague, friend or partner (though you may adopt a more formal manner in a work environment).

- ✔ **Spontaneous assertion:** This type of assertion applies to conflict situations about which you've no prior warning. Examples include being overcharged in a shop, asking your flatmates to clear up the mess they made in the kitchen, expressing your displeasure when a friend keeps you waiting in the pub, or voicing a difference of opinion during a team meeting.

The same basic guidelines for healthy assertion apply to both planned and spontaneous assertion (you just have very little time to prepare for the latter):

- ✔ **Make eye contact:** Keeping good eye contact conveys confidence in yourself and conviction in the points you're making. Hold your head up and meet the other person's gaze. Be careful to avoid staring at or 'eyeballing' the other person because this behaviour can be unnerving and appear aggressive.

- ✔ **Be clear in your head about what you want to say:** Get the points you want to make straight in your own mind. If you have time, jot down a few notes on paper.

- ✔ **Speak slowly and don't stray off the issue:** Try to keep an even pace when talking so that the other person can hear everything you say without you needing to repeat yourself. Speaking slowly and clearly also conveys confidence. Stick to the key issues and don't allow the other person to sidetrack you. Repeat your point again if the conversation strays into unrelated topics.

✔ **Avoid name-calling, abusive or accusing language:** Use respectful language even when you're feeling angry. You can be firm without resorting to aggression. The other person is more likely to be receptive to your point of view if treated courteously.

✔ **Take responsibility for your thoughts and emotional responses:** Be specific about the criticism you want to make. Avoid using global statements and structure your language so that you're taking responsibility for your reactions. Try using 'When *x*, I feel/think *y*' statements. Here are a few examples of this approach, with the more healthily assertive statement first:

- 'When you gave my appraisal I felt my hard work wasn't being acknowledged', instead of 'You don't appreciate my hard work.'

- 'When you hang up the phone abruptly I feel hurt', instead of 'You hurt my feelings.'

- 'When the company changes procedure without prior warning, it seems to me that the employees aren't being respected', instead of 'This company doesn't respect its employees.'

✔ **Make your point and give the other person a chance to respond:** When you've said your piece, allow the other person to answer. If you have more than one point to make, pause between each one so that the other person doesn't feel bombarded.

Use these tips to help you manage confrontational situations both at work and in your home or social life. Calm confrontation gets easier with practice. Although you may still feel nervous about being assertive, remind yourself that sometimes it can be worthwhile. You may not always get the result you want but at least you haven't allowed yourself to be pushed around or ignored.

Weighing up situations worthy of confrontation

Being able to assert yourself is good, but you need to decide when doing so is worthwhile. Walking away from a potential conflict situation can also be an assertive action. You may decide that getting dragged into a confrontation isn't a good idea or doesn't merit the effort.

Typically, people with low self-esteem are reluctant to assert themselves and may not do it at all. Never asserting yourself means that you probably put up with poor behaviour from others and rarely put your own point of view across. You may end up feeling resentful or bitter towards others and the world because your needs are frequently overlooked.

If you suffer from poor self-esteem, you may well avoid confrontation because:

✔ You believe that the opinions of others matter more than your own.

✔ You fear upsetting or offending others.

✔ You don't think you deserve to get what you want.

✔ You believe that your thoughts, feelings and opinions aren't significant.

✔ You fear being hurt emotionally or physically if you stand up for yourself.

✔ You think you'll look foolish, childish or pathetic if you try to assert yourself.

Beware of avoiding confrontation for the reasons just listed – that's low self-esteem talking.

Assertion takes practice and it can be done in all sorts of ways. You don't need to be running around squaring up to everyone who displeases you in some minor way. Sometimes merely standing your ground, maintaining eye contact or declining to agree with someone is ample assertive action. Starting to assert yourself is an important part of building healthy self-esteem. You don't always need to get what you want out of assertion: just saying your piece bolsters your self-esteem. On the other hand, people with healthy self-esteem don't go around asserting themselves willy-nilly. Generally, healthy self-esteem enables you to assess a given situation and decide whether or not you can gain anything through assertive action.

Asking yourself the following questions can help you to determine if being assertive is the best course of action in a particular situation:

✔ **Is this issue important enough to warrant a confrontation?** Consider whether you care enough about what's happening to put across your own point of view or challenge another person's actions. Think about whether you may regret avoiding confrontation later on.

   If the issue is personally important or if failing to assert yourself will lead to self-recrimination later, then it's probably worth getting your hands dirty, so to speak.

✔ **Is there anything to be gained by confronting this person?** Look for the point of asserting yourself. You may feel better about standing up for yourself and your beliefs in a situation even if the other person fails to agree with you or concede. Equally you may decide that asserting yourself won't make any appreciable difference to your own feelings or the situation. If you can't gain anything through confrontation and assertion then you may be best off simply walking away.

✔ **Is it safe to assert myself in this situation or with this individual?**
Sometimes it's just a bad idea to get into a confrontation with others.
When people appear to be very aggressive or hostile, assertive action is
usually ill-advised. Instead of putting yourself at risk, rise above it and
remove yourself from the situation.

As an example, Duncan has been working on getting more comfortable with
asserting himself when he thinks doing so is necessary. He doesn't run
around confronting everybody who annoys him, but he can stand his ground
on important issues. One day Duncan is going grocery shopping with his girlfriend. Just as he's about to pull into a parking space another car swerves in
front of him, taking the space and nearly causing an accident. Duncan swears
under his breath and starts looking for another space. His girlfriend says,
'Hey! You should go and tell that guy off! He nicked our space! I thought you
were trying to get more assertive. Why are you just letting this go?'

Duncan didn't bother confronting the person who stole the parking space
because although he found the situation pretty irritating, he decided that it
wasn't really worth getting into an argument over. Duncan came to this conclusion by asking himself a few simple questions:

Question	*Duncan's answer*
Is this issue important to me?	*Somewhat.*
Is it important enough to warrant a confrontation?	*No.*
Is anything to be gained by confronting this person?	*No. He's in the space and I can park elsewhere without trouble.*
Is it safe to assert myself in this situation or with this individual?	*Hard to say. People can be very unpre-dictable if they've got 'road rage'. The guy driving the car probably isn't going to attack me, but it's still not worth the hassle.*

Duncan didn't assert himself with the driver of the other car but he made an
assertive choice not to. He wasn't hiding away from the possibility, he just
didn't see much point in getting into a scene over a parking space. Although
Duncan didn't confront the driver, he did assert himself with his girlfriend by
defending his chosen course of action.

Standing up for what you believe in

When you act according to your values, you're standing up for what you
believe in. Whether the subject is recycling, not dropping litter, being
polite, tipping for good service, defending human rights or giving Christmas
cards to your neighbours, your actions all amount to standing up for what
you believe in.

You don't need to get up on a soapbox or be evangelistic in order to take a stand for your beliefs. The best method is to act in line with what's important to you.

You may find opportunities in the workplace to stand up for your beliefs. Being fair and polite or refusing to get involved in rumours and gossip are possible examples. Your self-esteem is likely to increase and strengthen with value-led actions. We discuss living according to your values in more depth in Chapter 15.

Offering your opinion

Let your opinions out! Give others the chance to hear what you think about things! Years of low self-esteem can lead you to bite your tongue and keep your views inside. You may fear that others are going to disagree with you or that your actions may lead to conflict. Perhaps you worry about being disliked for your opinions on certain issues.

The problem with not stating your opinion is that it reinforces negative ideas that you hold about yourself. Common fears about offering opinions include:

- No one else thinks the same way as I do about this issue.
- I don't know enough about this issue to offer an opinion; I'll sound stupid.
- Nobody cares what I think.
- Other people's opinions are more valid than my own.
- Offering my opinion is too risky – someone else may attack me verbally and I'll be humiliated.
- If I disagree with someone, they'll stop liking me.

Usually, these fears don't come true at all. If you think about it, people around you speak their minds all the time. Does anything terrible happen to them? The only difference between you and them is confidence. Be confident that even when others disagree with your opinion, you're going to survive.

Take the risk and speak your mind. Differences in opinion are common and healthy, and they rarely end friendships or result in ill-feeling. But you never see that first-hand unless you give it a try. Practise voicing your opinions in your social life and at work. You may be surprised at how good vocalising your opinion feels.

Part V
Living Like You Mean It

'Are you sure this is going to help me get rid of my depression, Frank?'

In this part . . .

Improving your self-esteem involves ongoing lifestyle changes. We guide you towards building a lifestyle that promotes and maintains positive self-opinion. You discover how to get in touch with your personal values and start living in a way that reflects what's most important to you. On top of that you find methods of keeping yourself moving in the direction of your goals even when the going gets tough.

Chapter 14

Honouring Commitments to Yourself

*P*ersonal commitments can take the shape of definite goals, such as changing jobs, getting a qualification or stopping smoking. They can also include on-going positive changes to your behaviour and overall lifestyle that don't necessarily culminate in reaching an obvious concrete end point. For example, the numbers on the scales let you know when you've reached a goal of losing 20 kilograms in weight. If you make a more general commitment to yourself to get fitter however, although you may notice improvements in your energy and stamina, the results are less measurable. Maintaining a good level of fitness is also part of a lifestyle change that you probably intend to keep going on with indefinitely. Weight loss, on the other hand, stops when you reach your target weight, although maintaining a healthy weight is likely to be an ongoing commitment. (Chapter 8 deals with setting personal goals, so we don't repeat ourselves here. You may benefit from looking at the material in that chapter as well.)

Your plan to behave consistently in ways that promote healthy self-esteem is another example of an ongoing personal commitment. In fact, making commitments to yourself and honouring them is a big part of building healthy self-esteem and living positively, making this situation a positive 'chicken and egg' scenario. You tend to feel better about your life and yourself when you stick to your personal commitments.

In this chapter we discuss different types of personal commitments you may choose to make and explore ways in which you can increase your chances of sticking with them through thick and thin.

Setting Goals

Getting where you want to go is difficult without a clear idea of where your destination is. You may already have a good idea of the goals and commitments you want to act on, which is great. Or, you may be still giving some thought to the types of changes that may improve your lifestyle and overall self-opinion.

Choosing an area to improve

The first step towards achieving any goal is making a definite plan and identifying concrete commitments.

If you're having difficulties in pinning down specific goals, you may find that considering the following questions is helpful:

✔ Do I want to do more of something in my life, such as exercising or socialising?

✔ Do I want to do less of something, such as working late or eating fast food?

✔ Do I want to stop doing something altogether, such as smoking or drinking alcohol?

✔ Do I want to start doing something new, such as studying or taking up a new hobby?

Your *personal goals* and *commitments* can centre around any area of your life. You may want to focus on actions that ultimately have a positive impact on your emotions, or you may be more interested in improving your physical health, relationships, work life or financial situation. The possibilities are pretty much endless.

Make sure that you choose commitments that are of personal importance to you. Choosing objectives because of pressure from others or in an attempt to impress is a common mistake. These goals may not reflect your true interests and values, and the result is that you can lose your impetus to reach them.

Also, trying too hard to please others can fundamentally undermine your own sense of self-worth. Let other people fulfil their own personal commitments while you fulfil yours. Trust your own judgement about what's right for you.

Identify the area of your life you want to target and choose a start date so that you're not tempted to procrastinate. Choosing a start date helps you to turn good intentions into actions.

Listing the possibilities

When you have a broad idea of the improvements or alterations you want to make in your life, you can start to fill in the details.

A *mini-goal* or *sub-commitment* is any behaviour that is likely to carry you towards your ultimate goal (see Chapter 8 for more on setting goals) and/or contribute to a positive lifestyle change. Depending on what your personal commitment is, you may have loads of mini-goals or as few as one or two. What's most important is outlining the steps involved along your journey to reaching a goal or honouring an ongoing personal commitment.

Be specific about your goal or personal commitment; for example, 'to improve my overall fitness'. Make a list of all the actions you can think of that may contribute towards fulfilling your personal commitments. A commitment to improved fitness may include specific points, such as walking to work and cooking organic food. These are your sub-commitments, mini-goals or commitment-honouring actions. Listing the possibilities points you in the right direction by helping you to identify individual behaviours that can be incorporated into your daily life.

Katrina's personal commitment is to live each day in a self-esteem-enhancing manner. In order to honour this personal commitment, she breaks her commitment down into specific behaviours or 'sub-commitments' that she can regularly act upon. Katrina knows that socialising more often, reducing her alcohol consumption and starting to date are likely to improve her mood and overall self-esteem. She also knows that her quest to maintain healthy self-esteem benefits from talking nicely to herself rather than engaging in negative self-talk and name-calling. Katrina's list of behaviours consistent with maintaining and promoting healthy self-esteem is as follows:

✔ Drinking only at weekends and in social situations rather than on my own in the evenings.

✔ Going out with friends at least once a week even when I feel low.

✔ Making an effort to strike up conversations with men in social situations even if I feel nervous. I can do this during lunchtime at work and at the pub quiz on Thursdays.

✔ Accepting invitations to social outings where I may meet someone suitable. I can aim to attend a party or concert at least once a month.

✔ Giving myself credit for my efforts and resisting calling myself names or putting myself down harshly and unfairly. I can do this every day.

Notice that Katrina identifies clear times to act on her self-esteem-enhancing sub-commitments. This approach helps to keep her personal commitment at the forefront of her mind and reduces the likelihood of her giving up or forgetting and lapsing back into old unhelpful habits. She can monitor the degree to which she honours her overall personal commitment by checking how regularly she adheres to her list of sub-commitments.

You can add to your list at anytime. You may find that with continued practice, you get very used to sticking to the commitment-honouring actions you originally outlined. Ideally they eventually become second nature and require little deliberate thought. When this happens you may want to review your personal commitment list and add on new sub-commitments that may further your progress toward commitment-consistent living.

Sometimes your mood can get in the way of honouring commitments to yourself. If you're feeling depressed or anxious you may be inclined to avoid doing things that seem overwhelming. Your energy may be low and carrying out even simple tasks may seem too daunting. Be compassionate and understanding with yourself when your mood is low but also urge yourself not to give into it entirely. Gently cajole yourself into sticking to your personal commitments and doing the things that make you feel better in the long run. (In Chapter 4 we offer ways to put an end to the type of abusive self-talk that Katrina is striving to give up.)

Maximising Motivation

Maintaining positive changes takes considerable effort and persistence. Sometimes your motivation wanes and at other times you feel like you've got plenty. People generally feel more motivated to pursue a course of action when they can really see the potential benefits. When you can remember why putting in the effort towards honouring your personal commitments is worthwhile, you can discover hidden reservoirs of motivation.

From time to time you may well fail to act in ways consistent with your personal commitments. Instead of giving yourself a really hard time and getting stuck in a rut, just try to get back on track as soon as you can.

Structuring a motivation-maximising statement

Building a motivation-maximising statement can help you to keep soldiering on even when you feel like stopping. The alliterative *motivation-maximising statement* is like a personal mantra to help you through struggle and fatigue en route to your goals.

Create your statement when you're in a positive frame of mind and feel like you've got plenty of motivation in the tank. Otherwise, your mood may interfere with your ability to think fairly and realistically about your personal commitment and the reasons why you need to honour it.

When you're feeling good and energised, write down a statement a paragraph or two long outlining all the potential benefits you can think of relating to your goal or commitment. Use compelling and vibrant language wherever you can to make the statement really come alive and speak to you.

Use these tips to help get you started at making a motivation-maximising statement:

✔ **Begin the statement by outlining your goal or personal commitment.** For example, 'My goal is to get a full-time job' or 'My personal commitment is to devote more time to my family'.

✔ **Record the benefits of sticking to goal/commitment-directed behaviours.** Be very clear about the positive effects of keeping your daily behaviour in line with your ultimate goals. Record the beneficial impact goal-led behaviour has on your feelings, on your productivity (at home and at work), on your relationships and on how you feel physically.

✔ **Record the negative consequences of giving up on your goal/ commitment-directed behaviour.** Write down in detail what you stand to lose by abandoning your personal commitments and goals. Identify the downside of behaviours that contradict your goals and values, like drinking to excess, working late every night or avoiding exercise. Record the impact destructive actions have on how you feel emotionally and physically, on your relationships and on how well you function in your overall life.

✔ **Use vibrant convincing language in your statement.** Remember that the purpose of the statement is to give you an extra boost of energy and motivation. Include lots of phrases that inspire you, such as 'I can do it' or 'It's worth doing because…' and 'All this hard work will pay off'. Your statement needs to make sense to you and immediately remind you of all the worthwhile reasons for sticking with your goals and commitments. So include enough detail to create a vivid picture in your mind when you re-read your statement.

✔ **Review your statement often and add to it as you journey along towards your goals.** Keeping the reasons for pursuing a goal or lifestyle change constantly in your mind can help ensure success. Try to re-read your statement at least three times per week. As you notice more benefits arising from your goal-led actions, add them to your statement. Equally, record new realisations about what you stand to lose by giving up.

Carry your statement with you in a pocket or handbag so you can readily refer to it whenever you feel the need to boost your motivation.

Katrina's motivation-maximising statement reads as follows:

> My overall personal commitment is to live each day in a self-esteem-enhancing manner. Sticking to the points on my list of 'commitment-honouring actions' is worthwhile because I feel happier about myself and enjoy my life much more when I do. When I drink alcohol moderately I avoid shocking hangovers and wake up energised instead of depressed. Everything looks brighter to me when I'm not suffering from a hangover. I also perform better at work and get more done around the house.

> Seeing my friends every week takes my mind off negative thoughts about myself and gives me proof that people like having me around. I laugh a lot and life seems far more positive for days afterwards. If I'm feeling low, going out with friends almost always cheers me up. Making conversation with men bolsters my confidence and I feel more optimistic about eventually finding a partner. Talking to myself in a respectful and positive way stops me getting depressed. Getting over everyday problems and difficulties is easier when I resist calling myself abusive names.

You can update and revise your motivation statement as you notice additional new benefits of sticking to your personal commitment.

Getting visual

An important aspect of maintaining your motivation to honour your personal commitments and attain your goals is to be able to see yourself doing so. When you create a strong image of yourself in the future, you're likely to have more confidence and faith in your ability to get to where you want to be.

Most people engage in daydreams from time to time. The following exercise encourages you to hone your daydreaming skills so that you can build a strong, positive and satisfying vision of yourself in the future:

1. **Clear your mind.**

   Imagine that you're wiping a blackboard clean or turning over a crisp, clean piece of paper.

2. **Focus on your personal commitment.**

   Be specific about what your commitment-honouring actions are and hold them clearly in your mind, whether they're about your self-esteem, work, study, relationships or personal lifestyle.

3. **Build a picture of how things may be when you're regularly honouring your personal commitments.**

   Explore how you're feeling, imagine your behaviour when you're working and socialising, picture the people in your life and speculate on how you're spending your free time.

4. **Fill in the picture with even more detail.**

   What previous worries have been resolved? Who are your friends? What's your daily routine? What time do you get up in the morning? What can you smell? Taste? Touch? What does the interior of your home look like? What are your hobbies? Add as many different details as you can to make the picture of your future complete.

5. **Indulge in this fantasy for at least a few minutes – longer if you prefer. Then re-focus on your personal commitments and the steps you need to take to honour them.**

Set aside time to do this exercise a few times each week or do it when you're out and about. For example, you may find time to daydream deliberately while in a waiting room, riding the bus, doing chores or walking somewhere.

Of course, when you get to where you want to be some things may be different from your daydream picture. However, a lot of the details from your vision of the future may be the same or similar in reality. You can't precisely predict the future, however vividly you construct it in your mind. But creating positive and enticing visions of your future life allows you to increase your chances of attaining a reasonable and gratifying facsimile.

Quoting quotable quotes

Many people find reciting quotes a good way of giving their motivation a turbo boost. Think of individuals you find inspiring and look up some powerful things that they've said. You can choose famous people or family members and friends as potential sources of inspiration. You can find words to motivate even in song lyrics!

Write down and commit to memory quotations that fill you with positive emotion, put things into perspective and encourage you to keep moving forward. Pin them to your wall or put them on the fridge – anywhere you frequently see them.

Lots of books contain famous quotations or you can find quotation websites on the Internet. Chapter 19 of this book discusses more potential sources of inspiration.

Drawing inspiration from other people's words

Quotes and song lyrics can lend you a inspirational hand when you feel like throwing in the towel. It's a good idea to dig out some of your own, write them down and maybe even commit them to memory; we offer you some here to get you started.

✔ 'To accomplish great things, we must dream as well as act.' Anatole France (1844–1924)

✔ 'Happiness depends upon ourselves.' Aristotle (384 BC–322 BC)

✔ 'The first step to getting the things you want out of life is this: Decide what you want.' Ben Stein (b. 1944)

✔ 'Most folks are about as happy as they make up their minds to be.' Abraham Lincoln (1809–1865)

✔ 'I was always looking outside myself for strength and confidence but it comes from within. It is there all the time.' Anna Freud (1895–1982)

✔ 'The man who has confidence in himself gains the confidence of others.' Hasidic saying

✔ 'Courage is fear that has said its prayers.' Dorothy Bernard (1890–1955)

✔ 'Courage is being scared to death but saddling up anyway.' John Wayne (1907–1979)

✔ 'I have never let my schooling interfere with my education.' Mark Twain (1835–1910)

✔ 'Education is the ability to listen to almost anything without losing your temper or your self-confidence.' Robert Frost (1874–1963)

✔ 'It does not seem to be true that work necessarily needs to be unpleasant. It may always have to be hard, or at least harder than doing nothing at all. But there is ample evidence that work can be enjoyable, and that indeed, it is often the most enjoyable part of life.' Mihaly Csikszentmihalyi (b. 1934) in *Flow: The Psychology of Optimal Experience*

✔ 'Plans are only good intentions unless they immediately degenerate into hard work.' Peter Drucker (1909–2005)

✔ 'I'm a great believer in luck, and I find the harder I work the more I have of it.' Thomas Jefferson *attrib.* (1743–1826)

✔ 'Work saves us from three great evils: boredom, vice and need.' Voltaire (1694–1778) in *Candide*

✔ 'If you can solve your problem, then what is the need of worrying? If you cannot solve it, then what is the use of worrying?' Shantideva (c. 700)

✔ 'A goal without a plan is just a wish.' Antoine de Saint-Exupéry (1900–1944)

✔ 'Success isn't permanent, and failure isn't fatal.' Mike Ditka (b. 1939)

✔ 'Success is the ability to go from one failure to another with no loss of enthusiasm.' Sir Winston Churchill (1874–1965)

✔ 'Eighty per cent of success is showing up.' Woody Allen (b. 1935)

And let's not forget song lyrics! A favourite Wiley editor of ours (Kathleen) loves Tom Petty: 'I won't back down. You can stand me up at the gates of hell, but I won't back down. Gonna stand my ground, won't be turned around, And I'll keep this world from dragging me down and I won't back down'.

Look for song lyrics and quotes or any sayings that give you gumption. Write them down and review them for a moral booster.

Taking Responsibility

You're the only person who can put in the hard work needed to make improvements to your life. No one else can honour your personal commitments for you. These cold hard facts, however, seem a bit warmer and softer when you realise that they also give you personal power.

Taking personal responsibility for your actions in response to negative events and undesirable situations is actually very good for your self-esteem. Remember that taking legitimate responsibility is not the same as blaming and condemning yourself. Instead, taking responsibility means recognising and accepting the role you play in deciding how to feel and act. This action promotes self-esteem by putting you into problem-solving mode rather than passive-victim mode. You can take charge of making changes in your life because you accept that you have some degree of control and influence. Taking responsibility also carries the added bonus of meaning that you can take full credit for your efforts and your successes.

Naming, blaming and shaming yourself, other people or even the whole darn universe is all too easy when things don't go your way. The trap is a sticky one to fall into and can be hard to escape from. The trick is to catch your blaming thoughts as early as you can and challenge them vigorously.

Follow these tips to catch those nasty thoughts and stop them in their tracks:

- **Write the thought down or isolate it in your mind.** Be clear about who you're blaming – yourself, someone else or the world. Also specifically identify what you're blaming yourself, others or the world for.

- **Take appropriate personal responsibility for what has happened.** Sure other people and events may have *contributed* to how you feel but ultimately your actions are of your own authorship. Review the situation and look for where your responsibility lies.

- **Exercise compassion and understanding.** If you *are* responsible (at least partly) for a bad event, you don't have to beat yourself up over it thereby making yourself feel even worse. Likewise, refuse to put the boot into others (and life in general) for failing to please. Recognise the role that life and other people may have played in a negative situation but stop short of metaphorically sentencing them to death.

- **Write down or mentally compose a balanced counter-argument to your original blaming thought.** Include all the factors that contributed to your emotions and actions; be *factual* rather than harshly judgemental. Highlight your part in the proceedings and decide what you want to do differently in the future to produce a more favourable outcome.

You may find it easier to challenge and restructure blaming thoughts by using the format shown in the following table. Sometimes, however, you can't easily get your hands on writing materials so you need to go through the same steps in your head. You can always write it down later if you want to keep a record of your blaming thoughts and counter-arguments.

Katrina fell off the wagon after a hard day at work and a lukewarm reception from a male colleague she quite fancies. She drank a bottle and a half of wine that evening at home on her own. The next day she felt pretty dreadful – not only physically but also emotionally. Katrina wanted to re-board the wagon, to revise her commitment to either controlled drinking or abstinence and return to honouring her personal commitment to living in a self-esteem-enhancing manner. But she found herself having a lot of blaming thoughts, so she sat down, put pen to paper and challenged them. Table 14-1 shows her blame thoughts – self-blaming, other-blaming and blaming the world – and her counter-arguments.

Table 14-1	Katrina's Blame Thoughts and Counter-Arguments
Blame Thought	*Counter-argument*
'I'm a useless waste of space for drinking so much. What a loser.'	'Okay, I did break my personal commitment by drinking. But I'm *not* a loser *or* a waste of space. I did a bad thing but I'm a worthwhile person who made a mistake. I can discover things from this setback and move on.'
'Paul was so aloof and offhand at lunch when I tried to talk to him. It's his fault for making me feel embarrassed. How rude of him; it's his fault that I bought wine and got trashed.'	'Come on Katrina, get a grip. Am I going to turn to the bottle every time someone is rude? Paul may not be interested in me and that's disappointing but he didn't *make* me drink. That was a poor choice that *I* made because I was feeling bad.'
'It was a terrible day. Paul rejected me, the trains were late and my boss loaded more work onto my plate. How can I be expected to stick to my personal commitments when the world is so unfair?'	'Okay, it was a bad day but going back to old destructive habits only makes me feel worse. I'm capable of weathering bad days while honouring my personal commitments but it's up to me to make the effort. The world doesn't owe me an easy ride all the time.'

Setting Optimum Conditions for Success

You want to give yourself the best possible chance of sticking to your personal commitments, right? Of course you do, and again success comes down to taking personal responsibility.

Sometimes people give themselves goals and make personal lifestyle commitments but neglect to structure ways to follow through on them. When you don't put some structure in place you leave your success almost entirely to chance.

In fact, luck isn't really involved in honouring your personal commitments; success is much more about concentrated effort and planning. To increase your likelihood of success you need to be prepared for motivation lags and obstacles that life may throw into the mix. You can also arm yourself against slip-ups by giving yourself realistic sub-commitments and a deadline to aim at.

Chewing off bite-sized chunks

When you're structuring goals and commitments, you need to think about your starting place. For example, if your overall personal commitment is to improve your fitness and the only exercise you currently get is a trip to the fridge, committing yourself to a eight-kilometre run every morning may be a little over-ambitious to start with. Your goal is where you want to end up eventually, and to improve your chances of getting there you need to be realistic about where you are now.

Choose commitment-honouring behaviours that you can be confident of achieving because you know that you have the skills and capabilities to do so. Otherwise you may be setting yourself up to fail and become discouraged and overwhelmed. Strike a balance between challenging yourself and being realistic about what you're able to achieve at this point in time. So instead of the eight-kilometre bound through the streets you may decide to start with a brisk twenty-minute walk every morning, stop buying snack foods and take up yoga.

Imagine yourself incrementally moving towards your goal or commitment. Identify small steps that will move you in the desired direction and aim to build them up over time (more on goal setting in Chapter 8). A basic rule of thumb is: Set yourself several smaller tasks leading to your main goal. Ensure that your mini-goals stretch you and urge you to develop tolerance for persistence and effort. Don't make it too easy or unduly hard for yourself. Strike a balance between the two.

Forming a time frame

Decide when, where and how often you're going to carry out the actions that reflect your personal commitment. Having a plan means that you're more likely to follow through on the intention and helps you to form healthy new habits quickly.

Getting into a routine really helps to keep your moods stable so that you don't have as many 'bad days' where you do nothing and good days where you go hell for leather.

Consistency and continuity are the hallmarks of sustainable lifestyle change. By scheduling specific times for ongoing tasks you condition yourself to carry them out regardless of how you're feeling on a given day.

In addition, give yourself a deadline for completing finite goals like cleaning out the garage, planting the garden or applying for a course. Having a clear idea of when you can reasonably expect to have reached a concrete goal helps you to keep moving forwards rather than putting off starting.

When deciding on a time frame for a task, try thinking about how long it took you to realise a similar pursuit in the past. Or you can draw from examples of other people you know who've achieved a similar goal to your own; consider how long it took them to reach their aims. Also take into account your personal circumstances and calculate how much time you've actually got to devote to goal pursuit. You may need to carve out extra time from your schedule for goal-related activities, which may involve re-juggling your priorities temporarily. (See Chapter 15 for more information about prioritising activities and responsibilities).

Charting changes

Chart your progress faithfully. Taking note of your progress and all the positive changes helps to encourage you if you're tempted to forgo your goals and personal commitments. Measure your progress on mini-goals and regard them as evidence that you're getting closer to your overall goal or positive lifestyle change. Every step you take counts, so be sure to take note of even the smallest of shifts forward.

Get yourself a notebook and regularly record your progress towards concrete goals. Also, make note of the ways in which you've honoured your ongoing personal commitments. Writing all this information down really helps to keep you motivated and on track.

In the case of ongoing lifestyle changes such as keeping fit or Katrina's commitment to maintaining healthy self-esteem (see previous sections), noting down benefits to your mood, relationships, daily functioning and quality of life is vital. If your goal is more concrete and finite such as 'I want to have the garden fully planted and tended by the first week in June', you can make a note of every task you do that brings you closer to a beautiful garden.

Chapter 15

Living According to Your Values

*W*e use the term *values* to refer to your principles and standards; what you hold to be important in life. Everyone's different, and so one person's values may not be in total harmony with those of someone else, although you may find that the people you're closest to share many of the same basic values that you do.

Most people feel better about themselves when they live in accordance with their values. When you uphold your values through action you get a sense of 'doing the right thing' and of being true to yourself. Chronic low self-esteem can prevent you from living according to your values or even acknowledging them in the first place, and you may act in ways that don't represent what you think is most important deep down. Taking stock of your personal values and making an effort to live daily in ways that reflect them is beneficial to your emotional well-being and your self-esteem.

Your values are different to your goals and personal commitments. Values are broader and more 'all-encompassing', although they frequently may be *reflected* in your goals and personal commitments, which we discuss in Chapters 8 and 14, respectively.

In this chapter we help you to identify your personal values and offer suggestions on how you can begin to act according to them.

Much of the material in this chapter is adapted from the 'valued living questionnaire' devised by Steven Hayes and Kelly Wilson. They also developed *acceptance and commitment therapy (ACT)*, a talking therapy that comes under the broad umbrella of cognitive therapy which is proving to be very helpful to people experiencing depression and chronic low self-esteem.

Looking at the Deprivations That Low Self-Esteem Causes

Low self-esteem can lead you to avoid many different sorts of things in your daily life. The effects of low self-esteem are so insidious and all-pervasive that you may not even be truly aware of how much your negative self-view dictates your actions. This situation may be particularly true when you've struggled with feelings of worthlessness and helplessness for many years. You may be so accustomed to living your life according to the negative beliefs you hold about yourself that the behaviour becomes a well-worn habit. We encourage you not to despair but rather to take hope: old habits can be reversed with diligent attention and practice.

Typically, low self-esteem leads to avoidance of any situation or activity that may trigger off your negative ideas about yourself. You may find that you stringently avoid entering into any activity that can potentially result in failure, rejection or disapproval from others.

Unless you urge yourself to try out activities that you generally avoid, your self-esteem will remain low. Doing things even though you fear them builds confidence and a sense of capability. You also discover that you can survive incidents of failure or rejection without any permanent damage. You may feel upset for a time but you'll recover.

In general it's far more damaging to your self-esteem to hide away from certain activities than it is to try them and fail.

The following statements are examples of reasons people with low self-esteem are reluctant to engage in new and unfamiliar activities. See if any of them resonate with you. If they do, your self-esteem is likely to benefit from challenging these ideas through action.

- ✔ I avoid trying new activities or launching new ventures because I fear failure, and negative responses or ridicule from others.
- ✔ I doubt my own ability to make a worthwhile contribution to groups or clubs.
- ✔ I don't think that I'm significant enough to make an impact on the world around me.
- ✔ My opinions aren't important and don't really count.
- ✔ Other people are more powerful and influential than I am and so I leave all the action up to them.

Evading new situations can seem to make sense because it saves you from the pain of negative feelings in the immediate and short term. In the longer term, however, this avoidance denies you fully experiencing your life, inhibits your personal expression, stops you acting on your personal values and prevents you from broadening your outlook with new experiences. If you think about this evasion objectively, you're paying one heck of a high price for a fairly meagre return. Inflicting long-term suffering on yourself in order to avoid short-lived pain is detrimental to your emotional health.

Pain is a normal part of life and unavoidable. Don't make things worse for yourself by causing yourself unnecessary and prolonged suffering in an attempt to avoid pain.

Look carefully at how you currently live your life and answer the following questions. (You may find this imagery exercise easier to do if you write down your discoveries.)

- ✔ What do I do to try to get approval from others?

- ✔ Do I go to extreme lengths to quell confrontation or avoid offending others? *Extreme lengths* means going beyond the dictates of social politeness. Examples may include: steering others away from contentious conversational topics, never disagreeing with anyone or offering a counter-opinion, becoming anxious if people around you argue and trying very hard to organise a reconciliation between them.

- ✔ Do I avoid anything that may call attention to myself?

Now vividly imagine what you would do differently if you had healthy robust self-esteem – if you truly believed that you could withstand failure, mistakes, difficulties, opposition or disapproval from others

- ✔ What activities would you be involved in?

- ✔ What opportunities would you seize?

- ✔ What causes or issues would you support?

- ✔ What groups would you be a part of?

The activities you imagine yourself doing point to your personal values.

The *vicious flower* is a popular technique used throughout Cognitive Behavioural Therapy (CBT) to illustrate the effects that attempting to cope with or avoid negative feelings has on the original problem. (You can read more about CBT in our book *CBT For Dummies* and we include other recommended reading in the Appendix). We adapt the vicious flower technique in Figure 15-1 to show you the unhelpful low-self-esteem cycle you may be caught up in. The figure illustrates how trying to save yourself from negative feelings actually feeds back into and reinforces your low self-esteem. Although you're probably doing it unwittingly, the effect is like laying down fertiliser and watering your low-self-esteem Venus flytrap!

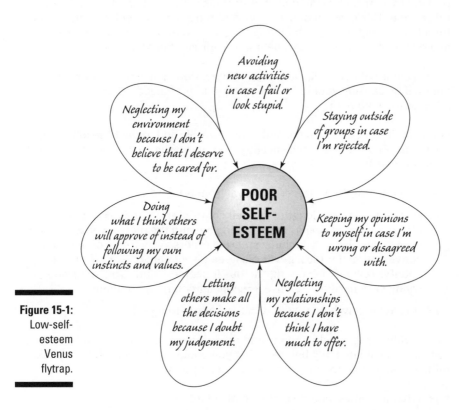

Avoiding new activities in case I fail or look stupid.

Neglecting my environment because I don't believe that I deserve to be cared for.

Staying outside of groups in case I'm rejected.

POOR SELF-ESTEEM

Doing what I think others will approve of instead of following my own instincts and values.

Keeping my opinions to myself in case I'm wrong or disagreed with.

Letting others make all the decisions because I doubt my judgement.

Neglecting my relationships because I don't think I have much to offer.

Figure 15-1:
Low-self-esteem Venus flytrap.

Acting as your low self-esteem dictates can cause many negative long-term effects, such as:

✔ Cheating you of enjoyable experiences

✔ Reinforcing negative and erroneous ideas about yourself

✔ Isolating you from the company and input of others

✔ Depriving you of experiences and information that may disprove your negative self-opinion

We suggest, however, an alternative. You can uproot and compost your Venus flytrap and then plant a fragrant healthy-self-esteem hyacinth in its place. Figure 15-2 demonstrates how healthy behaviours feed feelings of worth and ultimately help your self-esteem to flourish.

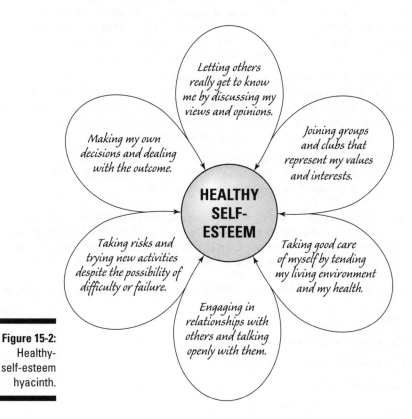

Letting others really get to know me by discussing my views and opinions.

Joining groups and clubs that represent my values and interests.

Making my own decisions and dealing with the outcome.

HEALTHY SELF-ESTEEM

Taking risks and trying new activities despite the possibility of difficulty or failure.

Taking good care of myself by tending my living environment and my health.

Engaging in relationships with others and talking openly with them.

Figure 15-2: Healthy-self-esteem hyacinth.

Taking Stock of Your Values

You may have spent so long with your low self-esteem in the driving seat that you're no longer sure how you lost direction towards your personal values.

To help you re-discover what you're all about as regards personal values, try these exercises:

✔ Speak to a close friend, your partner, a member of your family or your therapist (if you happen to have one) and ask what he or she thinks your personal values are, based on his or her knowledge of you.

The feedback and opinions of a trusted individual in your life can certainly point you in the direction of your personal values. However, don't place his or her opinion above your own. You're asking in order to gather useful information and to help you make up your *own* mind. Be sure to trust your own judgement as well as his or hers.

✔ Think back to when you were less consumed by low self-esteem and feeling more positive and more confident in your own self-worth: What were your personal values at that point. What were your interests? What basic principles did you hold, and what were your personal mottos? What causes or issues were you passionate about?

Don't worry if you can come up with only one or two answers to these questions. You may need to take some time before you can begin to think clearly about what's important to you in life.

Start by beginning a list of your personal values. Even if you only identify a handful, it's enough to be getting on with. You can add to your list at any time as additional ideas about what's important to you come to mind. From your list, you can identify particular behaviours and activities that reflect them.

To give you a bit of guidance, we include a list of broad possible values here:

✔ Career

✔ Causes and charities

✔ Community involvement

✔ Cultural identity

✔ Family life and relationships

✔ Friendship and being part of a group

✔ Knowledge and learning

✔ Nature and wildlife

✔ Politics

✔ Religion and spirituality

✔ Social responsibility

✔ Standards of social conduct such as politeness and respectfulness

✔ Travel

There are many more possibilities than those listed, so don't feel limited in your choices. The following example is designed to give you more ideas about how to dig deeper down into your values.

Jack has had a very poor self-opinion for many years, which became most problematic after his first year of college. When he realised that he eventually needed to enter a competitive job market, he developed anxiety about his abilities and skills and compared himself negatively against his fellow students. Although Jack has now finished his training and has a decent job, he's still dogged by low self-esteem. Here's how Jack answered the earlier questions:

✔ What were my earlier interests before low self-esteem clouded my thinking?

I've always been interested in animal welfare. I love nature and used to be interested in birdwatching. I'm still very interested in the effects of climate change on wildlife even though this has nothing to do with my job. I really enjoy TV programmes about nature and wildlife.

✔ When I was feeling better about myself, what were my principles and personal mottos?

I've always believed that people should treat others as they would like to be treated themselves. I've often thought that hard work pays off in the end. I still subscribe to the idea that we've only got one planet and we should all take personal responsibility for looking after it. Actually, I've got more personal mottos than I thought I did!

✔ When I was younger or at times when I'm not governed by low self-esteem, what issues or causes was I (or am I) passionate about?

When I was studying I was very into Amnesty International. I got really involved in discussions about human rights. I also got involved in an urban anti-litter campaign.

Jack found out that he has some strong personal values that he'd forgotten about due to the masking effect of his low self-esteem. Now he can focus on those neglected values and begin to plan ways in which he can live more in accordance with them.

Don't fall into the common low-self-esteem trap of assuming that other people's values are more valid or worthwhile than your own. Everybody is different, potentially holding different values to everyone else. You may be inclined to share your values with others or be inspired by some of the values that they hold, but try to remain true to what *you* really believe to be important.

Taking steps to live in line with your values

Living a life that reflects your basic values can be easier than you may think. It needn't involve grand gestures or obvious acts of goodwill. Living according to your personal values also doesn't require a lot of time. You can do it every day in small but significant ways, such as the following:

- ✔ Offering to do an elderly neighbour's shopping is an everyday action that reflects your personal value of looking after one another within the community.

- ✔ Recycling is a small daily gesture that reflects your value of being environmentally aware and responsible.

- ✔ Being considerate to other passengers on a busy tube journey by moving along or offering your seat to someone more in need of sitting down reflects your value of politeness and respectfulness.

- ✔ Regularly donating money to a charity reflects the value that cause holds for you.

As these examples demonstrate, you needn't aim for massive value-based actions that the entire world will be forced to notice. You can weave small, pertinent actions into your daily life. Your self-esteem will be nourished considerably when you consistently act in ways that you feel proud of because they are in keeping with your core values.

Start small and aim for consistency in your value-based behaviour. To get started, look at different areas of your life and think about the kind of values you hold for each of them. Small things that you can do to reflect your values may then become more obvious. Jack's example in Figure 15-3 may give you a better idea of how to develop value-based actions of your own. Using this exercise yourself may add some to structure to your personal values evaluation.

1. **Consider the broad categories of: family and relationships; work, career and study; recreation and hobbies; religion and spirituality; community and culture; mental and physical well-being; and your personal living environment. Record what's most important to you about those broad areas of your life.**

   With regard to family for example, it may be most important to you to spend plenty of time with your partner and children. Or perhaps you place emphasis on the importance of keeping in touch with relatives overseas. Your value statements are entirely up to you and your personal circumstances.

2. **Identify one or more actions that you can take to demonstrate your value in each category.**

   Start with small realistic actions like setting up a standing order for a valued cause, getting home from work earlier to eat with the family or joining a community-based initiative.

3. **Keep your values evaluation sheet handy and refer to it as a way of reminding yourself to stick with value-directed behaviour.**

   The more regularly you carry out value-led activities, the more readily they become positive habits.

This exercise can help you to become more focused on living in line with some of your basic values, increase your sense of purpose and involvement with the world around you and have a positive impact on your general self-esteem.

Jack wrote down his basic values and one or two actions to incorporate into his daily life to reflect those values, as shown in Figure 15-3.

Contributing to the kind of world you want to live in

We're not trying to send you out on a mission to right the world's wrongs all by yourself. If you sit down and think for a while, however, you probably have a good idea of the kind of world you ideally want to live in. Of course the reality is that the world is far from ideal in many respects. But instead of getting disheartened about that fact, you can do your bit to contribute towards a better world. The smallest of actions can make a powerful impact on those around you *and* on the world.

Because of your low self-esteem you may feel isolated from the rest of the world. You may feel like an outsider from society and spend much of your time with your head down simply 'going through the motions'. Re-evaluating your perspective and thinking of yourself as a fully fledged member of the human race can be very positive for your self-esteem. Understanding yourself as someone who has significance, simply by dint of being a living being, may empower you and help you to engage more fully with the world around you.

Making steady efforts to contribute towards the kind of world you want to live in also increases your awareness of personal responsibility, which again is good news for your overall sense of worth and purpose. Instead of thinking of yourself as a passive observer, taking personal responsibility for your behaviour and actions puts you in the position of being an active participant.

Jack's values evaluation exercise

Friendships

Value: *Friendships involve mutual support and a lot of 'give and take'.*

Action: *Call my best friend Billy once a week to see how he's doing. Try to see him more often.*

Family relationships

Value: *I believe that family shouldn't be taken for granted, even if we live far apart.*

Action: *Send mum a birthday card and a mother's day card every year. Give my sister a ring and invite her round with the kids for Sunday tea.*

Work, career, study

Value: *Hard work pays off. You're never too old to learn a new skill.*

Action: *Get in to work on time. Sign up for an in-house training course to improve my book-keeping skills.*

Recreation and hobbies

Value: *I think it's important to get enjoyment from my life and be able to unwind.*

Action: *Join a book club. Start doing carpentry in the garage at the weekends. Go bird watching once a month with Billy.*

Religion/spirituality

Value: *Spiritual practice enriches human experience and promotes self-discipline.*

Action: *Learn more about different types of religion that interest me. Spend a few minutes meditating or praying every day.*

Community/cultural community

Value: *Community spirit is great for society.*

Action: *Make an effort to say hello to my neighbours and have a chat when we bump into one another. Join the neighbourhood watch.*

Mental and physical well-being

Value: *Looking after my physical health makes me feel better about life generally. I can take personal responsibility for avoiding low moods by keeping in regular contact with friends.*

Action: *Keep going to the gym. Stop drinking sugary soft drinks and cut down on coffee. Eat some fruit every day. Keep seeing Billy, my sister and other friends every week.*

Personal living environment

Value: *A person's home should be a comfortable and welcoming place.*

Action: *Get those shelves put up in the front room. Keep the flat tidy and nice to come home to after work.*

Figure 15-3:
Jack's
personal
values
evaluation.

Your contributions to your world can be large, small or medium-sized. What's most important is that you recognise your ability to effect change on your environment. Contributions you can make include:

- ✔ Choosing not to drop litter
- ✔ Driving responsibly
- ✔ Being polite and cheerful to others
- ✔ Picking up and disposing of dangerous objects in a park
- ✔ Getting involved with a charitable organisation
- ✔ Doing volunteer work
- ✔ Voting in elections

Re-assessing Your Priorities

When you come to grips with your values, you may find yourself taking another look at how you currently prioritise different aspects of your life. Feelings of low self-esteem may have dictated your priorities for a long time, leading to avoidance. Or perhaps you allowed your low self-esteem to hurl you into pursuing approval from others at all costs. You may be very involved in work because you feel driven to prove yourself and compensate for feelings of worthlessness. In short, your priorities may be based almost wholly around trying to cope with low self-esteem to the expense of your values.

Have a look again at the previous sections in this chapter. You may also want to review your goals (which we address in Chapter 8) and personal commitments (covered in Chapter 14). Now put your healthy-self-esteem hat on. What *are* your priorities? Put pen to paper and draw up a new list of priorities based on your values and what's really most important to you.

Shifting priorities

You can expect your priorities to shift over time. Sometimes major life events such as buying a house, getting into a relationship or having a child can necessitate a change in your thinking about what things you prioritise. Also, negative events such as a change in your health or some other crisis may mean that you need to reshuffle your priorities for a period of time.

A change in your priorities doesn't always mean that your basic values have changed, just that your life circumstances have altered. If you can accept your need to adapt to new situations and still keep your values in sight, your self-esteem need not suffer in the process.

Conflicting priorities

Sometimes your priorities may conflict or contradict one another. Perhaps the most common examples of this situation are commitments to work and home life. Your main priority may be to spend time enjoying your family and yet work may be very busy and the bills need paying. The two things may not be happy bedfellows.

At times, you just need to do the best you can and accept that you're not superman or superwoman. You may need to prioritise work for a while until it's less demanding and you've paid off your debts. Then you can resume putting your family first.

To help preserve a positive self-opinion, give yourself permission to act according to what's most pressing at the time.

Resolving inconsistencies

Despite your best efforts to live in line with your values, low-self-esteem thoughts sometimes rear their ugly heads. Low self-esteem can slide back in like a slippery snake under a door frame or come charging in like a bull in a china shop. Either way, you may find yourself falling back into old low-self-esteem-driven habits.

You can do your best to prevent low self-esteem dictating how you live your life by keeping a regular check on your values and priorities. Ask yourself:

- ✔ Am I acting consistently within ways that reflect my basic values?
- ✔ Am I acting in ways that reflect my priorities?
- ✔ Am I doing small things that I think make a positive contribution to the world?

If the answers are 'No', consider what may be preventing you from doing so; have another look at Figure 15-1 earlier in the chapter.

If you decide that low self-esteem is starting to dictate your every move again, just stop. Re-visit your values and redouble your efforts to act according to whatever is most important to you.

Chapter 16

Developing Self-Discipline

· ·

· ·

Hard work spotlights the character of people: some turn up their sleeves, some turn up their noses, and some don't turn up at all.

— Sam Ewing, writer

Getting more of what you want out of life frequently involves determination, hard work and some short-term discomfort – that's just the way things are. No fairy godmother is going to wave a magic wand and raise your self-esteem level, and you can't take a pill and instantly get to your ideal weight.

A lot of people want to increase their fitness and lose weight. If you tell them that you have a fail-safe method of doing just that, they exclaim excitedly 'Great! What is it?' When they're told that the answer is to eat less and exercise more, their faces fall. Why? Because taking the steps necessary to improve fitness and lose weight require effort and deprivation.

Most people would rather get results without having to pay with blood, sweat and tears. Unfortunately, many of the things in life you desire are hard won. So being prepared to work your backside off, putting up with certain sacrifices (like giving up bacon double cheeseburgers) and keeping on slogging are all essential components of goal attainment. Self-discipline means being able to deprive yourself of gratification in the short term for long-term gain, as well as being able to get on with tasks that are difficult, tedious or distasteful because doing so is in your best interests.

In this chapter we explore some of the attitudes that can underpin poor self-discipline and offer some healthier alternative ways of thinking about persisting with hard work (and getting started in the first place!). We also include a few practical tips to help you stay motivated and focused.

Setting Yourself Up for Success

Don't leave achieving your goal to chance. Developing self-discipline is made somewhat easier by forward planning. The term is *self*-discipline after all, and so the responsibility is on you to make your goal a reality.

Many people decide that they want and need to become more disciplined but then sort of leave it in the lap of the gods. *Thinking* about making changes to your lifestyle, and then just crossing your fingers and hoping that the changes you want will magically occur, can be tempting, but this sort of passive approach flies in the face of everything that can help you actually realise your ambition. If you really want to develop your self-discipline, a proactive stance is required.

The tips outlined in the next sections can help you turn good intentions into actions.

Increasing your self-discipline

Many people struggle with exercising self-discipline even when they can clearly see the desirable outcomes of it.

The great thing about becoming more self-disciplined (apart from being able to realise goals and generally act in your best interests) is that it tends to make you feel good.

Being self-disciplined isn't just about being strict with yourself; it's also about nurturing yourself. Often self-discipline entails taking good care of your health – both mental and physical. For example, taking regular exercise or engaging in a course of study may be a step en route to a long-term goal and they also nurture your body and mind. You may lead a busy life and sometimes neglect to look after yourself (like many of us). It takes some serious self-discipline to make positive lifestyle changes.

The good news is that you probably already have some self-discipline skills but you may not be using them to move in the direction of your goals. For example, keeping your opinions to yourself and biting your tongue in social situations takes self-discipline. The trouble is that repressing your opinion feeds into low self-esteem if it springs from a feeling that your opinions aren't valuable or worth sharing. You can use the principle of self-discipline to urge yourself to engage socially even though you feel anxious about it in the first instance. So becoming more able to self-discipline has real benefits for how you feel in the long run.

The ability to employ appropriate self-discipline is a key characteristic of people with healthy self-esteem. Note the use of the word *appropriate*; we aren't recommending suffering for its own sake. Continuing to do things that give you pleasure while pursuing a goal or course of self-development is important. Short-term pleasure is a good thing, provided that it doesn't carry with it more profound longer-term negative consequences. We encourage you to be happy and to enjoy your life. However, we also believe that you get much more out of life if you're able to discipline yourself when necessary.

Allocating time slots for tasks

Procrastination has stopped many a plan for action dead in its tracks. Putting off onerous tasks is just all too easy. You may tell yourself: 'I'll wait to do it until I feel more like doing it'. Subscribing to this kind of attitude can keep you waiting for a very long time, maybe forever.

Ignoring and delaying unpleasant tasks, however, becomes that much harder when you allocate a specific date and time to them. Try getting out your diary and scheduling in stuff that you've been putting off. Make a commitment to yourself to carry out tasks at the specified time.

Don't choose a date too far in the future otherwise you may just be procrastinating in another manner. If you can complete a task in the next day or so, schedule it in for then: the sooner the better. You usually feel a lot better when you get something distasteful or tedious out of the way quickly.

If you're trying to eat better, schedule a definite time to shop – a time when you aren't hungry or rushed. And if one of your steps to getting fitter is going to the gym three times a week, choose the times, write them in your diary and keep those appointments with yourself.

When dealing with ongoing tasks, fixing definite times to carry them out helps: sticking to a schedule when you've actually *got* a schedule is far easier! So make things simpler for yourself and start timetabling your activities.

Troubleshooting obstacles

You're going to run into obstacles from time to time. These obstacles can make exercising your self-discipline difficult.

Although you can't always foresee trouble spots before you run into them, you can use your knowledge about yourself and your powers of imagination to prepare for possible difficulties. Forewarned is forearmed, as the saying goes.

With your goal or personal commitment in mind, sit down and write out some of the more obvious stumbling blocks you think you'll encounter. Then take time to write down possible ways of surmounting these obstacles when they arise.

When you're troubleshooting for obstacles, you need to consider both concrete events and psychological obstacles. A relatively simple solution often exists to a practical problem, but your thoughts and feelings are the real issue. So when you're developing strategies to surmount potential obstacles, pay close attention to the type of attitude that helps you remain self-disciplined.

Planning ahead for ways of dealing with adversity can help safeguard your good intentions and maintain your self-discipline.

Raj is trying to improve his overall self-esteem. Part of his plan is to take better care of himself through regular healthy eating and daily exercise. Raj also wants to get more socially involved with people from work, and so he's starting to eat with his co-workers at lunch and go out with them on Fridays after work for a drink.

Raj is kindly providing us with an example to show how to anticipate obstacles and plan strategies for dealing with them (see Table 16-1).

Table 16-1	Raj's Potential Problems and Solutions
Potential Obstacle	*Surmounting Strategy*
If I'm feeling very tired I may not have the motivation to cook myself a meal and end up ordering a pizza.	I can freeze some leftovers so that I always have something healthy that I can just reheat in the microwave for those times when I'm too tired to cook.

Potential Obstacle	Surmounting Strategy
If someone I don't know well joins our table for lunch I may feel anxious and be tempted to make an excuse and leave.	I can view this as an opportunity to further my social interaction. I can also talk to the people I do know and feel comfortable with, and yet still force myself to make some conversation with the new person.
We have early meetings some mornings and these may fall on a gym day and prevent me from working out as planned. I may use this as an excuse to miss a day at the gym that week.	I usually have at least a day's warning about early meetings. I can go to the gym on an alternative morning or go at the weekend.

Setting the scene

When you're making efforts to get to grips with self-discipline, getting your external environment in order is helpful. Bringing some organisation into a previously chaotic living or working environment can enable you to see more clearly what needs to be done and also give you the sense of being more on top of things.

Whatever you're trying to be more disciplined about, getting the decks clear can be a great starting point. Many people report feeling generally better and more motivated when their homes and work areas are under control.

Make a schedule of tasks to get your living environment in order over the next few days. Remember to include the points listed below if they're relevant to your situation:

- ✔ Clean your home 'spring clean' style

- ✔ Organise your affairs including filing and opening post

- ✔ Wash and organise your laundry

- ✔ Deal with any outstanding bills, letters and emails

- ✔ Go to the supermarket

- ✔ Decorate your home, hang pictures or change the lighting – whatever makes your living space feel organised and inviting

- ✔ Re-arrange furniture, if possible, to give you a fresh outlook

Also, if you're doing an office-based job or some form of study, think about making some changes to your workspace: turn it into a vibrant and pleasant place to be. Your workspace – be it an office (either within or outside your home), studio, garage or desk area – is ideally a place (or space) conducive to getting on with things. Take action on any relevant points in the following list:

- ✔ Clean your desk, office or workspace.
- ✔ Make sure that you have all the necessary supplies or tools for the task you want to get on with.
- ✔ Ensure that you have adequate lighting.
- ✔ Turn on a radio for some background sound and to prevent feeling isolated.
- ✔ Have some tea or coffee readily available for when you take a break from work or study.

Straightening out and freshening up your home or work environment is relevant even if your particular goal is completely unrelated to either of those areas. The idea is that you're more likely to be focused on your own specific self-discipline prerequisites when you're operating in a disciplined environment.

Even if you're sceptical, try tidying up a bit. Brushing the cobwebs out of the doorframes and giving your living/working areas a shaking up and dusting down can provide more of a boost than you may think.

You don't have to be a super-tidy person to develop self-discipline. But a little extra-imposed order can make a positive shift in your thinking.

Withstanding Your Own Attitudes

Having a low threshold for effort and persistence can derail your best intentions. You may start out on a course of action full of motivation and optimism but surrender the fight when things start to be painful, boring, repetitive and tough.

In your quest to improve your self-esteem you need to do things that are unfamiliar and uncomfortable. You may experience unpleasant emotions such as anxiety when you push yourself out of your comfort zone and into self-esteem enhancing activities. The chances are, though, that you get a sense of achievement from doing so. Your self-esteem benefits as you acquire more self-discipline because you come to realise that you have some control over your life. You're empowered when you realise that you can stand the discomfort associated with overcoming many of life's difficulties and pursuing your specific goals. Self-discipline is important not only for achieving concrete goals as discussed in Chapter 8, but also for living the kind of life you want on a day-to-day basis (for more on this aspect, see Chapter 15).

You may very much want to change an aspect of your lifestyle or reach a personal goal, and yet part of you just doesn't believe that you can see the process through. Some of your lack of confidence is likely to be caused by low self-esteem. Negative beliefs about yourself can certainly give rise to plenty of self-doubt and pessimistic predictions.

Certain attitudes you hold can blight your personal development plans. You may be aware of some of these ideas and not others. Have a look at the low-tolerance attitudes in the next sections; take note of those that apply to you and devise ways to combat them.

'I can't stand feeling like this'

Many people fail to stick with self-disciplined behaviour because they don't believe that they can endure uncomfortable feelings. Perhaps you think that you can't handle the pain of effort, deprivation or other types of unpleasant emotions.

Sure you can. You may not like the feeling but you can stand it. Deciding that you simply can't tolerate unpleasant emotions often leads to all sorts of problematic behaviours, such as overeating, spending money you don't have and misusing drugs or alcohol – just a few of the many behaviours people engage in when trying to escape negative emotions such as sadness, anxiety, anger or guilt.

Although trying to bury your feelings with unhelpful behaviour may provide you with some instant relief, it can cause you a lot of extra trouble down the road.

Most unwelcome feelings pass if you give them enough time. Instead of trying to dull, mask or eliminate strong feelings, give yourself a chance to tolerate them until they naturally subside.

Hold on to a more accurate and helpful attitude such as: 'I don't like feeling this way but I can stand it; it will get better.'

'I can't resist my cravings and urges'

This type of belief really sidetracks goals that involve doing *less* of something (or giving up something altogether), such as overeating or comfort eating, problem drinking, smoking and gambling.

Cravings and urges can certainly be very compelling, but keeping focused on what's most important to you can help you surf through these feelings. For example, is it more important to you to satisfy your immediate craving for a cigarette than to have healthy lungs? Is satisfying your urge to place a bet on a horse today actually more important than having some savings in the bank at the end of the month?

Weigh up the relative importance of giving into urges and cravings in the present against the future benefits to be gained through resisting them. Remind yourself to think beyond how you're feeling now and to consider how you want to feel in the future.

Getting through an intense craving without giving in to it produces very positive feelings of achievement, which can make resisting subsequent cravings and urges less difficult.

Think about cravings in this way: 'It's very hard to resist cravings and urges but I can do it; it's worth it in the long run.'

'This is too hard; it should be easier'

As we mention at the beginning of this chapter, many things worth doing aren't easy. If achieving your goal was *meant* to be easier, it probably *would* be easier.

If you think about it, why should things that are important to you come easily? Does any law of the universe say that good things should be easy to achieve? Sadly, no. And if you look at the evidence, you're likely to see many examples supporting the idea that most people have to put in a fair amount of effort to get what they want out of life.

So you're left with the reality that hard work en route to goal achievement is the norm rather than the exception. You can balk at this concept or roll up your shirtsleeves and get on with things. Holding an attitude that reaching your goals, making lifestyle changes or overcoming low self-esteem issues 'should be easier' is a sure-fire method of discouraging yourself. You may start to resent the whole process and throw in the towel.

Try re-adjusting your attitude to more along the lines of: 'I wish it were easier to achieve my goals but there's no reason it should be easier.' Holding this type of attitude is likely to help you feel more positive about exerting effort and may even enable you to get some enjoyment in the process.

'This is harder for me than for other people'

A grain or three of truth may well reside in this statement. Everyone is different and therefore people have varied skills, aptitudes and limitations. What comes pretty easily to one person may be far more difficult for someone else to achieve. You may find cooking or driving a car simple, whereas a friend may be famous for burning omelettes and failing practical driving tests.

The skills set that you have, naturally or through acquisition, makes completing specific tasks more or less difficult for you. But remember that just because someone else can socialise or study (or any other task for that matter) with more ease than you can, doesn't mean that you can't discover how to do it too.

In addition, bear in mind that we all have different personalities. Some people are more extrovert than others and find giving presentations or hosting a party less daunting than shy and more retiring personalities.

Comparing yourself to others isn't terribly useful. Instead, try to accept the level of difficulty you personally experience on the road to reaching your goals. Otherwise low self-esteem may rear its ugly head and start spouting a whole load of nonsense about others being 'better' or 'more competent' than you are. None of this low self-esteem claptrap is true or helpful.

You may be plain wrong in your assessment of how easy other people find achieving a given task. They may find it just as difficult as you do. You never know, so treat your guesses with a degree of scepticism.

Try taking on board a new belief such as: 'I'm finding this difficult and that's just the way it is. If others find it easier, that's good for them, but I'm allowed to have difficulty with it.'

'It's too boring'

Yep, lots of worthwhile activities can be pretty dull: going to the gym, cleaning the house or studying for an exam often cause you to be seized by a yawning fit. But we come back to the old question of whether putting up with the short-term tedium in the interests of long-term gain is worthwhile. We think such persistence is worthwhile in most cases and hope you will too if you persevere.

A lot of the stuff you have to do to keep your daily life ticking over is rather mundane. You probably don't expect daily chores and duties to be a rollercoaster ride of thrills. Therefore, why should the steps you tread along the path to improved emotional and physical health or other types of goals be a riot? The issue boils down to increasing your tolerance for persisting with boring but beneficial tasks.

Thinking about the problem in a more balanced way – such as 'this is boring but worth doing' – may help you to keep acting in your best interests, even when the task in question is far from interesting.

'This is too painful'

We know it hurts. You often need to push yourself into situations that provoke anxiety, especially when you're trying to overcome certain kinds of emotional problems (such as those we discuss in Chapter 2) or low self-esteem. And feelings of anxiety and the like aren't pleasant; in fact they're downright painful. Depriving yourself of familiar behaviours (such as social withdrawal or other types of avoidance) or something more concrete (such as a cream cake) stings a bit. The old adage contains more than a little truth: 'No pain, no gain'.

Keep reminding yourself that what feels good today may well hurt like anything tomorrow, or the next day. Many of the things you habitually do to make yourself feel better in the here and now have seriously negative knock-on effects in the future.

For instance, take your desire to improve your self-esteem. Avoiding speaking out socially tonight may be less painful in the moment, but what about the effects on your social confidence in the long run? Do you discover anything new? Do you give yourself a chance to see that nothing catastrophic happens?

And what about that cream cake? It tastes good on the way down and soothes your emotions temporarily, but do you give yourself a hard time about submitting to a craving later on?

Sabotaging your goals because persisting with new patterns of behaviour seems too painful is extremely common.

Don't make the common mistake of assuming that you're too fragile to deal with a bit (or a lot) of pain. Stop for a minute and just think about how much pain your low self-esteem or poor fitness (just two possible problems) cause you. The pain of change may be pretty acute but most of the time it's short-lived and less intense than the suffering you experience from your original problem.

Think of the pain associated with goal-driven behaviour as simply a different kind of pain instead of a more powerful or dangerous version of what you typically experience. Embracing the pain of positive action by telling yourself 'This is painful but ultimately it's good for me' can help you get through the discomfort without giving up.

'There must be an easier way'

This attitude can lead you to chop and change strategies without giving any single one a chance to be effective. As soon as the going gets tough (or boring) you can find yourself casting about for another method of getting to where you want to be. This searching around may seem to make sense, but in reality it's rather like blindly driving up and down unsigned roads without a map. These detours mean that you take a lot longer to reach your destination. (Enough with the driving analogies already!)

Remember that if you give a new behavioural or thinking strategy a decent trial run you may be surprised at how effective it can turn out to be. You need to exercise a little patience and a bit of faith.

Many of the techniques that your therapist (if you have one) may suggest and those that we recommend in this book (if we may be so bold) are tried and tested. That means that they've been scientifically tested or proven to be clinically effective – or both. If a technique works for other people with problems similar to your own, reason dictates that it may well work for you too.

Avoid the faulty belief that difficult equals ineffective. In many cases the opposite is true. Practise holding thoughts such as: 'This is tough but I'm going to stick with it until I get some results.'

'I want results right now'

Of course you do. And we'd like to give them to you, but unfortunately we can't. Positive change is cumulative rather than instantaneous; it's a process not an event. You need to be patient. Persistence and patience pay off in the end.

Goal-orientated behaviour involves delaying immediate gratification and waiting for the satisfaction that comes from working towards and eventually achieving your longer-term aims. In other words, after your little tantrum, pick up your rattle, get back in the pram and wait.

To put things a bit more compassionately, wanting to see immediate results for your hard work is understandable. You're likely to get some obvious benefits as you continue to act in accordance with your goals, but you may not get the great eureka moment that you yearn for (see the later section 'Taking things one step at a time' for more help combating impatience).

Think of your efforts as building blocks toward better self-esteem, improved lifestyle and so on. Try this sort of attitude on for size: 'I'd prefer to get positive results right now but I can tolerate waiting for them.'

'I don't want to have to do the same thing over and over again'

One arm curl does not a toned bicep make. Repetition is key to making permanent changes to the way you think and act. In order to bed down a new healthy habit you need to do it over and over again, like building a muscle.

After you adopt a new habit, the repetition seems less obvious and the whole thing takes far less thought and effort. You probably have loads of things you do habitually that you don't even notice, such as taking out the rubbish, doing some exercise or shaving. Discovering how to think and act consistently in goal-enhancing ways is not really that different from acquiring any other type of habit. When you've done something enough times, it becomes automatic.

So keep up the effort and hold on to this philosophy: 'Repetition is boring but if I keep it up it'll eventually become second nature to me.'

Paying Attention to Your Progress

Some of your goals may be finite, like getting a qualification or finding a new job. Once you achieve them you can move onto a different goal. Other goals are ongoing, like making a personal commitment to a healthier lifestyle. In both cases, monitoring your progress and keeping track of the steps you take towards reaching your goals can help keep you motivated and give you the opportunity to pat yourself on the back for a job well done. Being able to see that you're making progress is good for your general self-esteem.

Taking things one step at a time

Outlining steps that eventually lead you to where you want to be can help combat an 'I want results now' attitude:

1. **Write down your goal or ongoing personal commitment at the top of a piece of paper.**

2. **Break your overall goal down into smaller individual steps or sub-goals.**

   If you have an ongoing goal of getting fit, for example, think of milestones you can reach – walking up four flights of stairs without huffing or walking two miles in twenty minutes.

3. **Set realistic end dates for your overall goal and your sub-goals. Think about how long it's likely to take for you to reach your goal (or experience positive benefits in the case of an ongoing personal commitment).**

   Being realistic about how long it's going to take to get where you want to be can help increase your tolerance and patience.

4. **Write your sub-goals and end dates on your calendar and measure your progress.**

Be patient with yourself and be persistent. You'll get there in the end with some faith and hard work. You can give yourself small rewards when you complete essential steps on the way to your ultimate goal, to keep your spirits up. Just be sure that your rewards are reasonable and consistent with your goals.

Your hurry-up instinct can prevent you from sticking doggedly with a course of action because you rapidly lose patience. When you clearly select individual steps or tasks that are in line with your goals, you're more likely to find hidden reservoirs of patience.

The following sections show how to give structure to your pursuit of goals and reassure yourself that you're steadily moving in the right direction.

Making note of small changes

Hard work and self-discipline don't always produce immediate results. Often you're playing a waiting game and the substantial rewards are reaped some way off in the future. So make sure that you make a big deal out of the small positive changes and benefits that occur along the way to reaching your ultimate goal.

Change is frequently subtle and incremental. You can easily overlook small achievements and positive changes unless you make a deliberate effort to highlight them. Pay close attention to all the small steps you successfully take on your journey towards your long-term goals and personal commitments.

If you don't keep a record of your achievements, you may fail to notice that your game plan is actually beginning to work.

Raj understands that he's unlikely to suddenly wake up one morning brimming with healthy self-esteem. To keep himself on the straight and narrow, he's recording small changes, as shown in Table 16-2.

Table 16-2	Raj's Record of Small Changes
Achievement	*Benefit*
I shopped for the week and made myself a healthy meal every evening.	I feel better for eating healthily and have more energy.
I went to the gym three times this week.	I've lost a kilo and I'm proud of myself for sticking with my plan.
I went for a drink with everyone else last Friday.	People were glad that I joined in and I feel more part of the team.
I ate lunch with a few colleagues in the staff room today.	It was more interesting than eating on my own. I enjoyed the conversation and I feel less isolated.

By taking note of his achievements (however small) and the benefits, Raj is more likely to notice subtle improvements in his self-esteem. Recording changes in his mood and general wellbeing can help Raj keep motivated and disciplined.

Use the form in Figure 16-1 to note down what you've achieved, however small or subtle, under the heading 'Achievement'. Remember to be clear and specific. Next record any positive results arising from that particular achievement under the heading 'Benefit'. Again it's important to outline plainly what you've gained from your actions, otherwise it may just feel like a paper exercise. Getting into some detail tends to make the exercise more rewarding and valuable.

Achievement	Benefit

Figure 16-1:
Your record
of small
changes.

Remembering that it's worth doing

We can't emphasise enough the importance of understanding the worth of what you're doing. Why on earth would you continue to put yourself through toil and trouble if you didn't believe that a very good reason lay behind everything?

When exercising self-discipline you need to keep the reasons why your goal is worthwhile at the forefront of your mind, in order to improve your chances of success.

You can generate as many reasons as you like to remind yourself why sticking with your positive course of action is worthwhile. In some ways, the more reasons the better. However, these reasons need to be very compelling and convincing to you. So even if you've got only two or three reasons, as long as they're very strong ones, and as long as you're committed to these actions, they should be enough to pull you through.

Really being able to see the personal value of sticking with a positive course of action is what makes for success. Use your powers of imagination. Sit down, close your eyes and vividly imagine yourself having reached your goal or altered your lifestyle for the better. Identify what you have to gain by reaching your goal. Also identify what you stand to lose by giving up. Record both the positives of carrying on and the negatives of giving up as compelling reasons for goal-directed action.

Here are Raj's reasons why persevering is worthwhile:

✔ Looking after myself by eating well and exercising gives me more energy and I feel physically stronger. I also have a better body image, which gives me more confidence.

✔ Cooking and going to the gym imposes a routine that lifts my overall mood and I have fewer bouts of feeling depressed.

✔ Keeping up the socialising with co-workers proves to me that I can make interesting conversation and that I'm liked by others.

✔ Combining all these points gives me a stronger sense of self-worth.

Being your own cheerleader

'Two, four, six, eight! Who do we appreciate? Go Team!' Or words to that effect. Giving yourself a good dose of cheering can really boost your morale.

Think about the positive effect the roar of the crowd in the stands has on footballers. Giving yourself a vigorous pep talk can re-ignite flagging energy and motivation.

Other people may sometimes notice the positive changes and do the cheering for you, which is great. But even if others aren't aware of your hard-won achievements you can be your own cheering section.

Give yourself a big round of applause or even a standing ovation when you know that you deserve one. We mean this metaphorically. We don't actually expect you to stand in front of the mirror clapping ferociously (although you can if you want to). Simply saying to yourself 'I've done really well' may be your equivalent of cheering. The important thing is to give yourself credit when credit is due, however you choose to do it.

You may find keeping a record of positive comments that others have made about your progress useful. You can refer to it whenever you feel a lull in motivation. Also try writing down words of recognition and encouragement to yourself. If you have low self-esteem, you're probably not in the habit of paying yourself compliments but it's important that you do it. Writing positive self-messages down can help you really believe that you deserve praise.

Offering Yourself Rewards and Penalties

The satisfaction and benefits you get from achieving your aims are a reward in themselves. By the same token, the lack of benefits associated with not sticking to your guns and reaching your goals is a pretty stiff penalty. However, some people find that using a reward and penalty system helps them to remain self-disciplined.

You can decide for yourself whether or not rewards are likely to provide you with additional incentive and whether penalties are likely to work for you as an effective deterrent.

Treating yourself

If you decide to give yourself periodic rewards for sticking with goal-directed behaviour, we suggest that you do so in a structured way. A structure makes the reward more valuable to you and prevents you from overdoing it.

Decide on what your reward is going to be in advance and make it something that's in proportion to the nature of your achievement. Your reward needs to be something that you really want to get so that it serves the function of providing you with an incentive (kind of goes without saying), but not something that fundamentally undermines your self-discipline regime. Therefore, a dozen jam doughnuts is an inappropriate reward for losing 20 kilos. Similarly, a diamond ring is also a bit of an excessive reward for doing your tax return on time (maybe not for everyone, but you have to keep your personal financial situation in mind).

Also decide on when you get the reward. Remember you need to work for your reward for it to be valuable. If you give it to yourself too easily or quickly, the reward loses some of its appeal.

Here's how Raj structured his reward scheme:

- ✔ After one month of going to the gym three times each week, I'll reward myself with a new pair of trainers.
- ✔ After two months of eating lunch with my co-workers, I'll reward myself by going to a concert that I really want to see.

Giving yourself a fine

The most common form of self-imposed penalty is probably denying yourself a pre-planned reward. Raj doesn't get the trainers or the night out at the concert if he fails to meet the terms of his own agreement.

You can devise stiff penalties for yourself if you think this approach helps you to stick to your objectives, although you need to be wary of giving yourself fines that are so stiff that you don't honour them. You may end up letting yourself off the hook simply because the fine's self-imposed and you can.

You don't want to discourage yourself. The purpose of a fine is to deter you from reneging on your personal commitments, not to punish you.

As with rewards, keep your fines appropriate to the offence. Also be clear in advance about what the penalty is going to be and when it applies.

Here's Raj's penalty plan:

- ✔ If I fail to go to the gym for an entire week, I have to devote the weekend to weeding my sisters' jungle of a garden.
- ✔ If I avoid going out for Friday night drinks with my co-workers two weeks out of the month, I have to volunteer to take the minutes at the next two staff meetings.

Raj hates gardening and taking minutes at staff meetings and so these penalties are appropriate for him. His proposed penalties are neither too stiff nor too soft. They are also the sort of penalties that are tricky to back out of when he's committed to them. Neither of these penalties is going to do him or anyone else any damage (quite the opposite in fact – his sister will probably be delighted) and so this fact is also in their favour. If you're going to use fines make sure that they meet the criteria that Raj's do.

Part VI
The Part of Tens

'I'm sorry Norman isn't eating with
us but his low self-esteem
makes socialising almost impossible.'

In this part . . .

We collect a lot of core information about the principles underpinning healthy self-esteem in these chapters. We list ten key traits exhibited by people with solid self-esteem, ten habits that you can adopt to improve your own sense of worth and ten sources of extra inspiration that can also do wonders for your mood.

Chapter 17

Ten Hallmarks of Healthy Self-Esteem

In This Chapter

▶ Recognising the key characteristics of healthy self-esteem

▶ Understanding how behaviour and attitude affect self-esteem

Self-esteem is not something that you have or don't have. Happily, you can develop and improve your self-esteem through deliberate effort.

In this chapter we outline ten important characteristics that people with robust self-esteem exhibit. Albert Ellis, an American psychologist who founded a school of psychotherapy called 'Rational emotive behaviour therapy', considered many of the characteristics included in this chapter to be hallmarks of 'high-functioning' individuals. These people have an appreciation of their own intrinsic worth, derive satisfaction from daily life and deal effectively with problems.

When you recognise these characteristics of healthy self-esteem in yourself and others, you can then make a conscious effort to adopt and consolidate them through your attitude and behaviour (check out Chapter 18 for more on honing these habits in order to get optimum benefit).

Engaging in Vitally Absorbing Activities

If you have a healthy opinion of yourself you're likely to have one or more interests outside of your work and family life. You may be really passionate about these activities, such as immersing yourself in music or art, or just dip in and out of them, such as trying out various types of sport.

People with a healthy, realistic self-opinion are able to try out new things without worrying unduly about 'being good at them' or about the possibility of making mistakes. Taking the risk of starting a new sport, for example, helps you to realise that mistakes are part of the discovery and you needn't be ashamed of them. Finding out how to accept your mistakes and limitations is a major part of developing and maintaining healthy self-esteem. By the same token, developing competency at a new skill gives your confidence a real boost, proving that you have the ability to grow and change.

Engaging in activities that truly interest you also helps to relieve stress and maximise your enjoyment of life. Getting absorbed in hobbies allows you to take your mind off everyday concerns and give it (and your body) a much-needed break. Allocating time to enjoyable pursuits is a way of treating yourself with respect.

Being Genuinely Interested in Others

Healthy self-esteem gives you the freedom to really pay attention to people around you. Because your mind isn't occupied with constant worries about what others may be thinking of you, you have the mental space to really get to know others.

People are fascinating – you included! Being able to recognise yourself as a complex multi-faceted worthwhile person means that you can do the same with those around you. Instead of using other people's reactions to you as a gauge for determining your own self-worth, you can allow yourself to simply enjoy their company.

Try observing someone who has healthy self-esteem while he's engaged in a conversation. The chances are that he looks like he's really listening to the other person, making good eye contact and asking questions. He also probably remembers a lot about the conversation afterwards, because his attention is focused more on what he's doing and less on how well he's doing it.

Putting Yourself First – and Others a Close Second

Putting yourself first is not the same as being selfish or self-absorbed. Sayings such as 'looking out for number one' often carry the implication that you don't care about other people very much, but that isn't what we mean by putting yourself first. Having a healthy interest in yourself and your own well-being means that you strive to get your own needs met, though not at the expense of others.

How does this work as regards having partners and children or even friends? The answer is that unless you look after yourself, you don't have many resources to draw upon when looking after the people you love. The principle is the one that a flight attendant uses when advising parents to put on their own oxygen masks *before* putting on their child's. If you're suffering the effects of insufficient oxygen you're not going to be of much use to your child. Equally if you're exhausted from doing everything for other people, while ignoring your own needs, your ability to be a responsive parent, spouse and friend eventually suffers. Getting support when you need it, asking for help, saying 'No' to unreasonable or unmanageable requests, doing things that you want to do and generally taking good care of yourself are all hallmarks of healthy self-esteem.

These concepts may sound foreign and uncomfortable to you if you've suffered from low self-esteem for many years. Perhaps you've always believed that other people's needs and desires are more valid than your own. You may even think that regularly sacrificing your own needs for those of others around you is noble. The good news is that you can believe that your own needs are as valid as anyone else's *and* also make appropriate sacrifices for others. Of course, sometimes a person in your life needs a little more from you than usual – children and spouses need daily care, after all. The key point to remember is that although putting the needs of others before your own at certain times is wholly appropriate, you need to return to looking after yourself when the crisis has passed. You can't carry someone else for a while if you haven't got the strength to lift him.

You look after others because you care about them and recognise when they need your support. Therefore, if your goal is to develop healthy self-esteem, you need to treat yourself like someone who also deserves care and attention.

Taking Personal Responsibility

Personal responsibility involves acknowledging that you're the one who decides how to feel about events in your life. The way in which you think about what happens has a significant impact on your feelings (Chapter 2 has more on this connection between thoughts and feelings).

People with healthy self-esteem recognise that personal events contribute to how they feel, but also that the meanings they add to these events determine the quality of those feelings.

Of course, when bad things happen, you experience negative emotions. But you can practise thinking in ways that prevent negative feelings from becoming unnecessarily long-lasting and destructive.

Generally healthy and appropriate feelings such as disappointment and sadness lead to problem solving, whereas extreme emotions (for example, shame and depression) lead to problematic behaviours of withdrawal and giving up.

People who have robust self-esteem pick themselves up and dust themselves down when life gets tough. When they mess up they face up to the situation while continuing to think of themselves as basically okay individuals. This ability is in large part due to the fact that they're able to differentiate between making mistakes, failing or behaving badly, and *being* a 'failure' or a 'bad' person. (See Chapter 4 for more about discovering how to avoid judging the whole of yourself on the basis of one or two aspects.)

When you take personal responsibility for your thoughts, feelings and deeds, you empower yourself, moving out of a passive role into a proactive position. Thus, even if your boss criticises your work, he doesn't *make* you depressed and full of self-loathing. Instead, he provides a negative event and you decide how to think and feel about it. Taking appropriate responsibility for your thinking, behaviour and emotional reactions is therefore an optimistic standpoint, and shows that you have a degree of control over how you choose to respond to life events even when you have little or no control over the events themselves. Taking responsibility also means that your overall view of yourself is something that you can improve and enhance.

Harnessing your thinking takes time and practice. Feelings of depression, guilt and anxiety can be hard to shift on your own. Take a look at Chapter 2 where we discuss more fully the effects of low self-esteem.

Being a Flexible Thinker

Flexible thinking involves acknowledging and accepting that life doesn't always fulfil your personal preferences. However much you may want a particular event to happen (or *not* to happen), the universe sometimes refuses to co-operate. Frequently, people take a strong preference for personal performance or life conditions and turn it into a rigid demand leaving no room for error or deviation (see more on this in Chapter 4). Unfortunately, if you place demands upon yourself and you're unable to meet them, the result can be bad news for your self-esteem. Equally if you put demands upon your life conditions and random bad events happen, you're likely to be hit hard emotionally and have difficulty adjusting.

Thinking in a flexible way helps you to accept your own limitations and bounce back from undesirable life events. A flexible thinker understands that life is chock-full of uncertainty and that much of what happens is beyond human control.

Pursuing Personal Goals

Human beings tend to be happiest when they're actively pursuing personal goals. Working towards goals gives a purpose to everyday life that can fuel self-esteem. Although achieving goals can certainly be very satisfying and boost confidence, the journey *towards* a goal can itself be as important as the end result. En route to a specific long-term goal you're likely to reach smaller milestones (sub-goals), which is a rewarding experience. You may also discover more about what your interests and values are along the way.

People with healthy self-esteem have confidence in their ability to achieve realistic long, medium and short-term goals. Therefore, they can take risks, push themselves and tolerate short-term discomfort in the pursuit of longer-term gain. Giving yourself goals helps you to take a hopeful, optimistic attitude about your future. Put simply, setting goals means that you're investing in yourself and your future. Being engaged in pursuing a goal of personal or professional development (Chapter 8 speaks to this) helps you to feel like a fully fledged member of the human race, which is a vital aspect of healthy self-esteem.

Allowing Others to Have Their Own Opinions about You

Caring about what others think of you is part of being a socially well-adjusted individual. As social animals we strive for acceptance and like to feel that we belong. The reality is, however, that not everyone is going to like you all the time. Everybody faces rejection at some point in their lives.

If your self-esteem is low you probably place too much emphasis on being liked and accepted by others. You can find yourself surrendering parts of your personality in order to fit in with social groups or going to extreme lengths to try and gain approval. You worry when you sense that someone has a poor opinion of you and make strenuous efforts to get him to change his mind.

Placing more importance on what others think of you than on your own knowledge of yourself leaves you vulnerable to emotional disturbance at the first whiff of disapproval. Your self-esteem jumps up and down like a jack rabbit depending on the responses you get from others.

People with healthy self-esteem value the opinion of others and make efforts to be socially accepted. They stop short, however, of deciding that what others think of them is all-important. Accepting that other people are going to form their own opinions about you – and that you can live with whatever those opinions may be – contributes significantly towards healthy self-esteem.

Sharing Yourself with Others

Letting others get to know you through open conversation – expressing your opinions, tastes and interests – is the bedrock of forming friendships. Sometimes low self-esteem can really impair your ability to just be yourself. You may withhold personal information about yourself for fear of being rejected. You may be so worried about being liked that you bow to conformity and deprive others of getting to know the real you with all your idiosyncrasies. Sharing yourself with others may feel like a risky thing to do at first but with practice it becomes second nature. Remind yourself that you're unique and entitled to your own way of being – regardless of whether or not everyone else agrees with you. Give yourself and others the right to be different.

Getting Grateful

Gratitude is a wonderful thing, helping you to extract the good out of your experiences and find the silver lining around the clouds. Being grateful also contributes significantly to feelings of contentment and happiness. People with healthy self-esteem are grateful for positive aspects of themselves and their lives. If you suffer with low self-esteem you probably spend more time dwelling on your dissatisfactions with yourself and your life.

Try making a deliberate effort to gather things to be grateful for, however small or trivial they may seem. Put pen to paper and keep a running 'gratitude list'. Remember to include circumstances and personal traits that you may take for granted. Try to add a few items to your list every day over a period of two weeks. One of our clients from years ago had a real talent for 'gratitude gathering'. He included items on his list such as 'my wide smile and infectious laugh, the Rolling Stones, adequate street lighting on my road and healthy ready-made meals' (not surprisingly, he was also grateful for microwaves!).

Living with Laughter

The age-old adage 'laughter is the best medicine' contains a lot of truth. One of the hallmarks of healthy self-esteem is the ability to take a lighter attitude towards life. People with a healthy sense of their own worth frequently also have a good sense of humour. They are able to laugh at their own foibles and at the mishaps that life throws their way. (Not *all* the time of course – some things are no laughing matter.)

Laughter makes you feel better about yourself and pretty much everything else. A good sense of humour is also a very attractive trait. Try looking for the funny side in all sorts of situations and monitor the effect this response has on your mood and self-esteem.

Chapter 18

Ten Habits for Honing Healthy Self-Esteem

In This Chapter

▶ Developing habits that promote healthy self-esteem

▶ Committing yourself to daily practice

*W*e mention more than once throughout this book that healthy self-esteem requires effort and maintenance, and at the risk of being dull, we repeat this advice again here: If you want to maintain a healthy positive opinion of yourself, you have to work at it! There, we said it.

In this chapter we outline ten key habits for looking after your self-esteem. You may already possess some of these behaviours, whereas others may be new and require some getting used to. The important thing to remember is that you need to practise these behaviours deliberately and regularly in order for them to impact on your self-esteem. Practice and repetition is necessary to turn new healthy behaviours into habits.

Resisting Rumination

Rumination is the process of turning something over and over in your mind. You may take a recent event and rehash it again and again in your mind: 'Did I say anything stupid?' or 'I should have done things differently' are popular ruminations on the past. Or you may worry about an upcoming event and all the things that can go wrong.

Ruminations after an event are pointless because you can't do anything to change the past. They are also potentially damaging to your self-esteem because the tendency is to review your performance negatively. You usually end up feeling worse because you're likely to over-accentuate anything that didn't go smoothly.

Worrying excessively about an upcoming event is equally pointless because you can't change something that hasn't happened yet. The chances are that your future-focused ruminations dwell on possible disasters rather than on practical preparations for the task at hand.

Both past- and future-focused ruminations are faulty attempts at problem solving:

✔ Reviewing a past event over and over in your mind rarely helps you to avoid making the same mistakes in the future. In fact, you may simply magnify your errors and beat yourself up about them.

✔ Worrying about a future event doesn't prepare you for potential problems, but instead fills you with dread and undermines your confidence.

Neither rumination leads to effective problem solving and both lead to self-condemnation.

Instead of destructive rumination, strive to extract the good from a past situation and refuse to dwell upon the less-good or what may go wrong in the future.

Like everyone else, you have millions of random thoughts going through your mind everyday. Although you can't control which thoughts you have, you can choose to ignore some of them. You can choose *not* to seize upon destructive thoughts and instead practise letting them pass through your mind.

Giving Yourself Credit

Take time to give yourself a pat on the back for your efforts. When you work hard at something such as a project for work, gaining a new skill or on your psychological wellbeing (perhaps with a self-help book like this one), give yourself some credit. People with low self-esteem are often too quick to dismiss their efforts as 'not good enough' or 'not amounting to anything'.

Try focusing on the positive work that you put into a project and less on the outcome. Obviously outcomes are important and the idea is to try and elicit a good result, but remember that achieving your goals can take time, patience and persistence. Give yourself regular encouragement and even make a written record of your efforts. Also, remember to take note of small improvements and achievements, not just the big obvious ones. Sometimes the smallest changes can make the biggest difference.

People with low self-esteem frequently attribute success to other factors rather than to themselves. 'It was just luck', 'Someone else allowed me to achieve that aim' or 'Anyone can do what I do' may be familiar phrases to you. Stop deflecting your own contribution to your achievements and claim rightful credit. Doing so improves your confidence in your ability to reach goals and feeds into healthy self-esteem.

Lots of things are worth doing for their own sake – and not for a concrete outcome. Instead of looking solely for a 'success', recognise any discovery, growth, enjoyment or other benefits you experience through your pursuit of a given goal.

Treating Yourself with Respect

If you want to increase your self-esteem, treating yourself respectfully makes a lot of sense. All too often people with low self-esteem call themselves unpleasant (and unfair) names. You may find yourself thinking or saying out loud things like 'I'm such a loser', 'I'm so fat and ugly' or 'What an idiot I am!' Condemning your actions harshly may also be familiar to you: 'I totally messed that up' or 'Only a total waste of space like me would have made that mistake' are examples of damaging self-talk. You may also use more profane language (unprintable here) to describe yourself and your actions, the sorts of things you may never dream of saying to someone else (certainly not to someone you care about and respect). Put a stop to the abusive talk!

Bullying yourself is counterproductive. Perhaps you think that you deserve the abuse. Happily, you're wrong. Whatever the situation, you deserve to be treated with respect. Or maybe you believe that being cruel to yourself may bolster your motivation to succeed. Wrong again. You're more likely to end up feeling demoralised and depressed.

Think about how you speak to someone you care about. You probably strive to encourage rather than undermine. You're also probably fair and accurate with any criticism. Use the same tactic with yourself. By treating yourself respectfully you stand a much better chance of developing true self-respect. Instead of calling yourself 'a loser', fairly appraise your *actions*. Try saying: 'Okay, I made an error, but let's see how I can correct it or what lessons I can take from it.'

See Chapter 4 for more on speaking to yourself respectfully.

Engaging with Your Environment

Engaging with and tending to your personal environment are important parts of keeping your self-esteem healthy. Your environment includes your living space, workspace, community, other people and even the wider world in which everyone lives.

If your self-esteem is low, you may be tempted to shut yourself off from the rest of the world. You may feel like you're simply going through the motions and not taking in much that goes on around you. You may also neglect your living environment, allowing it to become chaotic and (in some cases) even filthy. Keeping your head down and living in a bit of a 'pit' frequently leads to (or worsens) feelings of depression and hopelessness. Think of how you tend to a person, pet or plant that you love and want to thrive. Try treating yourself with the same care that you bestow upon someone or something you love.

Investing in Your Relationships

Spending time with people who you like and are interested in does a lot to lift your mood. Other people may remind you of your good points or offer you support when you're going through a difficult time. Don't be afraid to lean on others a little every now and then. Your friends are probably very happy to provide a helping hand. If you keep your feelings to yourself, you deprive your friends and family of the opportunity to offer support.

You may want to stay away from people when your self-esteem is low and you feel as if you have nothing to offer socially. Or you may worry that other people don't like you or find you boring. The chances are, however, that you have more to offer than you think. You don't have to be super-entertaining; just being there is enough. Instead of focusing on your mood and negative thoughts, turn your attention towards the people you're with. When you find your mind wandering into dark thoughts, pull your attention back to the conversation. Asking questions and making eye contact can help you to stay mentally present.

Social withdrawal and isolation give you too much time to dwell on your negative thoughts about yourself. Your self-esteem is probably remaining low because you're not exposing yourself to contradictory evidence. Being in the company of others can provide proof that your negative thoughts about yourself are inaccurate. Invest time and energy in maintaining your current relationships via regular contact and open communication. You may also want to take newer relationships or acquaintances further. Being around others can really help to give you a brighter perspective on things. When your social life has been neglected for a long time, consider joining a group or a class. Meeting up with people who share your interests can provide a springboard into new friendships.

Making Time for Your Hobbies

Hobbies are important because they remind you who you really are and what you're all about, which can be a real boon to your self-esteem. They also give your life an extra sense of enjoyment and fulfilment. Too often hobbies fall by the wayside in favour of work and home-life obligations. True, during busy times or crisis periods, they may need to be relegated to the back seat, but given the busy lifestyles many people lead, hobbies never get a look in unless you purposely carve out time for them. Try claiming back time to pursue your hobbies and interests.

Even if you find your day-to-day routine and work life interesting (and if you do, great), they are often a means to an end. The mortgage or rent needs to be paid, mouths need feeding, laundry needs washing and so on. Plenty of satisfaction is to be had in performing your daily duties, but your less practical side may benefit from some attention as well. Even an hour or two at the weekend or half an hour during week-nights may be enough for you to indulge in a little 'hobby happiness'.

Recognising Your Strengths

People with a poor self-image generally spend much too much time thinking about their failings and weaknesses and completely ignore or discount their strengths. This way of thinking can become such an ingrained habit that you may no longer even be able to remember any of your strengths. No doubt you've got them but for the life of you, you just can't conjure up what they may be. In this situation, try paying attention to the positive things that others say about you. Write positive feedback down and force yourself to review it everyday. You may also benefit by taking a page from the positive psychology movement and complete a signature strengths questionnaire (such as the one online at www.authentichappiness.sas.upenn.edu). You may be very pleasantly surprised by what you find out about yourself!

Cherishing Your Uniqueness

No one else on the planet is quite like you. Everything about you – all your traits, behaviours, experiences, good, bad and neutral aspects – make you who you are. And you are unique. Maybe you compare yourself to others regularly and come off worst. Repeated negative self-comparison against others can really bash your self-esteem.

Try instead to value and hold dear your own individuality. By all means appreciate and value other people, but also remember to value your own input into this world.

Being Compassionate towards Others

Self-esteem is a double-edged sword. Being accepting and compassionate towards yourself necessitates doing likewise with others. After all, no one is perfect (think how weird and unnatural that would be).

Sometimes people with low self-esteem are also harsh critics of those around them. Yet being hard on others generally brings only temporary relief and is likely to make you feel worse in the long run. Recognise that what you're doing is trying to compensate for your own low self-opinion.

Resolve to be more fair and compassionate in your judgement of other people. By doing so you increase your chances of becoming more self-accepting. What's good for the goose is good for the gander.

Keeping Yourself Healthy

Looking after your physical health has a definite positive impact on your psychological health. Improving your diet and getting more exercise can help lift your mood. Animals that are kept in poor conditions, poorly fed and under-stimulated show signs of lassitude and depression. Human beings are animals and experience the same effects under similar circumstances. Through lack of exercise and eating junk food we become fatigued and apathetic.

If you're feeling depressed the last thing you may feel like doing is going for a brisk walk or fixing yourself a healthy meal. Far more inviting may be the idea of cracking open a bottle of wine, ordering a pizza and flaking out in front of the telly. No harm in doing this every now and then, of course, but when this behaviour becomes habitual you can become stuck in a vicious circle. The less you do to look after your physical health, the worse you feel emotionally.

Even though you feel dog-tired, you may be pleasantly surprised by how energised you feel after a workout. Exercise releases 'feel-good' chemicals in your brain called endorphins, which provide a sense of wellbeing and pain relief.

Review your lifestyle and make a determined attempt to follow these tips:

- ✔ Avoid excessive alcohol consumption (medical guidelines are a *maximum* of 14 units per week for women and 21 units per week for men).
- ✔ Drink plenty of water (a litre a day).
- ✔ Eat plenty of fresh fruit and vegetables.
- ✔ Exercise vigorously for around thirty minutes, three to four times per week.
- ✔ Reduce your caffeine intake (try decaf or herbal teas).

Monitor the effects that adhering to a healthier lifestyle have on your general mood and your self-opinion. If the effects are positive (and we bet they are) stick with it!

Chapter 19

Ten Ways to Give Your Self-Esteem a Lift

In This Chapter

▶ Buoying up flagging spirits

▶ Safeguarding your self-esteem

Despite your best efforts to truly appreciate yourself, some days are going to be harder than others. During these difficult times, when you may find yourself returning to old self-critical ways of thinking, seeking outside inspiration is useful. The suggestions in this chapter help you to get back on the road to healthy self-opinion. Using them more regularly can also keep your self-esteem robust and safe from self-sabotage.

Making the Most of Music

Music is an excellent form of inspiration, motivating you when you're running out of steam and calming you down when you're stressed. (Some studies claim that listening to upbeat music during exercise makes you think you're exerting less energy than you really are.)

Certain songs can make you feel more positive about yourself and your life because of their tempo or instrumental elements, or because the lyrics resonate and remind you that you're a worthwhile and significant individual. Other songs may remind you of pleasant times or people who are important to you.

Incorporate feel-good music into your everyday life. Using an mp3 player on public transport, putting on some background music while cooking, or tuning into some soothing classical when driving can make doing everyday tasks more pleasantly melodic and brighten your outlook. Seek out music that helps you feel good whenever you need an extra boost.

When you've got the blues, don't pull the blinds down and listen to Leonard Cohen tracks (not meaning to suggest that Leonard isn't a consummate song-writer.) When you're down, listening to music that you like but that isn't going to lift you into a more positive frame of mind can be tempting. Instead, leave your dirges and requiems for another day.

Reading Books and Stories

A whole load of literature from down the ages portrays stalwart characters who demonstrate confidence and genuine self-esteem. Reading about characters who are confident or who overcome adversity against the odds (real or fictitious) can remind you of how you want to act and feel yourself. Try imitating some of the attitudes or actions your favourite literary characters exhibit with a view to lifting your self-esteem.

I (RB) have a collection of Oscar Wilde short stories that I pull out from time to time. One of my favourite stories is *The Happy Prince*, because the two main characters demonstrate exceptional self-sacrifice in the interests of helping the poor. The prince is adored and beautiful but is truly humble, whilst the sparrow overcomes his initial selfishness and arrogance. The tale is a sadly beautiful little story that reminds me that ordinary individuals are capable of extraordinary acts of kindness.

Take some time to make a list of your best-loved pieces of literature; don't worry whether the list includes something as lofty as Shakespeare or a best-selling crime novel. What matters is what the writing means to you, not how grand the source. Think about stories that remind you to think of yourself as a complex multidimensional human being. Look for story lines or themes that inspire you to live according to your personal values (for more on this aspect, see Chapter 15). Keep your list of favourite reading material in a place where it's easy to find and refer to it when you need an inspirational boost. Pick a book from your list and re-read a few pages or passages.

Ask yourself the following questions as a guide when compiling your personal library of inspiration:

- ✔ What is the theme of the story, poem or passage that you like?
- ✔ What are the core values or philosophies in the story that resonate with you?
- ✔ What are the traits demonstrated by the characters that you also appreciate in yourself?

Collections of short stories or poetry are excellent to keep close at hand. Their brevity means that you can easily dip into them for instant inspiration. Alternatively, you can highlight and mark specific sections of novels or plays that you find useful and inspirational.

Reviewing Fantastic Films

Oh the fun, fascination, frivolity and fortitude found by film fanatics! (That sentence was an attempt to amuse ourselves with some alliteration.) Films and television programmes can be valuable sources of inspiration in your quest to adopt and maintain solid self-esteem. You can use them in the same way as literature (see the preceding section). The added bonus is that film also provides a visual component.

Compile a list of your top ten feel-good film favourites. Remember to choose films with positive themes and characters that model good self-esteem. You can pick a film to watch again (or even just a part of it) to remind and inspire yourself of self-esteem-enhancing actions and attitudes.

Mirroring a Role Model

You can take inspiration from people both real and fictional.

Choosing a role model can help you to act in accordance with your goal of achieving solid self-esteem. Your role model can be anyone – someone you know well, someone you know less well or even a character from a novel or film. Look for people who seem to embody true self-appreciation. By this we mean people who readily accept their limitations, flaws and errors without condemning themselves in the process. Look for people who are able to remain modest and yet accept compliments and acknowledge their strengths.

When you've selected one or more role models, observe how they act, what they say and how they carry themselves. Then try to incorporate these traits into your own daily life. Chapter 8 discusses the use of role models more extensively.

Good self-esteem is not about thinking of yourself as superior to others or above criticism; instead, healthy self-esteem involves truly believing that your human worth is on a par with everyone else's.

Taking Heart from Everyday Occurrences

You probably encounter many sources of inspiration in your everyday life. You may not notice them, however, because you're busy rushing about caught up in your own thoughts or because your low self-esteem prevents you from feeling part of the rest of the world.

In general, your mood responds positively to looking outside of yourself and becoming involved in your environment. Doing so can stop you feeling depressed and distract you from your worries.

Take a look around you as you go about your business and make note of the positive interactions you have with people. Did the shopkeeper make small talk with you? Did you receive a smile from someone in passing? Also look for caring behaviour between others. Notice someone helping a mother with her pram up the stairs or charitable acts that you may read about in the paper. Think about your day-to-day behaviour towards your family, friends and co-workers and their behaviour towards you. You can all too easily take these daily interactions for granted and forget the value they hold. Even the tiniest of occurrences where you treat others like worthwhile individuals and they act in kind are vastly important. You can make an effort to acknowledge these small events and use them as evidence to support the belief that you're an okay person.

By taking deliberate notice of humanity in action your belief that the world is largely a wonderful place may be bolstered. Taking an optimistic outlook towards others, the world and yourself is a vital part of building healthy self-esteem.

Acting Altruistically

Altruism is the practice of acting in a selfless way for the benefit of others. People tend to feel better about themselves when they behave in ways that do others good.

Altruistic actions may include small concessions such as giving way to another vehicle or picking up some shopping for an elderly relative. You may also choose to get involved in more far-reaching acts of altruism by becoming involved in a charity. Volunteering your time can be rewarding on many levels, not only through the benefit to your self-esteem but also because you may end up meeting like-minded people and forming new friendships. Research shows that active involvement in good causes that are consistent with your own personal values helps to prevent depression.

Spend a little time identifying your values (you may want to revisit Chapter 15) and investigate organisations whose aims correspond with them.

Engaging in Spiritual Pursuits

Spiritual pursuits don't necessarily have to be religion-based although many are. Mindfulness and other schools of meditation are quite popular at the moment and have spiritual elements to them. Meditative practice has also been shown to have positive effects on depression.

One of the main benefits of pursuing some form of spiritual practice is the emphasis placed on human worth. The majority of spiritual schools hold individual worth as sacrosanct and this aspect can be a very positive message for those battling with low self-opinion. Many religious schools also promote the principle of condemning the sin but forgiving the sinner, a message in keeping with taking responsibility for wrongdoing but also employing self-forgiveness and compassion. So give some thought to developing your spiritual side in whatever manner suits you.

Appreciating Art and Culture

You don't have to be a great artist or art buff to appreciate a sculpture or a painting. You can make your own decisions about a piece of art: right or wrong doesn't enter into it, your personal reaction is what's important.

Cinema, dance, public statues and comic book illustrations (to name but a few) are all forms of art, and so your options aren't limited to Monet or Dalí (to name but two). In addition, cultural displays of dance, food, dress or music can be both interesting and inspiring. Discovering other cultures, and often realising how similar everyone is in many respects, can be a great experience.

If you're someone who hasn't dabbled in the arts much, try pushing yourself into unfamiliar terrain and seeing what you think. If you love art, make more time for visiting exhibitions or galleries, all in the spirit of expanding your horizons and seeing yourself as one of many valuable people on the planet. You may even consider doing something creative yourself. Artistic pursuits can be fun and a great outlet for your thoughts and emotions.

Enjoying the Great Outdoors

Getting outside of your own head and out your front door can be very inspiring. Taking outdoor physical exercise makes everything look fresh again. Nature is great for making you feel part of the larger world and less focused on minuscule imperfections in yourself. So when you find yourself caught up in a cycle of self-battering, try thrusting yourself into nature. Even a walk in the park suffices when you can't easily get to the countryside. Train your attention on the trees, grass, sand, birds, rabbits or whatever, and breathe in the fresh air.

Animals can be very therapeutic as well. They're creatures of instinct and survival drives, and so they spend no time on self-denigration. Instead they just get on with the business of living. If you're an animal lover and your circumstances allow, consider getting a pet. When well treated, pets give you unconditional love. If you suffer from low self-esteem, the consistent enthusiasm of a dog or cat on seeing you come home from work can be fortifying (cats play it cool but they love you really). I (RB) have a West Highland terrier that looks at me with such unabashed adoration that I can't imagine I've ever put a foot wrong in my life. Bless her little furry head.

Getting Involved in Your Community

Belonging feels good. Human beings are social animals and like to be part of a larger group. Depending on where you live, getting involved with your local community may take a lot or hardly any deliberate effort. In big cities, remaining anonymous is easier than when you live in a small village. Regardless of where you live, however, getting involved with your community in one way or another is likely to be beneficial to your self-esteem.

Perhaps your low self-esteem tells you 'I won't fit in' or 'I've nothing to contribute'. Don't listen to those insidious carping voices in your own head. Just being you and being there is contribution enough. Showing your face at community meetings or gatherings allows people to recognise and get to know you. Your self-esteem is lifted when someone in your community says: 'Hey, where have you been? We missed you at the last meeting.'

Being part of a larger group can remind you that others don't share your own critical view of yourself. Getting involved also helps you to put social gaffes into a more realistic perspective. For example, perhaps you think you said or did something stupid when your group last met. Since then you've been going over it in your mind and calling yourself a host of unpleasant names. Despite your shame you force yourself to go back. To your surprise nobody seems to have thought twice about it and everyone treats you exactly the same as before your gaffe. Eureka! Or maybe someone mentions it in a jokey fashion. Perhaps you've blown the importance of the whole event out of proportion.

Even if you've actually done something memorable, you can still recover from the social embarrassment by getting back into the group sooner rather than later. Admit to your foot-in-mouth moment and allow others to treat you normally again. Maybe you wasted your time being so hard on yourself. Thinking of yourself as worthless is much harder when others around you are treating you as a worthwhile person. When you're considering getting involved with your community, think about looking for groups in local papers or on boards in your local shops; consider neighbourhood watch groups, regeneration projects, tenants associations, community meals, recycling initiatives and lots of other possibilities.

Appendix

Resources

• •

This Appendix lists organisations located in the United Kingdom that can offer further help, support and information.

Resources for Professional Help

Use the contacts here to find a therapist, discover where to browse the Internet and get in touch with organisations that can help with specific issues or problems.

CBT therapists

You can find a qualified CBT (cognitive behavioural therapy) therapist in Britain and Europe through the professional associations we list here. These organisations can also help you find CBT therapists in your area with experience and training specific to your individual problems.

✔ **Association for Rational Emotive Behaviour Therapy (AREBT)**, Englewood, Farningham Hill Road, Farningham, Kent DA4 0JR; phone 01322-862158; website www.arebt.org.

✔ **British Association of Behavioural and Cognitive Psychotherapies (BABCP)**, BABCP General Office, The Globe Centre, PO Box 9, Accrington, BB5 0XB; phone 01254-875277, fax 01254-239114; email babcp@babcp.com, website www.babcp.org.uk/.

✔ **European Association of Behavioural and Cognitive Therapies (EABCT)**, EABCT Office, Maliebaan 50B, 3581 CS Utrecht, The Netherlands; phone +31-30-2543054, fax +31-30-2543037; email eabct@vgct.nl, website www.eabct.com.

Other therapists

Many other types of therapy are available in addition to CBT. If you're looking for another type of therapist, or for information about the psychological treatments recommended for specific disorders, try contacting the organisations we list here. Remember that discussing other treatment options with your GP or psychiatrist, to ensure that you pursue a therapy that has been proven effective for your particular problems, is always a good idea.

- ✔ **National Institute for Health and Clinical Excellence (NICE),** MidCity Place, 71 High Holborn, London, WC1V 6NA; phone 0845-003-7780, fax 0845-003-7784; email nice@nice.org.uk, website www.nice.org.uk/.
- ✔ **United Kingdom Council for Psychotherapy (UKCP),** 2nd Floor, Edward House, 2 Wakley Street, London, EC1V 7LT; phone 020-7014-9955, fax 020-7014-9977; email info@ukcp.org.uk.

Online support

Websites devoted to specific disorders include:

- ✔ **The Mood Gym:** Developing CBT for treatment of depression. www.moodgym.anu.edu.au.
- ✔ **The Organization for Bipolar Affective Disorders:** www.obad.ca.

Organisations

Literally thousands of organisations devote themselves to helping people with various addictions, conditions and disorders. Some of the best include:

- ✔ **Action on Smoking and Health (ASH),** First Floor, 144–145 Shoreditch High Street, London, E1 6JE; phone 020 -7739-5902, fax 020-7729-4732; website www.ash.org.uk.
- ✔ **Alcoholics Anonymous**, PO Box 1, Stonebow House, Stonebow, York, YO1 2NJ; phone 01904-644026/7/8/9.
- ✔ **Anxiety UK (formerly the National Phobics Society)**, Zion Community Resource Centre, 339 Stretford Road, Hulme, Manchester, M15 4ZY; phone 0870-770-0456, fax 0161-227-9862; email nationalphobic@btinternet.com, website www.phobics-society.org.uk/contact.php.

✔ **Association of Post-Natal Depression**, 25 Jerdan Place, Fulham, London, SW6; phone 020-7836-0868.

✔ **The British Acupuncture Council (BAcC),** 63 Jeddo Road, London, W12 9HQ; phone 020-8735-0400, fax 020-8735-0404; website www. acupuncture.org.uk.

✔ **Depression Alliance**, PO Box 1022, London, SE1 7GR; phone 020-7721-7672 (recorded information).

✔ **First Steps to Freedom**, 1 Taylor Close, Kenilworth, CV8 2LW; phone 0845-120-2916 (freephone helpline 10 a.m.–10 p.m.); email info@first-steps.org, website www.first-steps.org/.

✔ **Manic Depression Fellowship**, 8–10 High Street, Kingston-Upon-Thames, London, KT1 1EY; phone 020-8974-6550 and 020-8546-0323.

✔ **MIND,** The National Association for Mental Health, Granta House, 15–19 Broadway, Stratford, London, E15 4BQ; phone 020-8519-2122.

✔ **No Panic**, 93 Brands Farm Way, Telford, TF3 2JQ; phone 01952-590005, freephone helpline 0808-808-0545 (10 a.m.–10 p.m.); email ceo@ nopanic.org.uk, website www.nopanic.org.uk/.

✔ **OCD Action,** Suite 506–509 Davina House, 137–149 Goswell Road, London, EC1V 7ET; phone 020-7253-5272; website www.ocdaction.org.uk.

✔ **Seasonal Affective Disorder Association (SADA)**, PO Box 989, Steyning, BN44 3HG; website www.sada.org.uk/.

✔ **Triumph over Phobia (TOP) UK**, PO Box 3760, Bath, BA2 3WY; phone 0845-600-9601; email info@triumphoverphobia.org.uk, website www.triumphoverphobia.com.

Further Reading

If you're interested in finding out more about dealing with the disorders described in Chapter 3 of this book, consult the 'Overcoming' series published by Constable and Robinson. The books in this series are widely available in larger bookstores and over the Internet.

For more information on cognitive behavioural therapy and how to apply it your own life, you can read *Cognitive Behavioural Therapy For Dummies* and the *Cognitive Behavioural Therapy Workbook For Dummies*. Both books are written by your faithful authors, published by Wiley and part of the *For Dummies* series (just like this book!).

Index

• I •

• P •

Notes

Notes

FOR DUMMIES®

Making Everything Easier!™

UK editions

BUSINESS

978-0-470-51806-9

978-0-470-77930-9

978-0-470-71382-2

FINANCE

978-0-470-99280-7

978-0-470-74324-9

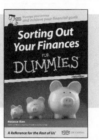

978-0-470-69515-9

HOBBIES

978-0-470-69960-7

978-0-470-77085-6

978-0-470-75857-1

Body Language For Dummies
978-0-470-51291-3

British Sign Language
For Dummies
978-0-470-69477-0

Business NLP For Dummies
978-0-470-69757-3

Cricket For Dummies
978-0-470-03454-5

Digital Marketing For Dummies
978-0-470-05793-3

Divorce For Dummies, 2nd Edition
978-0-470-74128-3

eBay.co.uk Business All-in-One
For Dummies
978-0-470-72125-4

English Grammar For Dummies
978-0-470-05752-0

Fertility & Infertility For Dummies
978-0-470-05750-6

Flirting For Dummies
978-0-470-74259-4

Golf For Dummies
978-0-470-01811-8

Green Living For Dummies
978-0-470-06038-4

Hypnotherapy For Dummies
978-0-470-01930-6

Inventing For Dummies
978-0-470-51996-7

Lean Six Sigma For Dummies
978-0-470-75626-3

FOR DUMMIES®

A world of resources to help you grow

UK editions

SELF-HELP

Cognitive Behavioural Therapy For Dummies
978-0-470-01838-5

Neuro-linguistic Programming For Dummies
978-0-7645-7028-5

Emotional Freedom Technique For Dummies
978-0-470-75876-2

HEALTH

Overcoming Depression For Dummies
978-0-470-69430-5

IBS For Dummies
978-0-470-51737-6

Low-Cholesterol Cookbook For Dummies
978-0-470-71401-0

HISTORY

British History For Dummies
978-0-470-99468-9

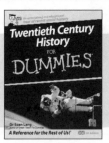
Twentieth Century History For Dummies
978-0-470-51015-5

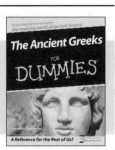
The Ancient Greeks For Dummies
978-0-470-98787-2

Motivation For Dummies
978-0-470-76035-2

Personal Development All-In-One For Dummies
978-0-470-51501-3

PRINCE2 For Dummies
978-0-470-51919-6

Psychometric Tests For Dummies
978-0-470-75366-8

Raising Happy Children For Dummies
978-0-470-05978-4

Reading the Financial Pages For Dummies
978-0-470-71432-4

Sage 50 Accounts For Dummies
978-0-470-71558-1

Study Skills For Dummies
978-0-470-74047-7

Succeeding at Assessment Centres For Dummies
978-0-470-72101-8

Sudoku For Dummies
978-0-470-01892-7

Teaching Skills For Dummies
978-0-470-74084-2

Time Management For Dummies
978-0-470-77765-7

Understanding and Paying Less Property Tax For Dummies
978-0-470-75872-4

Work-Life Balance For Dummies
978-0-470-71380-8

FOR

DUMMIES®

LANGUAGES

978-0-7645-5194-9

978-0-7645-5193-2

978-0-471-77270-5

MUSIC

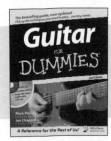

978-0-7645-9904-0

978-0-470-03275-6
UK Edition

978-0-7645-5105-5

SCIENCE & MATHS

978-0-7645-5326-4

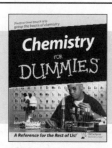

978-0-7645-5430-8

978-0-7645-5325-7

Art For Dummies
978-0-7645-5104-8

Baby & Toddler Sleep Solutions
For Dummies
978-0-470-11794-1

Bass Guitar For Dummies
978-0-7645-2487-5

Brain Games For Dummies
978-0-470-37378-1

Christianity For Dummies
978-0-7645-4482-8

Filmmaking For Dummies,
2nd Edition
978-0-470-38694-1

Forensics For Dummies
978-0-7645-5580-0

German For Dummies
978-0-7645-5195-6

Hobby Farming For Dummies
978-0-470-28172-7

Index Investing For Dummies
978-0-470-29406-2

Jewelry Making & Beading
For Dummies
978-0-7645-2571-1

Knitting For Dummies, 2nd Edition
978-0-470-28747-7

Music Composition For Dummies
978-0-470-22421-2

Physics For Dummies
978-0-7645-5433-9

Schizophrenia For Dummies
978-0-470-25927-6

Sex For Dummies, 3rd Edition
978-0-470-04523-7

Solar Power Your Home For Dummies
978-0-470-17569-9

Tennis For Dummies
978-0-7645-5087-4

The Koran For Dummies
978-0-7645-5581-7

FOR DUMMIES®

Helping you expand your horizons and achieve your potential

COMPUTER BASICS

978-0-470-27759-1

978-0-470-13728-4

978-0-471-75421-3

DIGITAL LIFESTYLE

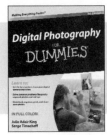
978-0-470-25074-7

978-0-470-39062-7

978-0-470-42342-4

WEB & DESIGN

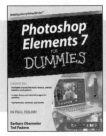
978-0-470-39700-8

978-0-470-32725-8

978-0-470-34502-3

Access 2007 For Dummies
978-0-470-04612-8

Adobe Creative Suite 3 Design
Premium All-in-One Desk Reference
For Dummies
978-0-470-11724-8

AutoCAD 2009 For Dummies
978-0-470-22977-4

C++ For Dummies, 5th Edition
978-0-7645-6852-7

Computers For Seniors For Dummies
978-0-470-24055-7

Excel 2007 All-In-One Desk Reference
For Dummies
978-0-470-03738-6

Flash CS3 For Dummies
978-0-470-12100-9

Green IT For Dummies
978-0-470-38688-0

Mac OS X Leopard For Dummies
978-0-470-05433-8

Macs For Dummies, 10th Edition
978-0-470-27817-8

Networking All-in-One Desk Reference
For Dummies, 3rd Edition
978-0-470-17915-4

Office 2007 All-in-One Desk Reference
For Dummies
978-0-471-78279-7

Search Engine Optimization
For Dummies, 3rd Edition
978-0-470-26270-2

The Internet For Dummies,
11th Edition
978-0-470-12174-0

Visual Studio 2008 All-In-One Desk
Reference For Dummies
978-0-470-19108-8

Web Analytics For Dummies
978-0-470-09824-0

Windows XP For Dummies, 2nd Edition
978-0-7645-7326-2

**Available wherever books are sold. For more information or to order direct go to www.wiley.com
or call +44 (0) 1243 843291**

05380_p4